THOMAS and VALERIE PAKEN4.
Thomas Pakenham is the auth   e
Great Irish Rebellion of 1798. H   of
Trees (2015), and Valerie Paken   1
Ireland (2017).

Praise for *Dublin: A Traveller's Reader*:

'Dublin is Pakenham territory, and no better compilers could have been found. Unforgettable: Yeats in action at the Abbey Theatre, Joyce conceiving 'stately plump Buck Mulligan' at the Martello Tower, and the staggering human tragedy conveyed by an eyewitness account of the Easter Rising'
History Today

'A collection of contemporary accounts, from the earliest days nearly to the present . . . A great help towards some understanding of "Irishness"; and of "Englishness" also'
P. J. Kavanagh, *Spectator*

'Dublin's past comes dazzlingly alive . . .'
Publishing News

'Erudite and practical simultaneously'
Gemma Hussey, *Irish Independent*

'Highly entertaining'
James Plunkett, *Irish Times*

'It is much more than a traveller's companion, to be enjoyed and appreciated by all who know and feel for this extraordinary city'
Contemporary Review

Other titles in the series

Dublin,
A Traveller's Reader

*Selected and introduced
by Valerie Pakenham
and Thomas Pakenham*

ROBINSON

ROBINSON
First published in the UK in 1988 as *Dublin: A Traveller's Companion* by Constable & Robinson

This edition published in 2018 by Robinson

10 9 8 7 6 5 4 3 2 1

Copyright © Thomas and Valerie Pakenham 1988, 2003

The moral right of the author has been asserted.

A CIP catalogue record for this book
is available from the British Library.

Every effort has been made to trace and contact copyright holders. If there
are any inadvertent omissions we apologise to those concerned, and ask that
you contact us so that we can correct any oversight as soon as possible.

ISBN: 978-1-47214-164-4

Typeset in Whitman by Hewer Text UK Ltd, Edinburgh
Printed and bound in Great Britain by CPI Group (UK) Ltd, Croydon CR0 4YY

Papers used by Robinson are from well-managed forests and other responsible sources.

Robinson
An imprint of
Little, Brown Book Group
Carmelite House
50 Victoria Embankment
London EC4Y 0DZ

An Hachette UK Company
www.hachette.co.uk

www.littlebrown.co.uk

In memory of Christine Longford

Contents

MARSH'S LIBRARY

THE LIBERTIES

KILMAINHAM

DUBLIN NORTH OF THE RIVER
PHOENIX PARK

THE ROTUNDA

CHARLEMONT HOUSE
(now the Municipal Art Gallery)

BELVEDERE HOUSE

O'CONNELL STREET
(called Sackville Street until 1922)

THE CUSTOM HOUSE

THE QUAYS

ST MARY'S PRO-CATHEDRAL

DUBLIN MOVES SOUTH-EAST
TRINITY COLLEGE

PARLIAMENT HOUSE, COLLEGE GREEN

ST STEPHEN'S GREEN

DUBLIN THEATRE

THE ABBEY THEATRE

THE APPROACHES TO THE CITY DUBLIN ON SEA
RINGSEND

DUBLIN BAY

CLONTARF

DUN LAOGHAIRE

SANDYCOVE

HOWTH

DUBLIN IN REVOLUTION
THE LARKIN STRIKE

THE EASTER RISING

THE CIVIL WAR

List of Illustrations

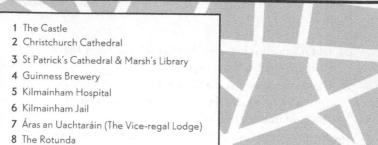

1 The Castle
2 Christchurch Cathedral
3 St Patrick's Cathedral & Marsh's Library
4 Guinness Brewery
5 Kilmainham Hospital
6 Kilmainham Jail
7 Áras an Uachtaráin (The Vice-regal Lodge)
8 The Rotunda
9 Charlemont House
10 Belvedere College
11 The General Post Office
12 St Mary's Pro Cathedral
13 The Custom House
14 The Four Courts
15 Trinity College
16 The Bank of Ireland (Parliament House)

Manor Street

Phoenix Park   7

Arbour Hill

River Liffey

25

25

Thomas Street

4

The Liberties

5 6

Grand Canal

MAP OF THE CITY
LOCATING THE PLACES DESCRIBED

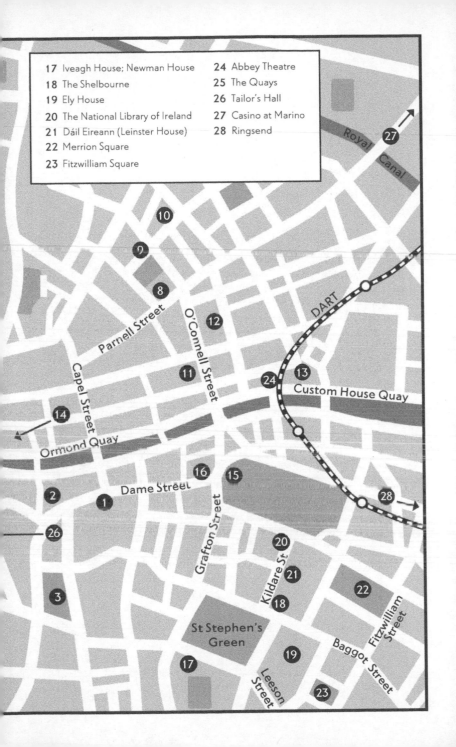

17 Iveagh House; Newman House
18 The Shelbourne
19 Ely House
20 The National Library of Ireland
21 Dáil Eireann (Leinster House)
22 Merrion Square
23 Fitzwilliam Square
24 Abbey Theatre
25 The Quays
26 Tailor's Hall
27 Casino at Marino
28 Ringsend

Royal Canal

Parnell Street

O'Connell Street

Capel Street

DART

Custom House Quay

Ormond Quay

Dame Street

Grafton Street

Kildare St

Fitzwilliam Street

St Stephen's Green

Baggot Street

Leeson Street

Acknowledgements

Anyone attempting the anthology of a city begins their search by consulting the historical experts who have gone before. In the case of Dublin, we were fortunate that many of them were also friends who offered generous bibliographical help with the original edition. Some of these are no longer with us, and we would like to remember them with gratitude, in particular Maurice Craig, the author of what is still probably the best history of Dublin and Professor Kevin Nowlan who helped not only with historical background but with selecting from a mass of undigested material. Desmond Fitzgerald, the Knight of Glin, was also hugely helpful with encouragement and suggestions. Other help and suggestions came from Desmond Guinness; Owen and Ruth Dudley Edwards; William Lefanu; William Garner and Anne Simmons, then working in the Irish Architectural Archive; and Peter Walsh, then Curator of the Guinness Museum. Most of the research for the book was done in the Irish National Library in Dublin or the London Library, whose librarians were unfailingly kind and patient with requests for rare books and little-known traveller's tales. For hospitality on many visits to Dublin, we would like to thank Moira Woods, Olda Fitzgerald, Barbara Fitzgerald, Bruce Arnold and Desmond and Penny Guinness. Last and most importantly, we would like to thank Laurence Kelly, who devised the series and gave us the original commission.

As with the other volumes in this series, we have prefaced each historical extract with short biographical notes on the writers themselves or in the case of writers too well-known to need them, a note on the context of a particular extract, or some necessary historical background.

With over a thousand years of Dublin history to choose from (or far longer if we are to take Richard Stanyhurst's date for the founding of the city, AD 155), it has been both pleasure and pain to choose the extracts themselves. Pleasure because Dublin itself has been so rich in producing talented writers or in attracting vivid descriptions from those who visited the city. Pain because we had to choose extracts that relate to a place or building readers can still find, and many have been swept away. We have also tried, as far as possible, to follow the brief for the series — that extracts should relate events rather than just describe buildings; there are many splendid books available on Dublin's architectural history. Finally, we have chosen, rather arbitrarily, with two or three exceptions, to end the timescale with the establishment of the Irish Free State in 1922.

We would like to make acknowledgement to the following for extracts used from their writings, editions, or where copyright permission was needed: Associated Book Publishers (UK Ltd) and Methuen for H. V. Morton's *In Search of Ireland*; Curtis Brown and the Estate of Elizabeth Bowen for *The Shelbourne*, and Virago and the Estate of Elizabeth Bowen for *Seven Winters*; Sphere Books for Oliver St John Gogarty's *As I Was Going Down Sackville Street* and *It Isn't This Time of Year at all*; Macmillan, London and Basingstoke, for Sean O'Casey's *Pictures in the Hallway* and *Drums Under the Window*; Simon & Schuster Inc., for Sean O'Casey's *Inishfallen Fare Thee Well*; The Educational Company of Ireland for Nora Connolly's *Portrait of a Rebel Father*; The Bodley Head, Random House and the Executors of the James Joyce Estate for *Ulysses*; Johnathan Cape, Viking and the Executors of the James Joyce Estate for *Portrait of the Artist as a Young Man*; John Murray for Walter Starkie's *Scholars and Gypsies*; Katherine Everett and Constable for *Bricks and Flowers*; Kate O'Brien and Batsford for *My Ireland*; Brendan Behan and Hutchinson for *Brendan Behan's Island*; Tom Kennedy and the Dublin Arts Federation for *Victorian Dublin*; Macmillan USA for Lady Gregory's *Seventy Years*; Austin Clarke and Routledge & Kegan Paul for *Penny in the Clouds*; Richard Ellmann and Oxford University Press for *The Selected Letters of James Joyce*; R. Pool and Batsford for *The Croker Papers*; the South Illinois University Press, Roger Hogan and Michael J. O'Neill for *Joseph Holloway's Abbey Theatre*; Joseph O'Brien and the University of California Press for *Dear, Dirty Dublin, a city in distress*; Linda Kelly and The Bodley Head for *The Kemble Era*; Molly Townsend and Sheed & Ward for *Not by Bullets and*

Bayonets; James Carty for *Dublin 1607–1872*; *The Dublin Historical Record*; Stephen Gwynn and Harrap for *Dublin Old and New*; Christine Longford and Methuen for *A Biography of Dublin*; Edward MacLysaght for *Irish Life in the Seventeenth Century*; Constantia Maxwell for *Irish History front Contemporary Sources, Dublin Under the Georges*, and *History of Trinity College, Dublin*; Christie's and the 6th Earl of Howe for the *Autograph Letters of Handel and Jennens*; A. P. Watt, Macmillan Publishing Company and Michael B. Yeats for 'Sixteen Dead Men' by W. B. Yeats; Sean MacBride for Maud Gonne Macbride's *Servant of the Queen*; Colin Smythe Ltd for James Stephens' *Insurrection in Dublin*; Hamlyn Publishing for Winston Churchil's *My Early Life*; Ernie O'Malley for *On Another Man's Wound*; and Desmond Ryan for *Remembering Sion*. Colin Smythe Ltd on behalf of Veronica Jane O'Mara for *It isn't This Time of Year at All* by Oliver St John Gogarty; Doubleday Broadway Publishing Group, for Mary Colum's *Life and the Dream*; The Anvil Press for Ernie O'Malley's *The Singing Flame*; The Collins Press for Cynthia O'Connor's *The Pleasing Hours*; Zwemmer for Edward McParland's *James Gandon: Vitruvius Britannicus*; The Boethius Press for *The Letters of Chief Baron Edward Willes* edited by James Kelly.

T.P.

V.P.

The editors have made every effort to locate all persons having any rights in the selections appearing in this anthology and to secure permission from the holders of such rights.

Introduction

Take the Holyhead ferry on a fine, summer morning, and you may be in for a surprise. Dublin or Naples? What are these calm blue waters, enclosed by the brown arms of two Italianate promontories, and that volcanic prong, sweeping up in two concave arcs two thousand feet from the bay?

Then you recognize it from its picture. The volcano is the Sugar Loaf, not Vesuvius, and the brown arms, freckled with white villas, are the arms of Killiney and Howth. Bay and mountain, they both belong to Dublin as Baiae and Vesuvius belong to Naples. How theatrical the setting, and how perfectly suited to the style of the city, even if Dublin turns out to have chosen the cool, north Italian stage-sets of Palladio, and shrunk from the exotic scenery of southern Baroque.

Soon the calm Palladian façades vanish in a fickle Celtic squall. That calmness is astonishing. Violence, as everyone knows, runs through Dublin's history like a jagged red seam in a carpet. How to reconcile the smooth eighteenth-century surface with the passions behind the brick-work – the passions bred by the invasions, rebellions, revolutions and counter-revolutions that have made the city what it is?

It was the narrow harbour, made secure by the generous bay and the sweep of the mountains that from the first attracted invaders. In the ninth century came Norse-speaking raiders from Norway, the Vikings. Theirs were the first long ships to come 'sniffing up the Liffey' (as a modern Irish poet puts it), ten days' hard sailing from bases in Bergen or Oslo. Apparently these Vikings found some kind of earlier settlements of wooden huts built by the Irish along the estuary: one at a Hurdle Ford (Ath Cliath) and the other at the Black Pool (Linn Dubh). Strung out on the coast either side of the Liffey were early Christian churches and monasteries, built and rebuilt in the previous three centuries, in the intervals between the fighting among local Irish chieftains. Their graveyards were punctuated with the high crosses and round towers that were a Celtic speciality. The Norwegians' speciality was a long ship and a battle-axe. For half a century they behaved like pirates, harrying the coastal plain from their lair beside the Liffey, looting for slaves and cattle, hunting for Irish souvenirs before burning the churches.

We know almost nothing about their pirate lair, the first Viking Dublin, except that they erected a great stone above the Black Pool, a stone about fourteen feet high, planted like a colonial standard. As the Steyne, it survived until the seventeenth century. Then in the early years of the tenth century, the Irish chieftains stopped fighting each other for long enough to make a successful counter-attack, and the Norwegian long ships sailed home with the survivors.

When the long ships returned they were manned by Danes, and this time the Viking toehold became a city. The Battle of Dublin gave them a permanent trading colony. It was a decisive battle fought in the harshness of midwinter, on 17 December 919. The Gaelic poet lamented:

> Fierce and hard was the Wednesday
> In which posts were strewn under the feet of the shields;
> It shall be called until Judgement Day
> The destructive memory of Ath Cliath.

If we took too seriously the laments of the medieval Irish scribes, we would think the whole of the next century was a Danish reign of terror. Brutal, ferocious, furious, untamed hordes: that is how the invaders were described. The invaders did not bother to leave their own version of events. Fortunately there is a mine of new archaeological evidence about Danish Dublin, and it is sober stuff. Day-to-day life in Dublin in the tenth century was doubtless brutish and short. It was also often dull. Commerce was the main preoccupation. There was more trading than raiding.

The most important archaeological discoveries were made from 1978 till 1980 and precipitated an unholy row. All the City corporation wanted to excavate was a hole for the foundations of a long-delayed new City Hall. This was to be a fashionable office complex in the shape of two eighty-foot-high pill boxes. They chose the best site in the heart of old Dublin, between Christ Church Cathedral and the Liffey, and stumbled on the core of the lost city of the Vikings. The row centred on whether the corporation should be allowed to destroy this core and go on with the pill boxes, or be told to look for a new site. They won the argument, unfortunately for posterity. But before the Viking city was lost again under the concrete (while the air was thick with missiles from the High Court) scholars had excavated thousands of artefacts, and added enormously to their knowledge of the way Viking Dublin and its successor – medieval Dublin – actually worked.

It turned out that the Vikings had built their walled city astride the ridge on the south bank of the Liffey. It was about a mile long and rather less than half a mile wide. The walls were built of stone about five feet thick and ten feet high. (One beautiful chunk was excavated along the line of the old river bank. Inside the masonry looked as fresh as when it was plastered.) Inside these imposing defences were hundreds of single-storey houses constructed of mud and wattle, with oak-framed doors and plastered walls. Even the floors were often made of plastered wickerwork. When the houses became insanitary, which they did very soon, they were levelled and replaced with new houses. It was a homely style of architecture, rather like the architecture of an African village today. There were no chimneys or windows. And it lasted in its essentials for several hundred years after the Danes had gone.

The narrow streets were full of workshops for craftsmen: bronze-smiths, tanners, weavers and blacksmiths. One possession that was most prized was a comb made from animal bone or antlers. Hundreds have been excavated, over two hundred in Wine Tavern Street alone. They were used for barter as well as for taming unruly Viking hair. Bronze working was also a speciality, and reached a very high technical standard. In the High Street area several hundred decorated bronze pins were excavated. Jewellery seems to have been common: bronze gilt brooches, gold armlets, gold and silver rings and so on. And the most striking evidence of the success of Dublin as a trading centre is the absence of weapons. Among all the tens of thousands of artefacts excavated, no arrows and only a few dozen weapons have been found.

By the eleventh century the local Danes had become half assimilated into the Gaelic world, and their power as an independent colony had ebbed away. (A similar fate overtook the Danish colonies at York, in Germany and elsewhere.) Increasing unity of religion – and a religion of one god – strengthened the bonds forged by the increasing diversity of trade. Norsemen took Irish wives. Gradually the terrifying Northern gods – Odin and Thor and Loki – lost their grip on Dublin's imagination, as Christianity came to dominate the whole of Europe. Squat wooden church spires rose on the southern bank of the Liffey, dedicated to both Irish and Danish saints. North of the river was built an outpost of the city, with a parish church dedicated to Danish Saint Michan, which was to be the only parish church north of the river for six hundred years. Two famous Danish kings of Dublin, Olaf Cuaran and Sitric Silkenbeard, retired to finish their days as holy men on the island of Iona.

One sympathizes with them. Odin or Thor or Jesus Christ: nothing seemed to alter the local appetite for fighting. Dublin was caught up in the three-way tug-of-war between Mael Sechnaill of Leinster, Brian Boru of the Midlands, and Ui Neill of the North. Brian claimed the high kingship but his armies were too weak to deliver it. The wars rumbled on, with Dublin periodically being captured and sacked. The contest reached its climax in 1014 when the combined forces of Leinster and the Danes were defeated by Brian Boru in the spectacularly bloody battle of Clontarf just outside the walls of Dublin. But it was a Pyrrhic victory for Brian. In Dublin it was soon business as usual. International trade had its ups and downs, and so did the city, sacked, rebuilt and sacked again with monotonous frequency.

When the Normans came in 1170, they came as a result of a local squabble, invited by a king of Leinster who had fled to England. Within a few years they had tidied up the confusion of centuries. Norman architecture and Norman institutions were imposed on Dublin and the Pale – the territory within about thirty miles. Two great stone cathedrals, Christ Church within the walls and St Patrick's just beyond, soon towered over the wooden houses of the city. Both were built in an uncompromising Anglo-Norman style, apt symbol that Dublin was and would be for the next seven hundred years a British garrison town in Ireland.

It is here that our Dublin tour should begin: on the dramatic ridge beside Christ Church Cathedral, averting our eyes from those concrete pill boxes now sitting on the site of the lost Viking city below us.

Picture this great colonial city in its heyday, the thirteenth century. The river has shrunk as the city has grown fat. Below us, at Cook Street, the medieval walls enclose new land reclaimed as the river has gradually silted up. The ships are moored further east. Streets have been laid out to assist trade, each with its own speciality: Fishamble Street for the fishmongers, and Wine Tavern Street for the wine merchants. Half a dozen stone churches have been built or rebuilt: St Audoen's, St Werburgh's, St Martin's, St Nicholas's and so on. Outside the walls there are ten abbeys or friaries, rich in tenant farms conferred on them by royal favour. But everything is dominated by these two cathedrals, and the great Castle commissioned by King John in 1204. Decorated with the heads of rebels, this must have been an awe-inspiring place, rather like an Irish Tower of London. There was a tower at each corner and a portcullis at the centre of the North Gate. In fact it was part fortress, part prison, part governor's palace, with a magnificent new hall modelled on Canterbury, and a fresco of the king and his barons, and other luxuries unheard of in Ireland, like piped water.

To get the colonial feeling of medieval Dublin, go to the north or south transept of Christ Church Cathedral. There, built in white stone imported from Dimdry in Somerset and worked by the rough hands of English craftsmen, is Romanesque architecture as the English knew it. There are four arches and the ghost of a Gothic arch in the triforium (for this is the age of transition). The walls bare their teeth at you: those

dogs' teeth – chevrons – loved by the Normans. Outside the south transept is an elegant doorway with more dogs' teeth and a pious portrait of
some ruler thrown in. It is all very orderly and conventional. Then you
descend to the crypt. Here the wild Celtic spirit has reasserted itself.
The plan is a strange muddle, and the chapels are lying abreast instead
of being separated behind the aisles.

By comparison, St Patrick's Cathedral has been scraped clean of all
medieval feeling. It is rich with associations of many other periods. In
fact, some would regard it as the principal national shrine (though the
prize of the Protestant minority). Yet so zealous were the nineteenth-
century restorers, that you can search in vain for a single medieval
stone today.

After Dublin's emergence in the thirteenth century as an Early
English colonial capital – a Gothic HQ for the governor of Britain's first
colony – Dublin's later medieval history forms something of an anti-
climax. There was no monumental building at this period. Not that
trade failed to increase. The wooden cranes of Merchants Quay and
Wood Quay creaked and rasped as they unloaded the bales of fine
English wool and in return loaded Bristol ships with Irish hides and
barrels of Irish butter. But Dublin was becoming increasingly isolated
from the rest of the country, as Anglo-Norman immigrants elsewhere
had become progressively Gaelicized – *ipsis Hibernis Hiberniores*. Only
a few miles south of the city, in the foothills of the Dublin mountains,
lived the wild Irish, O'Tooles and O'Byrnes, waiting to prey on the fat
of the colony. Indeed the pattern of the Viking age was beginning to
repeat itself. Making money demands different talents from making
war. Dublin's businessmen were better at buying off enemies than fighting them.

When an unexpected crisis loomed early in the fourteenth century,
they proved almost helpless. It took the form of the invasion of Robert
Bruce with six thousand Scottish knights. Bruce landed at Carrickfergus
in 1315 and fought his way south, looting the country as he went. By
1317 the campfires of his army at Castleknock were visible from the

tower of St Audoen's church. Desperate efforts were made to rebuild the city walls. Gaps along the quayside were hurriedly repaired. Down came the only bridge across the Liffey, the one linking the old Danish city on the north bank with the main city to the south. The mayor of Dublin, Robert le Nottingham, lost his head and tried a policy of scorched earth. He set fire to part of the suburbs. The fire quickly spread across the walls and burnt part of Christ Church itself. Fortunately for the English, Bruce had forgotten to bring a siege train. Dublin was saved, surrounded by the blackened ruins of the suburbs.

Bruce's raid set off the decline of the political power of the colony. The next crisis nearly wiped it out. This was the series of famines, plagues and cattle moraines culminating in the Black Death of the mid-fourteenth century. Of course famine was endemic. (At one time people were only saved from starvation by the stranding of a school of whales at Clontarf.) How the Black Death reached Dublin is not known. Perhaps it came, like other invaders, from Bristol, or perhaps it came direct from France. At any rate the Black Death bacillus travelled by flea, carried in turn on the fur of a black rat. It proved so devastating that people thought the world was coming to an end. According to the estimate of an Irish friar, John Clyn, four thousand people died in Dublin between August and December 1348. No doubt John Clyn, who died too, exaggerated the numbers. But Dublin, like all close-packed medieval communities, was especially vulnerable to disease. From England's point of view the plague had one good result. Dublin, wasted to a shadow, was more loyal than ever, more dependent on her powerful but over-burdened patron across the water.

Dublin's loyalty was not seriously tested till the end of the Middle Ages. It was then in 1534 that 'Silken Thomas' Fitz-Gerald (actually, the hot-headed), son of the Earl of Kildare, raised the standard of revolt in Dublin. His father, the king's deputy and the head of the Anglo-Norman aristocracy in Ireland, had been summoned to London to answer charges of maladministration, but Silken Thomas heard a story that he had been executed. He stormed in to the meeting of the Council, being held at St Mary's Abbey across the river, and renounced his allegiance to the Crown. Understandably confusion resulted. There was a Geraldine faction, eager to follow Silken Thomas. There was also plague within the walls and the O'Tooles were lurking outside them. So the authorities played for time. The rebels were allowed within the walls, provided they agreed not to harm the townspeople. And loyal officials were allowed to withdraw to the Castle, well stocked with food and the city's supply of gunpowder. It was a daft bargain for Silken Thomas. The castle proved impregnable. In due course a new deputy arrived from England and made mincemeat of the Geraldines. Silken Thomas was dragged off in chains to England, where he and five of his uncles came to a gruesome end at Tyburn.

Dublin businessmen had proved their loyalty in a fashion. In fact, they sensibly tried to keep out of politics whenever they could. This was no longer an option in the Reformation which followed within a few years. Suddenly the city found itself in the front line of a major war. Inside the walls the symbols of Popery were broken or burnt. A great bonfire was lit outside Christ Church to dispose of holy statues and other dangerous images. (One pre-Reformation treasure, a sixteenth-century wooden statue of Our Lady, survives today in the Carmelites' church in Whitefriars Street. A priest rescued it from a junk shop in 1824.) The monasteries, nunneries and friaries outside the walls were demolished, their gold plate melted down, their farmland taken by the Crown or handed over to the king's men. The townspeople of Dublin accepted this orgy of destruction without protest. There were dutiful celebrations to honour Henry VIII as head of the Church, and little enthusiasm either when the pendulum swung back to Catholicism in Mary's reign or when the Reformation was resumed in all its vigour by Elizabeth.

It was the brutal wars of Elizabeth's reign that propelled the city forward to a new prosperity. Soldiers flooded over from England, led by ambitious English noblemen or low-born adventurers – both equally anxious to make their name by exterminating Irish rebels. Dublin supplied the army with everything it could not bring for itself. The city still clung to its medieval walls, punctuated by thirty-two towers and gateways, with the five-towered Castle looming over the south-east corner. But the city of wattle and daub was at last changing to a city of stone and slate and regular architecture. Tudor Dublin must have looked like other large British cities (Chester is the best known example today) with black and white the predominant style, the larger houses constructed in a cagework of darkened oak beams and white plaster.

Life could be merry if you were a merchant with a line in imported linen or wool or wine. Dublin was already famous for its hospitality. Fresh English settlers waxed indignant at the way the alehouses were open at all hours of the day and night, run by 'idle housewives' of dubious morals. On the other hand, no one seemed to care that many of the public buildings, including churches of the Reformed faith, were becoming ruinous. Only one new public building was erected, but it was one of the highest importance. In fact, its huge open site still dominates Dublin today. It was Trinity College, founded by Elizabeth I on the site of an old abbey, whose land had been given to the mayor and the people of Dublin as a reward for their loyalty after the Reformation.

After the hurricanes of the late sixteenth century – rebellions, massacres, pogroms – came calmer weather at the beginning of the seventeenth. Dublin recovered its breath. Under a powerful governor, Lord Wentworth (later Earl of Strafford) business expanded rapidly. So did the city. And this time the expansion was to some extent planned. Wentworth decided to preserve a kind of green belt on the east, south-east and north-west of the city: College Green, St Stephen's Green, and Oxmantown Green. They were to be 'kept for the use of citizens to walke and take the open air by reason this cittie is at this present growing very populous'. Time was running out for Wentworth. In London he was thought too big for his boots, and he soon ended on the scaffold. As for Dublin, its citizens were not long in the mood for promenades. They found themselves cringing in the front line – or close behind it – of a disastrous new war.

In the great Catholic rebellion of 1641 the city became the main refuge for loyal English Protestants fleeing from the North and Midlands. In 1650 Cromwell marched into Dublin, hellbent on revenging himself against all Catholic rebels. The city had no doubts where its loyalty lay: with the winning side. Cromwell made it his base for his murderous sieges of Drogheda and Wexford. Then the smoke cleared. The agony of the civil war had opened the way for Dublin finally to slough off its medieval skin. The Restoration gave it back peace and prosperity. Of course that was the *sine qua non* for any conspicuous civic improvements. The city also needed someone with ideas to direct its expansion. And indeed it was now directed by the firm but benevolent hand of a great Viceroy, determined to reshape the city on a revolutionary new principle: splendour. Dublin would be the ceremonial capital of a centralized state, a symbol of power: his own, the King's and that of both peoples of Ireland, Protestant and Catholic.

The new Viceroy was an urbane Irish grandee, James Butler, first Duke of Ormonde, head of the great Anglo-Norman clan of Butler and no stranger to Continental ideas about replanning cities. He had learnt much, and suffered much, exiled in France with his royal master, Charles II. On 27 July 1662 he returned home like a Renaissance prince, Irish style. The Catholic peasantry came out to dance a welcome on the sands of Dublin Bay, singing *Thugamar féin an samhra linn* ('we have brought summer with us'). It was high time.

After a century of intermittent civil war, the people of Dublin must have felt as battered as their city. The Castle where Ormonde was supposed to live was described by one of his relations as 'the worst castle in the worst situation in Christendom'. Beside the Castle there were seventeen towers and gatehouses and two cathedrals, all verging on collapse. The population had shrunk to about nine thousand, most of whom lived in tumbledown cabins. From the distance the city might still sometimes look picturesque enough; it was a city of towers, decorated by the sails of windmills flickering in the sunlight. Inside, the place was, literally, a shambles: dead animals choked the narrow alleys.

One can imagine Ormonde's first reaction. Away with this disgusting anachronism. Let us build a great Baroque city instead; an Irish Paris, with a Tuileries and a Luxembourg Gardens crowning the banks of the Liffey. But Ormonde's master, Charles II, had still less spare cash for embellishing Dublin than he had for London. So Ormonde had to make do and mend with the Dublin authorities. He must cut his own cloth to suit their pockets. It was only well beyond the limits of the city, where the corporation's writ did not run, and where land was cheap, that he could make a splash. Inside the city, splendour must give way to compromise.

Ormonde's first great splash was to buy up 1,500 acres of open fields west of the city. In Phoenix Park he gave the people a royal deer park, bigger and more splendid than any royal park in London. From the first it was conceived as a park for the public to enjoy. His second great splash complemented it. Just across the Liffey at Kilmainham he constructed the Royal Hospital, a home for old soldiers modelled on the Invalides in Paris and anticipating the Royal Hospital at Chelsea by a few years. So imposing is the style, so skilful the work of the architect, that people came to attribute this building to the hand of Sir Christopher Wren. In fact it is now known to be the work of an Irishman, of Sir William Robinson, the Irish Surveyor-General. The first stone was laid by Ormonde in 1680, after his return for a new term as governor, the second stone by another great Irish grandee, the first Earl of Longford. The vast building was completed in 1684. Restored 1980s (for the vast sum of £20 million, or nearly a thousand times what it cost to build) it is now open to the public, and remains the most splendid monument in the whole of Ireland.

Meanwhile, inspired by Ormonde, the city began to pull up its socks. Taking up where Wentworth left off, the Corporation decided to enclose the ancient commonage on the south-east, at St Stephen's Green, and create a municipally owned square. It was to be a public pleasure ground, surrounded by four terraces of houses whose ground was leased to the builders on long leases. Not much now survives from this pioneering scheme but the vast scale of the layout and the public park. Each side of the square is nearly a quarter of a mile long, which makes Stephen's Green today larger than any square in London. The earliest and best houses on Stephen's Green now date from the eighteenth century.

But the foundations had been well laid: the broad, straight streets, and leafy public squares. They would be needed in Dublin's Golden Age, the eighteenth century. The guiding principle was Ormonde's: the cult of splendour. As the Corporation minutes put it, 'the whole designe of all persons concerned . . . is chiefly for the reputation, advantage and pleasure of the cittie'.

After pushing out to the south-east, the Corporation also channelled expansion in the opposite direction, to the open space across the Liffey on the north-west side, Oxmantown Green. Here their efforts were more prosaic. True, one fine public building was erected, the Bluecoat School (the forerunner of the current one which was built in the late eighteenth century). But there were no squares or gardens laid out on the north-west. It was here, on the muddy plain on the north bank of the Liffey, that the drovers' roads from the north and west converged on a new market called Ormonde Market. For centuries there had been only one bridge crossing the Liffey, so more bridges were now added: Bloody Bridge (named after the attempts to stop its construction), Ormonde Bridge, Essex Bridge and Arran Bridge.

Still more significant for the character of the city was Ormonde's decision to create a line of open quays beside the river. No doubt he was thinking of Paris again. The result was decisive. From Ormonde's Quay grew the main east–west axis that today bisects Dublin, a double line of roads and pavements along the river. So it was Ormonde who put the Liffey firmly in the foreground, and saved it (unlike so many rivers in British provincial cities) from being hidden away like a canal behind grimy factories and builders' yards.

Ormonde's long dazzling career finally ended with his recall in 1688, on the accession of James II, and soon the country was thrust on to the

centre of the European stage. Civil war resumed, a civil war the
Catholics this time seemed poised to win. Terrified Protestants fled to
England, and the Fellows of Trinity tried to sell their plate on the
English market. But it was seized in Dublin harbour and consigned to
the King's stores.

In March 1689 King James landed at Kinsale and marched rapidly
north to Dublin. His reception there moved him to tears of joy: 'the
Papists shouting' according to one hostile observer, 'the soldiers'
muskets, the bells ringing, and bonfires in all parts of the town'. But
soon the contradictions of the King's position became apparent. How to
reconcile the aims of loyal English Jacobites and wild Irish Catholics?
His Patriot Parliament sat in Dublin exuding toleration. Naturally the
Catholics wanted more: ascendancy. Meanwhile William of Orange
had landed in England and sent over Schomberg hot-foot to repossess
the sister kingdom. The Battle of the Boyne in 1690 and the Treaty of
Limerick in 1691 extinguished the political hopes of the Catholics,
whether English or Irish by origin. They were stripped of all public
office, humbled and kept humble by the penal laws. Now followed the
Golden Age of their enemies, the century of Protestant peace and
Protestant triumph.

No one would now defend their political ideals, nor the methods
they used to keep the Catholics out of power. Yet one thing has been
recognized by even their bitterest opponents. They had a style and a
sense of pride, a pride of community, colonial nationalism of a sort,
bigoted and narrow as it was, that set them apart from a mere English
garrison taking its orders from London. It was this relaxed colonial
pride that gave – and gives – the eighteenth-century streets of Dublin
their special feel. The self-confidence takes away one's breath. The men
who shaped Dublin were not content to imitate London. They would go
several times better. The streets would be wider, the squares larger, the
great monuments – Parliament, the Four Courts, the Custom House –
would all be more splendid. It took a century. And in the process the
city became a masterpiece. For all its glaring faults, including the

ghastly squalor of its slums, Dublin became one of the wonders of the eighteenth-century world.

Who were these men who found Dublin a shabby Englishstyle city of narrow alleys and dirty lanes, and left it a great European capital of broad streets and leafy squares? There was no single mind focused on the great design. There was something just as good: unity of purpose. Unity may sound odd to find in Ireland. For one thing, ultimate political control still remained in London. For another, the backbone of Ireland, judged by wealth and political power, was a bunch of redfaced squires, notorious for drink and duelling, the kind of men satirized in Goldsmith's Tony Lumpkin. Among them were the few hundred country gentlemen whose ownership of land gave them much of the landed rental and almost all the seats in Parliament. The Irish Tony Lumpkins seemed like a parody of their English counterparts. They came from the oddest backgrounds. Some could boast of hoary Catholic pedigrees; they were Gaelic like the O'Neills or 'Old English' like the FitzGeralds. They had adapted their religion, just as their English counterparts had done, to their political convictions. Others were pushy newcomers to Ireland, carpetbaggers of the recent wars and rebellions. Others again were Old Irish but new rich, men who had made a fortune out of pickled beef and bottled porter. Whatever their origin, they were now landowners and generally valued horseflesh above books on Palladio or other architects.

But the rising tide of agricultural rents had aroused them all. With the possession of wealth came the desire to make it conspicuous. Few of them up till then had town houses. A wig and a velvet waistcoat, and 'improvements' to your country house and estate, were all very well. But what about a new house in Dublin for the season, that is when the rents were safely harvested, hunting was over, Parliament sat and no man of fashion would be seen dead among his prize sheep and cows?

As the red-faced squires flooded into Dublin, the same fashionable tide floated a whole new fleet of whey-faced professional men – lawyers, engineers, land agents, surveyors, civil servants, doctors, as well as traders, builders and businessmen of all kinds. Few of them could afford a country house, unlike the squires. But their Dublin houses must be convenient and fashionable enough to impress their clients. Here was a common purpose that would bridge the gap between the middle class and the upper gentry. To supply this new democracy a new Dublin of tall, elegant, compact, plain (inexpensive without looking cheap) red-brick terraces sprang into life.

The architects, planners and financial backers were as diverse a bunch as their clients. Some like the great Palladian architect, Sir Edward Pearce, died mysteriously young. Many, no doubt, like the great James Gandon, were rather too keen on the bottle. Most of these designers were of humble origin and emerged only briefly out of the shadows. The two largest estates were concentrated in the hands of two rival families, the *nouveau riche* Gardiners, based north of the Liffey, and the old-rich Fitzwilliams, on the south side. It was to be a battle royal for the soul of fashionable Dublin, north versus south, that lasted for over a century.

At first it seemed that it would be a walk-over for Luke Gardiner. He was a banker by profession, and had married well. His wife was connected to the Mountjoys and Blessingtons. From 1714 he began to buy up the green fields north of the river, fields which had once belonged to St Mary's Abbey. Eventually he owned most of the building land north of the river. His first great work was a short street of palatial houses laid out in the 1720s, Henrietta Street, apparently named after the current Viceroy's wife. Today it is a palatial slum, for the great three-bay and four-bay terraced houses are marooned on the wrong side of Dublin. (In the early nineteenth century, a rascally Dublin alderman ripped out the staircases and sold the fireplaces on the London market before turning several houses into tenements.) But for a whole century Henrietta Street was the fashionable place for bigwigs of every kind, from gaitered bishops to gartered peers. No single street (except perhaps Lower Dominick Street nearby) could boast more magnificent plasterwork or richer panelling.

To the east, Luke Gardiner then launched an enormous tree-lined mall called Sackville Street, similar to the mall in London's Portland Place, built twenty years later. As O'Connell Street, this is now Dublin's best known thoroughfare. Better, perhaps, if it had been left forgotten in the background, to crumble away like Henrietta Street. O'Connell Street has passed, as Dublin's leading historian puts it, from neo-classic to neon classic. Ice-cream parlours and ketchup restaurants now decorate the sites of the houses of the hard-drinking squires. No doubt the street was doomed. Only forty years after Gardiner gave up the ghost, his quiet street was vandalized. The lower end was widened and what is now O'Connell Bridge was built and later widened, to turn the elegant mall into the main north–south axis, and shopping centre.

Meanwhile, on the south side, still grander and more enduring monuments – private and public – were being created. The forerunners of this new wave of building south and east of the historic centre were a pair of libraries, the gigantic library of Trinity College (designed by Burgh, the Surveyor-General, and finished by 1710) and the miniature library of Bishop Marsh, finished about the same time. Neither has suffered from too little – or too much – affection in the last 250 years, though Trinity's airy loggia was drowned years ago in the torrent of new books. The sardonic smile of the Great Dean floats over both – Swift, who baited the Fellows of Trinity and mocked poor Bishop Marsh (though he left him some of his own books, which you can still read, duly annotated in Swift's hand). Opposite the west façade of Trinity, dominating the traffic-choked oblong ironically called College Green, is Ireland's most spectacular monument after the Royal Hospital: the great Parliament House, designed by Captain (later Sir Edward) Pearce, in 1727.

Pearce was a dragoon officer by training, and a dilettante by temperament, a friend of Vanbrugh, who wandered round Italy in the footsteps of Grand Tourists like William Kent and Lord Burlington. His Parliament House was a great Palladian stageset: a pantheon behind, with two elegant arcaded wings thrust forward to catch the fitful Irish sun. It was this Palladian temple that housed the rotten-borough owners of the Irish Parliament, Commons and Lords, two Chambers of landlords, haggling over jobbery and bribery like a pack of crooked shopkeepers. How incongruous that a building of such Palladian purity should house the venal Parliament! Yet its theatrical qualities suited it admirably. The Irish Parliament was more theatrical than most parliaments: from many points of view a political sham. For a century they talked of independence from Britain with the same panache with which they transformed Dublin. Yet they could not make common cause with their Catholic compatriots. In fact the Catholic peasantry were still waiting, out beyond the Poddle and the Dodder, as they had waited so long, brooding on their ancient wrongs. The Protestant Ascendancy needed Britain as much as Britain needed a loyal garrison. Soon enough the bluff of independence would be called and the theatre in College Green close its doors forever.

But this is to anticipate. By the mid-eighteenth century the city was pushing south-east, as the battle for the soul of fashionable Dublin was fought out over tea-cups and claret mugs. The pioneer of the drive south-east was the young James FitzGerald, Earl of Kildare and later first Duke of Leinster. He bought some cheap land east of Coote Lane, which he renamed Kildare Street, and here on the seedy eastern flank of the city built himself a great mansion in 1745. Town house or country house? It was both. Leinster House, as it became, was designed by Richard Cassels, Pearce's successor as the leading Palladian architect, and a specialist in country houses. Cassels made no bones about the fact that he preferred doing country houses. So Leinster House is incongruous enough; a great long, stone-built Italian country house, with flanking wings and no 'back', marooned among the red-brick terraces and tall chimneystacks. Today it flies the tricolour and has a new role, no less incongruous than the one Cassels designed for it. This is the Dáil and Senate, the current Irish Parliament.

When the Duke of Leinster was asked whether this site was not somewhat remote, he is supposed to have replied, 'They will follow me wherever I go.' It was the cue for Lord Fitzwilliam of Merrion to begin his campaign to steal fashionable Dublin from the Gardiners. First Fitzwilliam built a magnificently broad street, Merrion Street, part of whose west side was kept open by the lawn of Leinster House. Then he launched into a still more magnificent square, Merrion Square, which took thirty years to fill with terraced houses. Some of these have rich plasterwork, and all their façades have been preserved more or less as designed. The great disaster occurred in Fitzwilliam Street, the street that leads southwards out of the east side of Merrion Square. This was once the most elegant piece of axial planning in Dublin, framing the blue Dublin mountains far to the south. But in 1958 the Electricity Supply Board insisted on replacing thirty-two perfectly sound red-brick houses with a long pink concrete office block, making mockery of the vertical pattern of the windows in the rest of the terrace. Sixty years later, the original façades are being rebuilt with a discreet office block behind.

The eighteenth-century battle between two private landlords – Fitzwilliam and Gardiner – ended in victory claimed by both sides. By the 1790s fashionable Dublin was split roughly half and half between the north side and the south side. At the same time the State had been encouraged to help replan the city. Intervention took two forms: commissioning new public buildings and knocking out kinks in the city's street plan. The public buildings did not favour either side as they were built on the Quays: the Custom House (completed in 1791 for the unheard-of sum of £400,000) and the Four Courts (completed in 1802 for £200,000). Both these giants came from the drawing-board of James Gandon, the young English architect shipped over specially for the job. The choice of Gandon was inspired. He brought the new style of Palladianism pioneered by Sir William Chambers in England, a style where delicate neo-classical detail is used to contrast with massive Palladian modelling. Each of Gandon's public buildings is a masterpiece fit to challenge Pearce on his own ground. In fact Gandon ingeniously added a new front door to the House of Lords on the east side of the Parliament House. His great Corinthian colonnade shakes hands with Pearce's great Ionic colonnade to the south. As for the Custom House, this had a dramatic and permanent effect on the direction of the city's growth. The old Custom House was at Essex Bridge, below which the river was still open to shipping. Now the ships were pushed firmly downstream, and a new bridge (Carlisle Bridge, the future O'Connell Bridge) was built just above the new Custom House, which was itself built on slob land won back from the sea. It was this new bridge that gave the Wide Street Commissioners the chance to create the main north–south axis across the river.

In 1800 the Protestant Ascendancy finally got its come-uppance. Dublin's Golden Age was over. Britain imposed a legislative union, and Dublin's venal Parliament, bought out from the red-faced squires, was sold very fittingly to be a bank, as it remains today. The Union with Britain was precipitated by the threat of a rival union, expressed in the United Irish Rebellion of 1798. This in turn was inspired by the twin revolutions in America and France. Protestant enthusiasts like Wolfe Tone and Lord Edward FitzGerald (one of the younger sons of the first Duke of Leinster) dreamt of an Irish republic, and planned to use the ancient grievances of the Catholic peasantry and the dissenters to break the British connection. The dream evaporated on bloody battlefields from Antrim to Wexford. Thirty thousand died. Dublin proved loyal enough, although the United Irish had counted on a rising within the city coordinated with attacks from outside.

After the Union some people predicted that grass would grow in the streets of Dublin. The future was to be less theatrical. Dublin continued to expand, but more slowly than before, growing towards the two recently founded canals and filling the squares, like Fitzwilliam Square in the south and Mountjoy Square to the north. Some fine public monuments were added on the north side: the GPO (completed in 1818) and Nelson's Pillar (built in 1808–9, half a century before the London column, and unfortunately dynamited in 1966 by Republicans to celebrate the fiftieth anniversary of the Rising). There were also some fine Catholic churches built, notably St Andrew's, St Nicholas', and the Pro-Cathedral. But the city was no longer a capital.

It was not so much the absence of the red-faced squires, some of whom now had seats in Westminster. Parliamentary reform would soon make them irrelevant. The Four Courts were not short of well paid lawyers, nor the city hospitals of well paid doctors. The most obvious effect of the Union and the 1798 Rebellion was that Dublin had lost its pride. The city began to look and feel as ordinary as an English commercial town.

At the same time fewer better-off people wanted to live in the centre, once the railway had brought the delightful southern seaside within half an hour of the city. Dublin's loss was the suburbs' gain: Donnybrook, Blackrock, Dun Laoghaire, Killiney and Howth. It was the north side that suffered worst. Here the fine houses were abandoned to the poor, and under the great plaster ceilings could be found some of the most shameful slums in Europe. On the south side of the core, the great houses suffered more from prosperity than neglect. Those in Grafton Street and Dawson Street were to become department stores, hotels and finally office blocks. Neon classic pays better than neo-classic. These were the forces of the market already identifiable in the nineteenth century. The city corporation, overwhelmed with social problems, and losing much of its rateable income to the independent boroughs in the suburbs, had neither the means nor the will to save Dublin.

But if nineteenth-century Dublin was running out of cash, it was to strike it rich in another field – literary talent. In October 1891 Ireland's great political chieftain, Charles Stewart Parnell, had died in England. On a day of lashing wind and rain his coffin was borne through the streets of Dublin, packed with vast silent crowds, to a final burial at Glasnevin. Ireland's hopes for political independence seemed at their nadir. It seemed at this moment, claimed the poet W. B. Yeats long after, that the national spirit burst out in a new channel, and Ireland's 'modern literature' began – the movement now known as the Irish Literary Renaissance.

Like many Irish movements, it began with a group of expatriates. Early in 1892, some of Yeats's friends gathered at his father's house in

Chiswick, London, to found the Irish Literary Society. But what marked the real birth of the movement was an impassioned speech given by Douglas Hyde to its Dublin branch a few months later. Hyde was a Protestant clergyman's son, straight out of the old Ascendancy world, but he had spent his boyhood learning Irish and absorbing Gaelic myths and folklore from the peasant farmers around his father's rectory; and he had already made a reputation for himself as a poet and Gaelic scholar. Now he warned his Dublin audience that the only way Ireland would find her true self was by purging herself of English influence and going back to her own cultural roots. Yeats enthusiastically agreed. Between them then they soon recruited other enthusiasts – many of them, like Hyde, from the Ascendancy. How surprised the eighteenth-century red-faced squires would have been. There was Edward Martyn, a Catholic landowner from Galway; Lady Gregory, widow of another Galway land-owner; and the novelist George Moore, who had left his estate in Mayo fifteen years before to live in Paris and London, but now returned to Dublin to play, he hoped, a key role in the new movement. Half a generation behind them was to emerge a string of equally talented young writers and poets: Sean O'Casey, James Stephens, Seamus O'Sullivan, Oliver St John Gogarty – and Dublin's most famous exile, James Joyce. (Joyce had no sympathy with Hyde's Celtic Revival, but he later described Dublin's literary gyrations of the period with sardonic humour.)

By 1899 the Irish Literary Society had become the Irish Literary Theatre; a few years later still it was to become the Irish National Theatre with a permanent home at the Abbey. Suddenly it seemed as if all Dublin was stage-struck. The Abbey's new productions became the focus of fierce political debates, with Yeats himself often rising white-faced, black hair thrown back, to lecture his audiences on their short-comings. With the production of J. M. Synge's *Playboy of the Western World* in 1907, the theatre became a nightly battlefield between those who saw the play as an insult to Irish morals and the Trinity College students who defended the cast. Even a clash of cultures could end in broken heads.

In the next decade Dublin was to experience far more serious clashes. First, in 1913, there was the great tramway strike organized by Jim Larkin and James Connolly, which looked (to authority at least) like a Socialist revolution in embryo. It culminated in a bloody street battle in O'Connell Street, when the police charged strikers with batons and sabres. Sean O'Casey's account still makes harrowing reading, and a government enquiry into the strike revealed once again the appalling condition of the Dublin poor.

The Dublin Rising three years later caught everyone by surprise. On Easter Monday 1916, Dubliners woke to find the city centre taken over by Volunteers of the Irish Republican Army. They were only a few hundred men, ill-armed and led by a strange mixture of poets, school-masters and one veteran of Larkin's strike, James Connolly. Their aim was to save the soul of Ireland, even if they had to sacrifice their own lives. At the time, the Rising seemed a forlorn hope. British troops were rushed across to Dublin and stamped it out within a week, gutting much of central Dublin – including the Post Office – in the process. But in the days that followed it was clear the insurgents had won a moral victory. And the execution of the leaders transformed them post-humously into national heroes.

In 1921, after several years of guerrilla warfare, Ireland finally won its independence. An official treaty was signed with England. Ireland became the Irish Free State. Even then the fighting was not over. In the Civil War that followed, a duel between the Free State army and the Republicans who would not accept the terms of the treaty, another of Dublin's finest public buildings was gutted by shell-fire: the Four Courts on the Quays. The Four Courts had housed the Irish State papers which made a spectacular bonfire, 'all the records of the country, processes, leases, testimonials . . . chronicled since Strongbow came to Ireland flying up', wrote Sean O'Casey, 'to come down scorched and blackened in every Dublin backyard and front garden!'

The new State, though desperately short of funds, then acted most generously. By the 1930s the damaged architectural masterpieces had been carefully restored in almost every detail. But by the '60s, prosperity had again begun to take its toll. The next fifty years saw many disasters. Far more buildings of the eighteenth century were destroyed by the planners and developers than were ever knocked down in the fighting. Soon it became apparent that some sort of miracle would be needed if Dublin were to be saved. And perhaps we are now seeing that miracle: the discovery that so many people in Dublin care about what is happening to their city and have enough pride – pride like that of their eighteenth-century forebears – to fight to try to preserve what is left.

THOMAS PAKENHAM

Dublin: the Old City

Previous page:
The Normans build a new church in Dublin; woodcut from
The History of Ireland in Holinshed's *Chronicles*

The old city

*Richard Stanyhurst (1547–1618) was the son of the Speaker of the Irish
House of Commons. His Description of Ireland was written especially for
Holinshed's Chronicles, first published in 1577, and like most Elizabethan
history is firmly on the side of the English conquerors. Soon after, however,
he became a Roman Catholic and fled to Spain, where he became one of
Philip II's advisers.*

Dublin the beautie and eie of Ireland, hath beene named by Ptolome, in
ancient time, Eblana. Some terme it Dublina, others Dublinia, manie
write it Dublinum, authors of better skill name it Dublinium. The Irish
call it, Ballee er Cleagh, that is, a towne planted upon hurdels. For the
common opinion is, that the plot upon which the ciuitie is builded,
hath beene a marish ground; and for that by the art or invention of the
first founder, the water could not be voided, he was forced to fasten the
quake mire with hurdels, and upon them to build the citie. I heard of
some that came of building of houses to this foundation: and other hold
opinion that if a cart or waine run with a round and maine pase through
a street called the high street, the houses on ech side shall be perceiued
to shake: This citie was builded, or rather the buildings thereof inlarged,
about the yeare of our Lord 155. For about this time there arrived in
Ireland three noble Easterlings that were brethren, Avellanus, Sitaracus,
and Yuorus. Avellanus being the eldest brother builded Dublin,
Sitaracus Waterford, and Yuorus Limerike. Of the founder Avellanus,
Dublin was named Avellana, and after by corruption of speach Eblana.
This citie, as it is not in antiquitie inferiour to anie citie in Ireland, so
in pleasant situation, in gorgious buildings, in the multitude of people,
in martiall chivalric, in obedience and loialtie, in the abundance of
wealth, in largenesse of hospitalite, in maners and civilitie it is

superiour to all other cities and townes in that realme. And therefore it is commonlie called the Irish or yoong London. The seat of this citie is of all sides pleasant, comfortable, and wholesome. If you would traverse hils, they are not far off. If champion ground, it lieth of all parts. If you be delited with fresh water, the famous river called the Liffie, named of Ptolome Lybnium, runneth fast by. If you will take the view of the sea, it is at hand.

Henry II's seal

[2] A CHARTER FOR NORMAN DUBLIN FROM HENRY II; FROM *STRONGBOW'S CONQUEST OF IRELAND* BY F. P. BARNARD.

Henry II of England had taken formal possession of Ireland in 1172 from his vassal, Strongbow, Earl of Pembroke who had invaded Ireland three years before. The Norman settlement at Dublin was intended to follow the same pattern as Bristol, a highly successful trading city, and many of the new settlers came from there.

*   *   *

Henry, king of England, duke of Normandy and Aquitaine, and count of Anjou, to his archbishops, bishops, abbots, earls, barons, justices, sheriffs, officers, and all liegemen, French, English, and Irish, of all his land, greeting:

Know ye that I have given and granted and by the present charter confirmed to my men of Bristol my city of Dublin to dwell in.

Wherefore I will, and steadfastly enjoin, that they have and hold it of me and of my heirs, well and in peace, freely and undisturbed, entirely and fully and honourably, with all liberties and free customs which the men of Bristol have in Bristol and throughout all my land.

Witnesses: William de Braos, Reginald de Curtenai; Hugh de Gundeville; William Fitz-Aldelm; Ralph de Glanville; Hugh de Creissi; Reginald de Pavilli. At Dublin.

The Castle

[3] KING JOHN COMMANDS THE BUILDING OF DUBLIN CASTLE IN
1205; FROM *STRONGBOW'S CONQUEST OF IRELAND* BY F. P. BARNARD.

*The need for a stronghold in Dublin had become acute by the reign of Henry
II's son, King John (John had mortally offended the Gaelic lords as a young
prince by pulling their beards) – and for the next 800 years, the castle was
to remain the centre of British power in Ireland, part fortress, part palace,
part government offices. The massive walls of the Record Tower still survive
from the original Norman building, which occupied roughly the space of the
present Upper Yard.*

To Meiler Fitz-Henry, Lord Justice of Ireland – Greeting.

You have given us to understand that you have not a convenient place
wherein our treasure may be safely deposited, and forasmuch, as well for
that use as for many others, a fortress would be necessary for us at Dublin,
we command you to erect a castle there in such competent place as you
shall judge most expedient, as well to curb the city as to defend it if occasion shall so require, and that you make it as strong as you can, with good
fosses and durable walls. But you are first to finish one tower, unless
afterwards a castle and palace and other works that may require greater
leisure may be more conveniently raised and that we should command
you so to do: for which you have our pleasure, according to our desire – at
present you may take to this use 300 marks from G. FitzRobert, in which
he stands indebted to us. GEDDINGTON, *21st August* 1205.

[4] A GAELIC POET LAMENTS HIS LORD, IMPALED ON
THE WALLS OF DUBLIN CASTLE; FROM *THE LITERARY
HISTORY OF IRELAND* BY DOUGLAS HYDE.

*The Gaelic poet is Angus O'Daly (1309–1350), bard to a Wicklow chieftain
killed during one of the many battles against the Norman Pale. The beautiful*

*English translation is by Douglas Hyde (1860–1949) who devoted his life to
the restoration of the Irish language and culture, was founder of the Gaelic
League, and, in old age, first President of Ireland.*

> O body which I see without a head,
> It is the sight of thee which has withered up my strength.
> Divided and impaled in Ath-cliath,
> The learned of Banba will feel its loss,
> Who will relieve the wants of the poor?
> Who will bestow cattle on the learned?
> O body, since thou art without a head,
> It is not life which we care to choose after thee.

[5] THE FATE OF IRISH TRAITORS – THE UNREPENTANT VIEW OF
AN ELIZABETHAN ENGLISHMAN; FROM RICHARD STANYHURST'S
DESCRIPTION OF IRELAND IN HOLINSHED'S *CHRONICLES*.

> These trunckles heddes do playnly showe
> Each rebelles fatall end
> And what a haynous crime it is
> The Queen for to offend.

[6] TRIAL BY COMBAT IN THE CASTLE YARD,
1584; FROM HOLINSHED'S *CHRONICLES*.

During these continuall troubles in Mounster, the two lord iustices
which laie at Dublin were much eased from all martiall affaires elsewhere, and were troubled but with the clamorings, exclamations, and
brabling of the Irish people, not woorth the remembring: saving that a
certeine combat was fought and tried before them in the castell of
Dublin, betweene two Oconhours [*O'Conors*], verie neere coosens &
kinsmen: the one was Teig mac Guill Patrike Oconhour appellant; the

other was named Con mac Cormake Oconhour defendant. One of these appealed and charged the other for sundrie treasons in the late rebellion, and which could have no other triall but by combat, which was granted unto them. Whereupon, according to the lawes and orders of England for a combat to be tried, all things were prepared, the daie, time, and place appointed; and according to the same, the lord iustices, the iudges, and the councellors came and sat in the place appointed for the same, everie man in his degree and calling. And then the court was called, and the appellant or plaintife was brought in before the face of the court, being stripped into his shirt, having onlie his sword and target (which were the weapons appointed) and when he had doone his reverence and dutie to the lord iustices and to the court, he was brought to a stoole set in the one of the ends within the lists, and there sat. After him was the defendant brought in, in the like maner and order, . . . and . . . placed in the other end of the lists. Then were their actions and pleadings openlie read, and then the appellant was demanded whether he would averre his demand or not? . . . who did answer as did the other, that he would averre it by the swoord.

Upon this their severall answers, they were severallie called the one after the other, everie of them taking a corporall oth that their quarell was true, and that they would iustifie the same both with sword & blood. . . . And then when by the sound of a trumpet a signe was given unto them . . .; they arose out of their seats, and met ech one the other in the middle within the lists, and there with the weapons assigned unto them, they fought: in which fight the appellant did prevaile, and he not onlie did disarme the defendant, but also with the sword of the said defendant did cut off his head, and upon the point of the same sword did present it to the lord justices, and so with the victorie of his enimie he was acquitted. Thus much I thought good to saie swhat of much, of the maner of a combat, which . . . is now for want of use almost cleane forgotten, and yet verie necessarie to be knowne. And as for this combat it was so valiantlie doone, that a great manie did wish that it had rather fallen upon the whole sex [sect] of the Oconhours, than upon these two gentlemen.

Sir Henry Sidney, Lord Deputy of Ireland, rides out from Dublin
Castle. The heads of Irish 'traitors' are impaled above the gate; detail
from a late sixteenth-century woodcut by John Derricke

[7] HUGH ROE O'DONNELL ESCAPES FROM DUBLIN CASTLE,
CHRISTMAS EVE, 1592; FROM LUGHAIDH O'CLERY'S LIFE
OF HUGH ROE O'DONNELL, IN CONSTANTIA MAXWELL'S
IRISH HISTORY FROM CONTEMPORARY SOURCES.

*Hugh Roe O'Donnell, the fifteen-year-old son of the Prince of Tyrconnell,
was kidnapped by a merchant ship from Lough Swilly and brought to
Dublin as hostage for the Ulster Gaelic lords' good behaviour. He finally
escaped from a cell in the Record Tower. After his ordeal and rescue in
the Wicklow Mountains, he made his way back to Donegal, and duly
succeeded his father as clan chieftain. He proved an able ally to Hugh
O'Neill in the last uprising of the Gaelic lords, but after their defeat at
Kinsale by Mountjoy in 1602, he fled to Spain and died of poison soon*

*after. His escape route from Dublin Castle is still commemorated by
Dubliners with an annual Christmas hike through the Wicklow
Mountains.*

[1587.] As for the ship of which we have spoken and her crew, when
they had finished the business for which they had come, and taken with
them the most desirable of the hostages . . . they sailed . . . after that
with the strength of the north-west wind along the shore of Ireland . . .
till they landed in the harbour of Dublin again. It became known immediately throughout the whole city and to the Lord Justice and the
Council, especially that they had come after this manner, and that
Hugh O'Donnell was in their custody. They were glad of his coming, yet
it was not at all through love of him, and they summoned him to them
without delay so that he was face to face with them, and they proceeded
to converse with him and ask information of him, and they were chiefly
bent on searching out and discovering his character. In the end they
ordered him to be put in a strong stone castle, where the nobles of the
sons of Milesius were in chains and captivity, expecting slaughter and
death, together with some of the nobles of the white foreigners who
had come to the island long before, and had entered into amity and
friendship with the Irish against the English . . . It was their solace and
entertainment day and night in the close prison where they were, to be
lamenting over the intolerable hardships and relating the great cruelty
which was inflicted on them both, English and Irish, and listening to
the unjust sentences pronounced, and the dishonour and ill-treatment
done against the high-born nobles of the sons of Milesius and of the
white foreigners alike.

As for Hugh O'Donnell, he was, just like the rest, in chains for the
space of three years and three months, hearing of the ignoble bondage
in which the Irish were. It was anguish and sickness of mind and great
pain to him to be as he was, and it was not on his own account, but
because of the unbecoming helplessness of his friends and kinsmen, his
gentlemen (*urradha*) and leaders, his sanctuaries and holy churches,

his poets and learned men, his subjects and people, expelled and banished to other territories throughout Ireland. He was always pondering and thinking how he might find a way of escape. This was no easy thing for him, for he was put every night into a well-closed apartment in the castle for security, and until the hour of tierce on the morrow. That castle was situated thus. There was a broad deep trench of water all round it, and a compact bridge of boards over it, opposite the door of the castle, and the grim-visaged host of the English outside and inside the gate to guard it . . .

[1592] When it seemed to the Son of the Virgin time that he should escape, he and some of his companions found the keepers off their guard in the very beginning of the night before they were taken to the refectory, and they took their fetters off. They went after that to the privy, having a long rope, and they let themselves down by means of the rope through the privy, till they came to the deep trench which was around the fortress. After that they climbed to the opposite bank, till they were on the edge of the trench at the other side. The hostages who escaped with Hugh were Henry and Art, the two sons of Shane, son of Con Bacach, son of Con, son of Henry, son of Eoghan. There was a certain faithful servant who visited them in the castle, in the guise of a horseboy, to whom they imparted their secret, so that he met them face to face when need was, and became their guide. They went off after that through the crowded street near the fortress, without being known or overheard by any one, for they were no more noticed than any one else of the city people, as no one stopped to converse with or visit any one in the houses of the stronghold at that hour, for it was the beginning of the night exactly, and the gates of the city were not yet closed. They went out beyond the city in that manner. They leaped over the rough and rugged parts of the huge moats and of the strong, firm palisades which were outside the city, until they came to the slopes of Slieve Roe [*the Three Rock Mountain*], over which Hugh had crossed at the time he first escaped. The darkness of the night and the hurry of the flight separated the oldest of the party from them. This was Henry O'Neill. Hugh was the youngest of the nobles. They were not pleased at the separation. They went on, however, their attendant leading the way. The night came on with a drizzle and downpour, and a venomous shower of rain and thick smooth snowflakes, so that it was not easy for the highborn nobles to walk on account of the storm and the scanty clothing, for they were without overmantles, having left them in the privy through which they had come.

This hurried journey, strange and unusual, was more severe on Art than on Hugh, and his gait was feebler and slower, for he was corpulent, thick-thighed, and he had been a long time confined in prison. It was not so with Hugh, for he had not passed the period of boyhood, and he had not ceased to grow in size and his gait was quick and nimble. When he perceived Art growing weak and his step heavy, what he did to him was to place one hand of his on his own shoulder and the other hand on the shoulder of the servant. They went on in this way across the upper part of the level mountain. They were tired and weary then, and they could not bring Art further with them. As they could not, they rested under the shelter of a lofty cliff on the moor which was in front of them. After halting there, they sent the servant with news of them to Glenmalure, the place where Fiach MacHugh was. This was a secure impregnable valley, and the English of Dublin were accustomed with their engines of war to besiege and assault it, in order to plunder and lay it waste. This Fiach maintained it valiantly against them, so that many heads were left behind with him, and they could do nothing against him . . . So, too, the hostages aforesaid made a tryst with him, and sent their servant to him. When [the servant] came to where Fiach was, he told his story to him and the state in which he left the youths who had escaped from the city, and that they would not be found alive if he did not go to their assistance quickly.

Thereupon Fiach selected a party of his picked men, and bade them go with the servant to the youths. They rose up at once as they were ordered, and went off, one having food and another ale and beer, until they came to the mountain, the place where the men had been left. Alas! truly the state and position of these nobles was not happy or pleasant when the soldiers who had come to seek them arrived. They had neither coverlets nor plaids nor clothing about their bodies to protect them from the cold and ice of the sharp winter season, but the only bedclothes around their fair skins, and pillows under their heads, were high-fenced bed-rails, white bordered of hail, freezing all round them, and attaching their light tunics and shirts of fine linen thread to their bodies, and their long shoes and sandals to their shins and feet, so that they seemed to the men that had come not to be human beings at all, but their shapes in sods of earth covered up by the snow; for they did not perceive a stir in their limbs, but just as if they were dead, and they were nearly so. Thereupon the soldiers raised them from where they lay and bade them take some of the food and ale, but they failed in this, for every drink they took they let it out of their mouths again. Even so, Art died at last and was buried in that place. As for Hugh, he retained the beer after that, and his strength was on the increase after drinking of it, except in his two feet, for they were like dead members without motion, swollen and blistered from the frost and snow.

[8] THE DEFEAT OF THE 'OLD ENGLISH' NOBILITY; FROM
A LETTER BY SIR CHRISTOPHER PLUNKETT TO HIS SON
IN 1622, IN *DESIDERATA CURIOSA HIBERNICA*.

The 'Old English' were the descendants of the original Norman settlers, most of whom had remained Catholic after the Reformation. At the first Parliament held in Dublin Castle since the Elizabethan wars which had finally brought all Ireland under English rule, they find themselves outnumbered by the new settlers of the Tudor and Stuart plantations, and a ludicrous struggle ensues. Christopher Plunkett, the letterwriter, later became Earl of Fingal. His son, a Catholic, joined the 1641 rebellion and died a prisoner in Dublin Castle.

*   *   *

The Great Courtyard at Dublin Castle, aquatint by James Malton from
Picturesque Views of Dublin, 1794

And upon the 8th day of May, being Tuesday, the lord deputy, with all
the peers of the realm, and the noblemen, the clergy, both bishops and
archbishops, attired in scarlet robes very sumptuously, with sound of
trumpets; the lord David Barry, viscount Buttevant, bearing the sword
of estate; the earl of Thomond, bearing the cap of maintenance: and
after all these, the lord deputy followed, riding upon a most stately
horse, very richly trapped, himself attired in a very rich and stately robe
of purple velvet, which the king's majesty had sent him, having his train
borne up by eight gentlemen of worth: and thus, in most stately and
sumptuous manner, they rode from the castle of Dublin, to the cathedral church of St Patrick, to hear divine service.

But as many of the nobility of Ireland, as were of the recusant
faction, went not into the church, neither heard divine service or
sermon, notwithstanding that they were lords of the parliament house,
and rode towards the church with other lords of estate, yet they stayed
without during the time of service and sermon. Now when service was
done, the lord deputy returned back to the castle, those recusant lords

joined themselves again with the rest of the estate, and rode to the castle in manner as before they came from thence.

Now the lord deputy, with all this honourable assembly, being entered into the castle, ascended up into the high house of parliament . . .

And when the whole high court of parliament was set, the lord chancellor made a grave and worthy speech, . . . and among many other things, his lordship declared the king's majesty's pleasure, concerning Sir John Davis, his majesty's attorney-general in Ireland; and how his highness was pleased, that he should be the speaker of the lower parliament house . . .

The next day, being the 19th of May, and the 2nd of the parliament, the said Sir John Davis was brought into the parliament house, to be presented, and to take his place according to his majesty's good meaning, and thereupon arose a great tumult, because there were two elections, viz. those of the recusants sect had chosen Sir John Everard knight, for the speaker, and therefore, would in no wise accept of Sir John Davis, and in this division grew an uncertainty who had most voices; whereupon Sir John Davis, with all those of the protestancy, went out to be numbered, and before they came in again those of the recusancy had shut the door, and had set Sir John Everard in the chair of the speaker; but when the protestants saw that, they quietly pulled Sir John Everard out of the chair, and held Sir John Davis therein; and thus, with great contention, the 2d and 3d days were spent: but the recusants prevailed not, for Sir John Davis was maintained in the place, according to his highness's good meaning. Then did the recusants of both houses of parliament withdraw themselves, and resorted not thither any more, notwithstanding that they were often sent for by the lord deputy. And now they began to invent new projects, whereupon they had sundry secret meetings among themselves. . . .

[9] A RAMBLE ROUND THE CASTLE IN 1698; FROM JOHN
DUNTON'S LETTERS QUOTED IN EDWARD MACLYSAGHT'S
IRISH LIFE IN THE SEVENTEENTH CENTURY.

*John Dunton (1659–1733) was a highly eccentric London bookseller, who had
first tried emigrating to New England, then come to Dublin to escape domestic
troubles. He later published an account of his rambles as* The Dublin Scuffle.

Another of my inquisitive rambles is to the castle, the place of residence for the chief governor. It is encompassed with a wall and dry
ditch over which is a drawbridge and within that an iron gate, opposite
to which in the inner court are two brass field pieces planted, as also
some others on top of one of the towers, and yet it is no place of great
strength, I mean such as is able to endure the battery of great guns,
though it can command all the city from its towers. It has an handsome
guardhouse for the soldiers and other rooms for the officers, for a foot
company with three commissioned officers daily mount the guard, and
whenever the government go out or come in they are received with
colours flying and drums beating as the King is at Whitehall, and indeed
the grandeur they live in here is not much inferior to what you see in
London if you make allowances for the number of great men at court
there. The building is handsome without much magnificence on the
outside, you enter the house up a noble stairs and find several stately
rooms one of which is called the Presence chamber and has a chair of
state with a canopy over it. One part of the house stands over a large
stone gallery supported by several pillars of stone.

At the back of the house lies a broad terrace walk the length of the
building the walls covered with greens and flower pots, from hence on
a stone arch over a little river you descend by two spacious pair of stone
stairs into the garden, which is handsomely laid out into grass plots
with green and gravel walks, and at the north side there are two rows of
flourishing lime-trees, beneath which lies another grass walk. This
garden was made by that great man the Lord Sidney, now earl of

Romney, when he was chief governor. To the castle belongs an officer called the Constable of the Castle, who receives prisoners of state when committed, as the Lieutenant of the Tower does. To the north side lies the chapel to which the lord Galway goes constantly every morning to prayers, and at his return spends sometime in receiving petitions, which he answers with all the sweetness and readiness that any petitioner can wish for in so great a man.

Next the chapel is the office of the Ordinance, near which the King's gunsmiths and armourers work, before these buildings lies a large piece of ground called the Stable-yard, on one side of which are the King's stables, which as they are not extraordinary so they are no way despicable, but convenient and big enough; in this yard two companies of foot parade every morning, one of which mounts the town guard and the other that of the Castle. The little river which I now mentioned runs here, on the other side of which stands the coach-houses, and biggest hay-stacks that ever I saw.

[10] A CASTLE BALL IN 1732; FROM THE AUTOBIOGRAPHY AND CORRESPONDENCE OF MRS DELANY.

Mrs Delany, a niece of Lord Lansdowne, came to Dublin on a prolonged visit as a young widow in 1730, and later returned to marry Dr Delany, a famous Dublin preacher and close friend of Dean Swift. Their house, Delville at Glasnevin, became a centre of hospitality and her letters (mainly to her brother and sister in England) give sparkling vignettes of eighteenth-century Dublin society.

Dublin, 7th March, 1731–32.

MY DEAR BROTHER,

May your assemblies increase at Wells, and every agreeable entertainment that can give you any pleasure. A thousand thanks to you for your last letter. I will not defer my answer, though I am in a monstrous hurry.

'Tis fit in return for the account you give me of your amusements, that I let you know what we do here. Why, on the first of March we went to Court in the morning, heard a song of Dubourg's, (not so pretty as the last,) after that compliment was over and we had refreshed ourselves by dinner, we went again at seven. The ball was in the old beefeaters hall, a room that holds seven hundred people seated, it was well it did, for never did I behold a greater crowd. We were all placed in rows one above another, so much raised that the last row almost *touched the ceiling!* The gentlemen say we looked very handsome, and compared us to Cupid's Paradise in the puppet-show. At eleven o'clock minuets were finished, and the Duchess went to the basset table.

After an hour's playing the Duke [*of Dorset*], Duchess, and nobility marched into the supper-room, which was the council chamber. In the midst of the room was placed a holly tree, illuminated by an hundred wax tapers; round it was placed all sorts of meat, fruit and sweetmeats; servants waited next, and were encompassed round by a table, to which the company came by turns to take what they wanted. When the doors were *first* opened, the hurry burly is not to be described; squawling, shrieking, all sorts of noises: some ladies lost their lappets, others were trod upon. Poor Lady Santry almost lost her breath in the scuffle, and fanned herself two hours before she could recover herself enough to know if she was dead or alive. I and my company were more discreet than to go with the torrent; we staid till people had satisfied their curiosity and hunger, and then took a quiet view of the *famous tree*, which occasion'd more rout than it was worth.

[11] THE WIT AND WISDOM OF LORD CHESTERFIELD;
FROM 'SKETCHES OF IRISH HISTORY' QUOTED IN
IRISH CAVALCADE BY M. J. MCMANUS.

The Earl of Chesterfield was a scholar and a man of wit, as well as an elegant courtier; his government of the country proves him not only a man of enlightened understanding, but of the most benevolent disposition. He came over in the year 1745, a period remarkable for the rebellion which raged in Scotland, and made it necessary to have an able and prudent statesman at the head of affairs in Ireland. By the wisdom and levity of his measures, the Catholics remained perfectly quiet; before his arrival, those in power had shut up their chapels in Dublin, and their priests were commanded to leave the country by proclamation. These severities were offensive to Lord Chesterfield; convinced that harsh treatment alienates the heart, but that gentle usage inspires confidence and gains the affections, he permitted them the undisturbed exercise of their religion. To accusations to their preju- dice, resulting from dislike, he paid no regard; rumours of plots and insurrections were listened to by him with calm indifference.

One morning prior to the battle of Culloden, Mr Gardiner, the Vice- treasurer, abruptly entered his bedchamber with tidings that the Papists were rising. 'Rising?' said his lordship, yawning and looking at his watch; 'it is time for every honest man to rise; it is past nine o'clock, and I will rise myself.'

[12] CUSTARD-PIES AT THE LORD LIEUTENANT'S DINNER, 1757; AN UNPUBLISHED LETTER (IN THE BRITISH MUSEUM) FROM CHIEF BARON WILLES TO HIS FRIEND, THE EARL OF WARWICK.

Chief Baron Willes, originally from Warwickshire, rose through the Irish legal system to become head of the Irish Exchequer. He lived partly in Monkstown.

Upon state days when some of the Nobility, Bishops, Privy Councils, and Judges dine with the Ld. Lieutn. he is attended with great state. Behind his chair stand his two pages. Behind them in the middle stands his Gentleman of the Bedchamber & on each side the steward and Controller of the Household with their white wands. When the 2nd course is set on the Table the King at Arms preceded by a pursevant at

Arms & the King with his Crown on his head is attended into the Room & goes to the upper End & proclaims the Kings Stile in Latine, French, & English, & then the pursevant pronounces the words Largess Largess. And formerly the doors were then thrown open & the Crowd entered to see the Ld. Lieutenant at dinner. And the Company at the Table used to give the Sweetmeats &c to those that stood behind them. Some few years ago the Crowd grew troublesome & used to seize what was at Table [and throw it] over the Gentlemans heads. And it happening that a woman seized a large Custard in paste & in getting it over a Bishop's head it fell directly upon his face & robes, & he made so ridiculous a figure that it was thought proper to prevent such rudeness for the future that the Crowd would not be admitted till the Ld. Lieutenant was rose from Table. Accordingly now so soon as the Company rises from Table the Servants show all the Sweetmeats & Oranges &c on the Table & take away the Glass & Ornaments of the dessert & then the Mob enters & scramble for it. The Lord Lieutenant & Company retiring up one End of the room to see the diversion of the Scramble.

The ballroom upon the Kings Birthday is a prodigious fine sight. Tis a noble room Much larger than the Ballroom at St James. The Ld. Lieutenant & Lady duchess sit on two chairs of State at the upper end of the room, And behind them stand peers, Lord Justices & privy Councillors. There are 4 rowes of benches raised one above another the whole length of the room. A bar is made across the room about mid space between that & the door stand the gentlemen. The four rows of Benches on each side are filled with Ladies only. And nobody dances but who the Gentleman Usher directs & takes out. As I stood by the side of the Lady Duchess Chair & had a fine view of the rows of Ladys I thought it the finest sight I ever saw. There were I believe about 400 Ladies, many of them extremely handsome. All of them very richly dressed, but not many that had any great quantity of Jewels, but the blaze of Beauty was superior to the sparkling of diamonds.

[13] THE UNITED IRISHMEN FAIL TO CAPTURE THE
CASTLE, 23 MAY 1798; FROM *THE RISE AND FALL OF
THE IRISH NATION* BY SIR JONAH BARRINGTON.

*In 1798 the United Irishmen – a revolutionary movement largely inspired by
the example of the American and French Revolutions – launched the first
serious rising against English rule since the seventeenth century. Many of
their leaders, including Lord Edward FitzGerald (see p. 77 and p. 192) were
arrested before the rising, betrayed by the Castle's network of spies; and the
attack on the Castle by rebel forces from the surrounding villages was confused
and unco-ordinated. In this extract, the loyalist forces crouch in the cattle-
market north of the Castle.*

*Sir Jonah Barrington (1760–1834), who wrote this account ten years later,
is a racy though highly unreliable historian of eighteenth-century Ireland.
Son of a squire from Co. Leix, he sat as MP in Grattan's Parliament, which he
later saw as the highpoint of the 'Irish Nation' (the Protestant Ascendancy
version); he became an Admiralty judge after the Union; and was eventually
deprived of office for embezzlement.*

The danger was considered imminent, the defence impracticable, yet
there was a cheerful, thoughtless jocularity with which the English
nation, under grave circumstances, are totally unacquainted; and plain
matter-of-fact men can scarcely conceive that renovating levity which
carries an Irish heart buoyantly over every wave, which would swamp,
or at least water-log, their more steady fellow subjects. All the barristers, attorneys, merchants, bankers, revenue officers, shop-keepers,
students of the University, doctors, apothecaries, and corporators, of an
immense metropolis, in red coats, with a sprinkling of parsons, all
doubled up together amidst bullock stalls and sheep pens, awaiting, in
profound darkness (not with impatience), for invisible executioners to
dispatch them without mercy, was not (abstractedly) a situation to
engender much hilarity – scouts now and then came, only to report
their ignorance – a running buzz occasionally went round, that the

videts were driven in – and the reports of distant musketry, like a twitch of electricity, gave a slight but perceptible movement to men's muscles. A few (faintly-heard) shots on the north side also seemed to announce that the van-guard of the Santry men was approaching. In the mean time, no orders came from the general, and if there had, no orders could have been obeyed. It appeared, at break of day, that both Santry and Rathfarnham rebels had adjourned their assault to some other opportunity. . . .

The rebels had learned that the yeomanry were ready to receive them, and contented themselves with shooting some mail coachmen, and burning some houses, till morning dispersed them. The rebels on the south intended to take the castle by surprise, whilst the Santry men assailed the barracks; but their plan was disconcerted by Lord Roden, at the head of his dragoons (called the fox hunters, from their noble horses). His Lordship marched rapidly upon them, and surprised the few who had collected; and, being supported by a small number of light infantry, the attack completely succeeded. A few rebels were sabred, and some few made prisoners; but the body dispersed with little resistance. Lord Roden received a ball on his helmet, but was only bruised, and some dragoons were wounded; the other (county of Dublin) rebels retreated to join the Kildare men; the southern marched to unite themselves with those of Wicklow. Their plan had been excellent – had they acted steadily on it success was not improbable; however, the metropolis for some time had no further dread of molestation.

A new, disgusting, and horrid scene was next morning publicly exhibited; after which military executions commenced, and continued with unabating activity. Some dead bodies of insurgents, sabred the night before by Lord Roden's dragoons, were brought in a cart to Dublin, with some prisoners tied together; the carcasses were stretched out in the Castle yard, where the Viceroy then resided, and in full view of the Secretary's windows; they lay on the pavement, as trophies of the first skirmish, during a hot day, cut and gashed in every part, covered with clotted blood and dust, the most frightful spectacle which ever disgraced a royal residence, save the seraglio. After several hours' exposure, some appearance of life was perceived in one of the mutilated carcasses. The man had been stabbed and gashed in various parts, his body was removed into the guardroom, and means were taken to restore animation; the efforts succeeded; he entirely recovered, and was pardoned by Lord Camden; he was an extraordinarily fine young man, above six feet high, the son of a Mr Keogh, an opulent landholder of Rathfarnham; he did not, however, change his principles, and was, ultimately, sent out of the country.

[14] THE CASTLE GUARDROOM; FROM *JACK HINTON, THE GUARDSMAN* BY CHARLES LEVER

Charles Lever (1806–1872) originally studied medicine but in 1842 gave up work as a doctor to write and edit the Dublin University Magazine. *He became one of the most popular writers of the Victorian age, producing a stream of rollicking novels mainly of Anglo-Irish life; Jack Hinton was one of his earliest. Set in the early 1800s, it is the story of 'an exceedingly young English guardsman coming over to Ireland at the time of the Duke of Richmond's viceroyalty when every species of rackety doings was in vogue'.*

When I next came to my senses, I found myself lying upon a sofa in a large room, of which I appeared the only occupant. A confused and misty recollection of my accident, some scattered fragments of my voyage, and a rather aching sensation in my head, were the only impressions of which I was well conscious. . . . The room, I have already said, was large; and the ceiling, richly stuccoed and ornamented, spoke of a day whose architecture was of a grand and massive character. The furniture, now old and time-worn, had once been handsome, even magnificent. Rich curtains of heavy brocaded silk, with deep gold fringes, gorgeously-carved and gilded chairs, in the taste of Louis XV; marble consoles stood between the windows, and a mirror of gigantic proportions occupied the chimney-breast. Years and neglect had not only done their worst, but it was evident that the hand of devastation had also been at work. The marbles were cracked; few of the chairs were available for use; the massive lustre, intended to shine with a resplendent glare of fifty wax-lights, was now made a resting-place for shakos, bear-skins, and foraging-caps; an ominous-looking star in the looking-glass bore witness to the bullet of a pistol; and the very Cupids carved upon the frame, who once were wont to smile blandly at each other, were now disfigured with cork moustachoes, and one of them even carried a pair of spurs in his mouth. Swords, sashes, and sabretashes, spurs and shot-belts, with guns, fishing-tackle, and tandem whips, were hung here and there upon the walls, which themselves presented the strangest spectacle of all, there not being a portion of them unoccupied by caricature sketches, executed in every imaginable species of taste, style, and colouring . . .

The owner of this singular chamber had, however, not merely devoted his walls to the purposes of an album, but he had also made them perform the part of a memorandum-book. Here were the 'meets' of the Kildare and the Dubber for the month of March; there, the turn of duty for the garrison of Dublin, interspersed with such fragments as the following: Mem. To dine at Mat Kean's on Tuesday, 4th – Not to pay Hennesy till he settles about the handicap – To ask Courtenay for Fanny Burke's fan: the same Fanny has pretty legs of her own – To tell Holmes to have nothing to do with Lanty Moore's niece, in regard to a reason! – Five to two on Giles' two-year-old, if Tom likes – NB–The mare is a roarer – A heavenly day, what fun they must have! – may the devil fire Tom O'Flaherty, or I would not be here now. These and a hundred other similar passages figured on every side, leaving me in a state of considerable mystification, not as to the character of my host, of which I could guess something, but as to the nature of his abode, which I could not imagine to be a barrack-room.

[15] GEORGE IV KISSES THE GIRLS; FROM *THE CROKER* *PAPERS 1808–1857*, EDITED BY R. POOL.

King George IV made his visit to Dublin in August 1821 (in an unusually
affable mood, having just heard the news of his wife's death) and was
received with enormous enthusiasm – which soon evaporated when he failed
to approve Catholic Emancipation.

John Wilson Croker (1780–1857) was a close friend of the King since
Regency days. Born in Galway and educated at Trinity College, he wrote
several drily satirical sketches of Irish life while in his twenties, and went on
to found and edit the famous Quarterly Review and make a highly successful
career in Tory politics. In old age, he was satirized himself as the unpleasant
Rigby in Disraeli's novel Coningsby.

August 20th. – The King held a *levée*, and previous to it received the
addresses of the Synod of Presbyterians, the Quakers, and the Catholic
bishops in the closet. He also had an investiture of St Patrick and the
Bath. Lord Graves, proxy for the Duke of Cumberland, and Lords
Donegal, Ormond, Meath, Roden, Fingal, and Courtown, were invested.

The address of the Catholic bishops was in bad taste; it talked too
much politics, and said that they were four-fifths of the population.
Everybody observed how unseemly this tone was at this time. Some
days after, Lord Donoughmore told me that he had written this address,
and he took great credit for having inserted these very passages. . . . I
cannot conceive how a man can be so blinded by vanity or party as not
see that his address is at least a thing not to boast of.

The *levée* which ensued was wonderfully crowded. I reckoned 1500
names, and was told there were 2000. I know not how many guineas
were offered for the loan of a dress sword, and I know two people who
were kept away by the want of this article of court dress. Some who
came had most incongruous swords, and there were many ludicrous
figures, but they were lost in the immense crowd, and many passed the
King without seeing or recognising him.

August 21st . . . Dressed for the drawing-room. By opening a large suite of rooms, and by publishing the King's desire that no gentlemen should come except in attendance on ladies, the crowd was not so inconvenient as at the *levée* though the numbers were greater. I should suppose that above 1000 ladies were presented . . . and their dresses were both rich and in good taste. When the rooms began to thin, about twelve o'clock, I walked about with Lord Lovaine, making our observations, and we both agreed that it was a drawing-room quite equal, except as to jewels and titles, to any we had seen at St James's. By some interruption, about one-third of the company were cut off and prevented coming up with the stream. The attendants thought there were no more to be presented, so the door of the presence chamber was shut, and the King made his bows and retired. In a few minutes it was found that the anterooms were again full (the interruption in the train of carriages having been obviated). What was to be done? The King had retired and was undressed. On the other hand, the ladies were dressed and had no mind to retire; after a good deal of *pourparlers*, the King was told of the circumstance, and with great good nature he put on his fine coat, came back to the presence chamber, and went through the ceremony of kissing about 300 ladies more.

[16] THE VICE-REGAL COURT IN THE 1870S; FROM *RECOLLECTIONS OF DUBLIN CASTLE AND DUBLIN SOCIETY* (ANON), 1902.

The castle remained the centre of the Dublin social season until the First World War. The State apartments have now been splendidly restored and are used for public receptions.

The Castle, where this Card King lived, was a great centre of the city. In my childhood, boyhood, youth, manhood, I suppose no word rang out more loudly or more frequently in one's ears, or inspired such an awesome feeling. Often I passed it; often was I in it. There were held the 'levys,' 'draw'n rooms,' 'Patrick's balls,' dinners, concerts, and dances *galore*. You went from Westmoreland Street – often sounded West*more*-land Street – to the Royal Exchange, a rather stately building, which brought you to the steep 'Cark Hill,' *i.e.*, Cork Hill, on the top of which was the awful enclosure. It was rather an imposing place, with a great gateway and a guard-house adjoining, out of which – for what reason Heaven knows! – a large sort of church steeple rose. But everything in Dublin is more or less unaccountable. The older churches are mostly without steeples, while a guard-house *has* one. Within, there is a large and stately court-yard, and on the left an archway, opening on a second, viz., 'The Lower Kestle yard'; though it seems undignified to call these august enclosures 'yards.' Round the first court were the residences of the high and mighty officers – the Chamberlain (minus 'Lord') – Comptroller, all squeezed, sorely cribbed and cabined into little sets of rooms, much as those of smaller degree are at the Ambassadors' Court, St James's Palace. It was often a pitiable thing for those poor creatures, wives and children – who had all to 'cram' into these straitened apartments. Their wage was miser-able enough, but there was free lodging, with occasional board, and it may be coals; consequently, these offices were much sought after by the broken down peer or baronet, to whom such quarters were an object; while the Lord Lieutenant was glad to have persons of title about him. The aides-de-camp lived on their very position – on the strength of which they might have been at free board every day of their life. The *paid* aide – this was much insisted on – had, I believe, about £100 a year, with quarters; the extra, nothing.

And the household! – that awe-inspiring word! There was the 'Private Secretary,' the 'additional Private Secretary,' and, odd to say, 'Assistant Private Secretary,' State Steward, Comptroller, Gentleman Usher, Chamberlain, and actually a 'Master of the Horse,' who looked after the job-master-hired animals mentioned already. Then came three paid aides and four unpaid ditto. There were also 'gentlemen at large,' and 'gentlemen-in-waiting.' There was the 'Physician in Ordinary,' 'Surgeon in Ordinary,' 'Surgeon to the Household,' 'Surgeon Oculist,' and 'Surgeon Dentist.' These last were entitled to appear at the levees and to be so announced, and, for aught I know, to walk in the tag, rag, and bob-tail procession.

A nice lady friend of my own, suffering from toothache, hurried to her dentist, and sent in her name. 'Is it see you today, Ma'am? It's quite impossible. Isn't he upstairs undressin' himself to go to the levy?'

Christ Church Cathedral

[17] THE MIRACULOUS CRUCIFIX AT CHRIST CHURCH CATHEDRAL;
FROM THE *TOPOGRAPBIA HIBERNIA* BY GIRALDUS CAMBRENSIS,
IN *STRONGBOW'S CONQUEST OF IRELAND* BY F. P. BARNARD.

*The original Christchurch or the church of the Holy Trinity was built in wood
during the reign of King Sitric around 1038. Giraldus Cambrensis, the first
Norman historian of Ireland, had come to Ireland in 1184 with Prince John,
Henry II's ten-year-old son, and was offered but refused an Irish
archbishopric.*

Of the cross at Dublin which spake and bore testimony to the truth.
We come now to treat of occurrences in modern times. There is a cross
possessed of great virtues in the church of the Holy Trinity at Dublin,
and having the features of a crucifix. Not many years before the arrival
of the English, namely, in the time of the Ostmen, this crucifix opened
its sacred mouth and spoke in the presence of many persons who heard
the words. The circumstances were these: one of the citizens had
invoked the crucifix as the sole witness, and a kind of surety, in a
contract which he had entered into. In process of time, however, the
party with whom he had contracted repudiating his engagements, and
persisting in denying his obligation for the money which the other had
lent him on his credit, his fellow citizens, rather ironically than seriously, tried the case before the cross, and having assembled in the
church for that purpose, the crucifix, on being adjured and called to
witness, gave testimony to the truth in the presence of many persons
who heard the words.

How the same cross became immoveable
At the time that earl Richard [*Strongbow*] came first with an army to
Dublin, the citizens, having a presage in their minds of the many evils
which were impending, and fearing that the city would be taken, as

they despaired of its defence, were contriving how they could make their escape by sea, and wished to carry away this cross with them to the islands. They used every effort in their power to effect this; but the whole population of the city failed to move it from its place either by force or contrivance.

[18] THE NORMANS REBUILD CHRIST CHURCH CATHEDRAL, AND A DESCRIPTION OF STRONGBOW; FROM *THE DESCRIPTION OF IRELAND* BY RICHARD STANYHURST IN HOLINSHED'S *CHRONICLES*.

Strongbow, the Norman conqueror of Ireland, was buried 'with great state', Giraldus relates, in the chancel of Christ Church in 1176. But the so-called Strongbow Monument is in fact a misnomer. His tomb was so badly damaged by a collapse of the Cathedral roof in 1562 that Sir Henry Sidney substituted the tomb of one of the Earls of Desmond.

In the yeare one thousand two hundred and foure score, Robert Uffort came the third time to occupie the roome of lord chiefe iustice in Ireland, resuming that roome into his hands againe. . . . And about the same time, the citie of Dublin was defaced by fire, and the steeple of Christs church utterlie destroied. The citizens before they went about to repare their owne privat buildings, agreed togither to make a collection for reparing the ruines of that ancient building first begun by the Danes, and continued by Citrius prince of Dublin at the instance of Donat sometime bishop of that citie, and dedicated to the blessed trinitie.

At length Strangbow earle of Penbroke, Fitzstephans, & Laurence, that for his vertue was called saint Laurence archbishop of Dublin, and his foure successors, John of Evesham, Henrie Scortchbill, and Lucas, and last of all Iohn de saint Paule finished it.

The earle [Strongbow] was somewhat ruddie and of sanguine complexion and freckle faced, his eies greie, his face feminine, his voice small, and his necke little, but somewhat of a high stature: he was verie liberall, courteous and gentle: what he could not compassae and bring to passe in déed, he would win by good words and gentle spéeches. In time of peace he was more readie to yéeld and obeie, than to rule and beare swaie. Out of the campe he was more like to a souldior companion than a capteine or ruler: but in the campe and in the warres he caried with him the state and countenance of a valiant capteine. Of himselfe he would not adventure anie thing, but being advised and set on, he refused no attempts: for of himselfe he would not rashlie adventure, or presumptuouslie take anie thing in hand. In the fight and battell he was a most assured token and signe to the whole companie, either to stand valiantlie to the fight, or for policie to retire. In all chances of warre he was still one and the same maner of man, being neither dismaid with adversitie, nor puffed up with prosperitie.

[19] FOUR IRISH KINGS ARE KNIGHTED IN CHRIST CHURCH CATHEDRAL IN 1395; FROM *FROISSART IN BRITAIN* BY SIR HENRY NEWBOLT.

This account in Froissart's famous fifteenth-century Chronicles comes from Henry Castide, an English squire who had been taken hostage as a youth while fighting in Ireland and married his Irish captor's daughter. As a fluent Irish speaker, he is commanded by Richard II in 1394 to 'give attendance' on four Irish kings who had agreed to swear fealty to the English crown and bring them 'to reason and to the usage and customs of England'.

They had a fair house to lodge in in Dublin, and I was charged to abide still with them, and not to depart; and so two or three days I suffered them to do as they listed, and said nothing to them, but they followed their own appetites; they would sit at the table and make countenance neither good nor fair; then I thought I should cause them to change that manner. They would cause their minstrels, their servants and varlets, to sit with them, and to eat in their own dish and to drink of their cups, and they shewed me that the usage of their country was good, for they said in all things (except their beds) they were and lived as common.

So the fourth day I ordained other tables to be covered in the hall after the usage of England, and I made these four kings to sit at the high table, and their minstrels at another board, and their servants and varlets at another beneath them; whereof by seeming they were displeased, and beheld each other and would not eat, and said how I would take from them their good usage wherein they had been nourished.

Then I answered them, smiling to appease them, that it was not honourable for their estate to do as they did before, and that they must leave it and use the custom of England, and that it was the king's pleasure they should so do, and how I was charged so to order them.

When they heard that they suffered it, because they had put themselves under the obeisance of the king of England, and persevered in the same as long as I was with them. Yet they had one use, which I knew well was used in their country, and that was, they did wear no breeches. I caused breeches of linen cloth to be made for them.

While I was with them I caused them to leave many rude things, as well in clothing as in other causes. Much ado I had at the first to cause them to wear gowns of silk furred with minnever and gray; for before, these kings thought themselves well apparelled when they had on a mantle. They rode always without saddles and stirrups, and with great pain I made them ride after our usage.

And on a time I demanded them of their belief; wherewith they were not content, and said how they believed on God and on the Trinity as well as we.

Then I demanded on what pope was their affection.

They answered me, on him of Rome.

Then I demanded if they would not gladly receive the order of knighthood, and that the king of England should make them knights according to the usage of France and England and other countries.

Four Irish kings are instructed in English manners in Dublin before being knighted in Christ Church Cathedral, 1395; from Froissart's fifteenth-century *Chronicles*

They answered how they were knights already and that sufficed for them.

I asked where they were made knights, and how, and when.

They answered that in the age of seven year they were made knights in Ireland, and that a king maketh his son a knight, and if the son have no father alive, then the next of his blood may make him knight; and then this young knight shall begin to joust with small spears, such as they may bear with their ease, and run against a shield set on a stake in the field, and the more spears he breaketh, the more he shall be honoured.

I knew their manner well enough, though I did demand it. But then I said that the knighthood that they had taken in their youth sufficed not to the king of England, but I said he should give them after another manner.

They demanded how.

I answered that it should be in the holy church, which was the most worthiest place. Then they inclined somewhat to my words.

Within two days after, the Earl of Ormond came to them, who could right well speak the language, for some of his lands lay in those parts: he was sent to them by the king and his council. They all honoured him, and he them: then he fell in sweet communication with them, and he demanded of them how they liked me.

They answered and said, 'Well; for he hath well shewed us the usage of this country; wherefore we ought to thank him and so we do.'

This answer pleased well the Earl of Ormond. Then he entered little and little to speak of the order of chivalry, which the king would they should receive: he shewed it them from point to point, how they should behave themselves, and what pertained to knighthood.

The Earl's words pleased much these four kings, whose names were these: first, the great O'Neal, king of Meath; the second, O'Brien of Thomond, king of Thomond; the third, Arthur MacMorrough, king of Leinster; the fourth, O'Connor, king of Connaught and Erne: they were made knights by King Richard of England in the cathedral church of Dublin, dedicate of St John Baptist [Christ Church] it was done on our Lady Day in March; it fell on a Thursday.

These four kings watched all the night before in the church, and the next day at high Mass time with great solemnity they were made knights, and with them Sir Thomas Ourghem, Sir Jonathan Pado, and Sir John Pado his cousin.

These kings sat that day at the table with King Richard: they were regarded of many folks, because their behaving was strange to the manner of England and other countries, and ever naturally men desire to see novelties.

[20] LAMBERT SIMNEL IS CROWNED IN CHRIST CHURCH, 1487; FROM HOLINSHED'S *CHRONICLES*.

England has just emerged from the Wars of the Roses, Henry VII is King, but his justiciar in Ireland, Garret More, the Great Earl of Kildare, chooses instead to crown a ten-year-old boy, claimed to be the Yorkist heir. The coup failed; Lambert Simnel was spared to turn spits in the royal kitchens, and Kildare – still safe on his own ground in Dublin – was granted an unconditional pardon.

To (the) earle (Gerald, Earl of Kildare) came the wily priest, Sir Richard Simon, bringing with him a lad that was his scholar named Lambert, who he feigned to be the son of George, Earl of Clarence, lately escaped from the Tower of London. And the boy could reckon up his pedigree so readily and learned of the priest such princely behaviour that he greatly moved the said earl, and many of the nobles of Ireland . . . either to think, or to feign, that the world might believe they thought, verily this child to be Edward, Earl of Warwick, the Duke of Clarence his lawful son.

And although King Henry more than half marred their sport in showing the right earl through all the streets of London, yet the lady Margaret, Duchess of Burgoyne, sister to Edward the Fourth, her nephew John de la Pole, the Lord Lovell, Sir Thomas Broughton, Knight, and divers other captains of this conspiracy, devised to abuse the colour of this young earl's name, for preferring their purpose.

Wherefore it was blazed in Ireland, that the King, to mock his subjects, had schooled a boy to take upon him the Earl of Warwick's name, and had showed him about London, to blind the eyes of the simple folk, and to defeat the lawful inheritor of the good Duke of Clarence, their countryman and protector during his life, with whose lineage they also derived title in right to the crown.

In all haste they assembled at Dublin and there in Christs Church they crowned this idol, honoring him with titles imperial, feasting and triumphing; raising mighty shouts and cries, carrying him from thence to the castle on tall men's shoulders that he might be seen and noted, as he was surely an honourable child to look upon.

Herewith assembling their forces together, they provided themselves with ships and embarking therein, they took to the sea and landing in Lancashire pressed forwards till they came to Newark upon Trent. Thereupon ensued the battle of Stoke commonly called Martin Stuarts Field, wherein Lambert and his master were taken, but yet pardoned of life and were not executed. The earl of Lincoln, the Lord Lovell, Martin Stuart, the Almail Captain and Maurice Fitzthomas, Captain of the Irish, were slain, and all their power discomfited as in the English history it may further appear.

St Patrick's Cathedral

*St Patrick's, Dublin's second great Norman cathedral, dating from the mid-
thirteenth century, stood just outside the medieval city walls. Gerald, Earl of
Kildare is the famous 'Garret More' who had tried to crown Lambert Simnel
king (see p. 54). Twenty-five years on, the rivalry between the Yorkist
Geraldines and the Lancastrian Ormondes is still raging. The two armies meet
at St Patrick's and Kildare is persuaded to 'chance his arm'. The chapter-house
door can still be seen at the west end of the nave leaning against a column.*

Girald Fitzgirald earle of Kildare, son to Thomas Fitzgirald, of who
mention hath beene made in the latter end of the former storie, a mightie
man of stature, full of honor & courage, who had beene deputie & lord
iustice of Ireland first & last 33 yeeres, deceased at Kildare the third of
September, & lieth intoomed in the queere of Christes church at Dublin,
in a chappell by him founded. Betweene him & Iames Butler earle of
Ormond (their owne gelousies fed with envie & ambition, kindled with
certeine lewd factious abettors of either side) as generallie to all noblemen, so especiallie to both these houses everie incident, ever since the
ninth yeare of Henrie the seventh, bred some trouble in Ireland. The plot
of which mutuall grudge was grounded upon the factious dissention, that
was raised in England betweene the houses of Yorke & Lancaster, Kildare
cleaving to Yorke, and Ormond relieng to Lancaster. To the upholding of
which discord, both these noble men laboured with tooth and naile to
overcrow, and consequentlie to overthrow one the other. And for somuch
as they were in honour peeres, they wrought by hooke and by crooke to
be in authoritie superiours. The governement therfore in the reigne of
Henrie the seventh, being cast on the house of Kildare; Iames earle of
Ormond a deepe and a farre reaching man, giving backe like a butting
ram to strike the harder push, devised to inveigle his adversarie by

submission & courtesie, being not then able to overmatch him with stoutnesse or preheminence. Whereupon Ormond addressed his letters to the deputie specifieng a slander raised on him and his, that he purposed to deface his governement, and to withstand his authorities. And for the cleering of himselfe and of his adherents, so it stood with the deputie his pleasure, he would make his speedie repaire to Dublin, & there in an open audience would purge himselfe of all such odious crimes, of which he was wrongfullie suspected.

To this reasonable request had the lord deputie no sooner condescended, than Ormond with a puissant armie marched towards Dublin, incamping in an abbeie in the suburbs of the citie, named saint Thomas court. The approching of so great an armie of the citizens suspected, and also of Kildares counsellors greatlie disliked, lastlie the extortion that the lawlesse souldiers used in the pale by severall complaints detected: these three points, with diverse other suspicious circumstances laid and put togither, did minister occasion rather of further discord, than of anie present agreement. Ormond persisting still in his humble sute, sent his messenger to the lord deputie, declaring that he was prest and readie to accomplish the tenour of his letters, and there did attend (as became him) his lordship his pleasure. . . .

Kildare with this mild message intreated, appointed the meeting to be at saint Patrike his church: . . . the citizens and Ormond his armie fell at some iar, for the oppression and exaction with which the souldiers surcharged them, With whom as part of the citizens bickered, so a round knot of archers rushed into the church, meaning to have murthered Ormond, as the capteine and belwedder of all these lawlesse rabble. The carle of Ormond suspecting that he had beene betraied, fled to the chapiter house, put to the doore, sparring it with might and maine. The citizens in their rage, imagining that everie post in the church had beene one of the souldiers, shot hab or nab at randon up to the roodloft and to the chancell, leaving some of their arrowes sticking in the images.

Kildare pursuing Ormond to the chapiter house doore, undertooke on his honor that he should receive no villanie. Wherupon the recluse craving his lordships hand to assure him his life, there was a clift in the chapiter house doore, pearsed at a trise, to the end both the earles should have shaken hands and be reconciled. But Ormond surmising that this drift was intended for some further treacherie, that if he would stretch out his hand, it had beene percase chopt off, refused that proffer; until Kildare stretcht in his hand to him, and so the doore was opened, they both imbraced, the storme appeased, and all their quarrels for that present rather discontinued than ended.

[22] THE GREAT EARL OF CORK'S TOMB IS PUT IN
ITS PLACE, 1635; FROM *THE LIFE AND LETTERS OF THE
GREAT EARL OF CORK* BY DOROTHEA TOWNSHEND.

Richard Boyle, the Great Earl of Cork, was the most successful of all the Elizabethans who came to Ireland to seek their fortune. He acquired vast estates and became Lord Treasurer of Ireland. In 1630 his 'dearest, dear wife' Catherine Fenton, who had borne him fifteen children, died suddenly and was buried in St Patrick's. The tomb he commissioned as her monument was to become the first battlefield in a power struggle between the aged Earl and the new Lord Deputy, Thomas Wentworth, later Earl of Strafford.

In May the Pursuivant-at-arms completed a design for a magnificent tomb, which was to commemorate Lady Cork's parents and grandparents as well as herself. The stonecutter of Chapel Izod, who was already at work on the restoration of Maynooth Castle for the Earl of Kildare, was intrusted with this important piece of work, and it was estimated that the cost, including painting, gilding, and iron railings, would be £300. Eventually, between the cost of the iron supplied from the Earl's own forges, fees to the Dean and Chapter, and 'liberalities among the workmen,' the expense rose to £400. But the tomb was to cost him dearer than a few hundred pounds. By a strange irony of fate his troubles began at his wife's grave, and it was that stately marble erection that gave Strafford his much-desired opportunity to humiliate the Great Earl.

Richard Boyle, the Great Earl of Cork, engraving from a portrait at
Hardwick Hall

The tomb was not completed till January 1633; then the Earl wrote:
'This night the bones of my wife's grandfather, Dr Weston, sometime
Lord Justice and Lord Chancellor of Ireland, of her father, Sir Geoffrey
Fenton, Kt, principal secretary of state in Ireland, and the coffin
wherein my lost wife's dead body was enclosed, were all removed out of
the old tomb wherein they were all three buried in St Patrick's church,
and all placed in the new vault of my wife's tomb by me made and
erected at the upper end of the chancel of the said St Patrick's church,
expecting a joyful resurrection.'

And then arrived the great Lord Deputy. . . . In the eyes of
[*Strafford*] he [*the Earl of Cork*] was but a doting old Polonius, and
not an honest dotard either. It was very convenient for Wentworth
that Archbishop Laud had already a complaint against Cork which
would be a good opening for the course of humiliation that the
Deputy was preparing for the Great Earl, and would also give

opportunities for a little plain speaking to several archbishops and deans.

To Laud's mind the black marble tomb which Cork had erected in St Patrick's Cathedral was nothing less than a scandal. Laud's trusted emissary Bramhall had written of it in horror as soon as he arrived in Dublin, telling that the tomb was 'erected in the proper place of the altar as if it were contrived to give it worship and reverence which the chapter and whole church are bound by special statutes to give towards the east.'

This commotion at first merely astonished the Earl of Cork, and he sent over letters to explain that his tomb, although it certainly stood at the east end of the cathedral, so far from standing on the site of the communion table, was placed in front of a blocked-up doorway. But protests and explanations were of no avail; Laud was determined that the tomb should be removed, and Wentworth was delighted to be the instrument of such a humiliation to Cork. . . .

It is true that commissioners were appointed to view the tomb before sentence was given, but the matter was really settled before they set foot in the cathedral. Lord Cork wrote that the commission examined some weak aged people as to where the altar had stood, but they spake by hearsay and to very little purpose. Wentworth, however, thought there was no need of human witnesses when the tomb itself spoke so much to the purpose. He wrote to Laud:

'I have issued a commission according to my warrant for viewing the Earl of Cork's tomb; the two archbishops and himself, with four other bishops and the two deans and chapters, were present when we met and made them all so ashamed that the Earl desires he may have leave to pull it down without reporting further with England; so I am content if the miracle be done, though Mahomet do it, and there is an end of the tomb before it came to be intombed indeed.'

And then the next spring, March 1635, Wentworth wrote triumphantly:

'The Earl of Cork's tomb is now quite removed: how he means to dispose of it I know not, but up it is put in boxes, as if it were march-panes and banquetting stuffs going down to the christening of my young master in the country. The wall is closed again, and as soon as it is dry and fit to be wrought upon, it shall be decently adorned or else – ! It costs me at least one fifty pounds for my share.'

Cork could but submit with the best grace he could muster up. Even in his diary he only records that it cost him £68 to remove the tomb to the side of the cathedral, and so the struggle ended, and the first triumph was scored to the Lord Deputy.

[23] JONATHAN SWIFT DESCRIBES HIS LIFE AS DEAN OF ST PATRICK'S IN 1733; FROM *THE CORRESPONDENCE OF JONATHAN SWIFT* EDITED BY ELRINGTON BALL.

Jonathan Swift (1667–1745), poet, satirist and philanthropist, was born in Dublin, and returned there to live full-time in 1713 when he was appointed Dean of St Patrick's. In black moods he regarded the post as banishment: during his years in London he had irretrievably offended the Whigs with his lampoons. In this extract he is writing more philosophically to one of his oldest friends, Alexander Pope.

Only a fragment of his Deanery remains, as part of the police station opposite the Cathedral.

I am told, to my great misfortune, that a very convenient offer happening of a coach with one gentleman and his sister coming to Ireland from their elder brother, your friend and neighbour, you waived the invitation pressed on you, alleging the fear you had of being killed here with eating and drinking; by which I find that you have given some credit to a notion of our great plenty and hospitality. . . .

If you had ventured to come over you should have had a very convenient warm apartment more open than usual in great cities, with a garden as large as your green plot that fronts the Thames, and another about two hundred yards further, larger than your great garden and with more air, but without any beauty. You should have small dinners of what you liked, and good wine, and you eat and drink so little that I could well afford it, considering how often you would be invited either with me or without me. The conveniences of taking the air, winter or summer, do far exceed those in London; for the two large strands just at two edges of the town, are as firm and dry in winter, as in summer. There are at least six or eight gentlemen of sense, learning, good humour and taste, able and desirous to please you, and orderly females, some of the better sort, to take care of you. These were the motives that I have frequently made use of to entice you hither; and there would be no failure among the best people here, of any honours that could be done you.

As to myself, I declare my health is so uncertain that I dare not venture among you at present. I hate the thoughts of London, where I am not rich enough to live otherwise than by shifting, which is now too late. Neither can I have conveniences in the country for three horses and two servants, and many others which I have here at hand. I am one of the governors of all the hackney coaches, carts and carriages, round this town, who dare not insult me like your rascally wagoners or coachmen, but give me the way; nor is there one Lord or squire for a hundred of yours, to turn me out of the road, or run over me with their coaches and six. Thus, I make some advantage of the public poverty, and give you the reasons for what I once writ, why I choose to be a freeman among slaves, rather than a slave among freemen. Then, I walk the streets in peace without being justled, nor ever without a thousand blessings from my friends the vulgar. I am Lord Mayor of one hundred and twenty houses, I am absolute lord of the greatest Cathedral in the kingdom, am at peace with the neighbouring Princes, the Lord Mayor of the city and the Archbishop of Dublin; only the latter, like the King of France, sometimes attempts encroachments on my dominions, as old Lewis did upon Lorraine.

[24] A VISIT TO SWIFT'S DEANERY IN THE 1730S;
FROM *THE MEMOIRS OF LETITIA PILKINGTON.*

Letitia Pilkington (1712–1750), the pretty young wife of a penniless Irish parson, met Dean Swift when his eccentricities had already become marked. Swift befriended the young couple generously and found Letitia's husband a job in England. The marriage soon broke up, Letitia returned to Dublin, destitute, and was supported by Swift's friend, Dr Delany. Her memoirs were published-in 1748, three years after Swift had died, probably from Menière's disease which had produced his apparent insanity.

On our return to the Deanery House, we found there waiting our coming Dr Delany and Mr Rochford, to whose wife A *Letter of Advice to a new-married Lady* (published since in the Dean's works) was written, and which, by the by, the lady did not take as a compliment, either to her or the sex, Mr Pilkington, Dr Sheridan, author of *The Art of Punning,* with two or three other clergymen (who usually passed Sunday evening with the Dean). Mr Pilkington, and I were for going home, but the Dean told us: 'He gave us leave to stay to supper'; which from him was a sufficient invitation. The Dean then pulled out of his pocket a little gold runlet, in which was a bottle-screw, and, opening a bottle of wine, he decanted it off; the last glass being muddy, he called to Mr Pilkington to drink it: 'For', says he, 'I always keep some poor parson to drink the foul wine for me.' Mr Pilkington, entering into his humour, thanked him, and told him: 'He did not know the difference, but was glad to get a glass at any rate.' 'Why then', says the Dean, 'you shan't, for I'll drink it myself: why p–x take you, you are wiser than a paltry curate whom I asked to dine with me a few days ago; for upon my making the same speech to him, he told me he did not understand such usage, and so walked off without his dinner. By the same token, I told the gentleman who recommended him to me that the fellow was a blockhead, and I had done with him.'

The Dean shewed me into a little street-parlour (where sat his housekeeper, a matron-like gentlewoman, at work). 'Here', says he; 'Mrs Brent, take care of this child (meaning me) and see she does no mischief, while I take my walk out within doors.' The Deanery House has I know not how many pair of back-stairs in it, the preceding Dean who built it, being it seems extremely fearful of fire, was resolved there should be many ways to escape in case of danger.

The Dean then ran up the great-stairs, down one pair of backstairs, up another, in so violent a manner that I could not help expressing my uneasiness to the good gentlewoman lest he should fall and be hurt. She said: 'It was a customary exercise with him, when the weather did not permit him to walk abroad.'

I told Mrs Brent 'I believed the Dean was extremely charitable.' 'Indeed, Madam', replied she, 'nobody can be more so; his income is not above six-hundred pounds a year, and every year he gives above the half of it in private pensions to decayed families; besides this, he keeps five-hundred pounds in the constant service of the industri- ous poor: this he lends out in five pounds at a time, and takes the payment back at twelve-pence a week; this does them more service than if he gave it to them entirely, as it obliges them to work and at the same time keeps up this charitable fund for the assistance of many. You cannot imagine what numbers of poor tradesmen, who have even wanted proper tools to carry on their work have by this small loan been put into a prosperous way and brought up their families in credit. The Dean (added she) has found out a new method of being charitable, in which however, I believe, he will have but few followers; which is, to debar himself of what he calls the superfluities of life, in order to administer to the necessities of the distressed: you just saw an instance of it; the money a coach would have cost him he gave to a poor man, unable to walk. When he dines alone, he drinks a pint of beer, and gives away the price of a pint of wine; and thus he acts in numberless instances.'

[25] Dean Swift's final descent into insanity, 1740s; from *The Memoirs of Letitia Pilkington*.

The first proof he gave of his incivility was affronting the Lord Lieutenant at the Lord Mayor's table, who, because he had not paid his compliments to him in due form, he very civilly accosted by the extraordinary title of 'You fellow with the Blue String'. Some little time after this he invited two clergymen to take the air with him, and when he got them into a coach, he did so belabour them and knock their heads together, that they were obliged to cry out for assistance.

From this he fell into a deep melancholy and knew nobody. I was told the last sensible words he uttered were on this occasion: Mr Handel, when about to quit Ireland, went to take his leave of him. The servant was a considerable time before he could make the Dean understand; which, when he did, he cried, 'Oh, a German and a genius! A prodigy! Admit him.' The servant did so, just to let Mr Handel behold the ruins of the greatest wit that ever lived along the tide of time, where all at length are lost.

[26] Swift's death and the rape of his locks, 1745; from *The Life of Doctor Swift* by Thomas Sheridan.

Thomas Sheridan (1719–1788) was Swift's godson and the first to publish his collected writings. He made his name as actor-manager of Dublin's Smock Alley Theatre (see p. 204). His son, Richard Brinsley Sheridan, brilliantly continued the family tradition in London.

The behaviour of the citizens on this occasion [*Swift's death*], gave the strongest proof of the deep impression he had made on their minds. Though he had been, for so many years, to all intents and purposes dead to the world, and his departure from that state seemed a thing rather to be wished than deplored, yet no sooner was his death announced, than the citizens gathered from all quarters, and forced their way in crowds into the house, to pay the last tribute of grief to their departed benefactor. Nothing but lamentations were heard all around the quarter where he lived, as if he had been cut off in the vigour of his years. Happy were they who first got into the chamber where he lay, to procure, by bribes to the servants, locks of his hair, to be handed down as sacred relicks to their posterity. And so eager were numbers to obtain at any price this precious memorial, that in less than an hour, his venerable head was entirely stripped of all its silver ornaments, so that not a hair remained.

[27] SIR WALTER SCOTT VISITS ST PATRICK'S, 1825; FROM
THE LIFE OF SIR WALTER SCOTT BY J. G. LOCKHART.

The famous Scottish novelist visited Dublin accompanied by his son-in-law and future biographer Lockhart (who is here writing to his wife). Scott was enthusiastically lionized by Dubliners, and reported to his friend, Maria Edgeworth, that he found the city 'splendid beyond my expectations'.

. . . one thinks of nothing but Swift there – the whole cathedral is merely his tomb. Your papa [*i.e. Scott*] hung long over the famous inscription, which is in gilt letters upon black marble; and seemed vexed there was not a ladder at hand that he might have got nearer the bust (apparently a very fine one), by Roubilliac, which is placed over it. This was given by the piety of his printer, Faulkener. According to this, Swift had a prodigious double chin; and Peveril remarked that the severity of the whole countenance is much increased by the absence of the wig, which, in the prints, conceals the height and gloom of the brow, the uncommon massiveness and breadth of the temple-bones, and the Herculean style in which the head fits in to the neck behind. Stella's epitaph is on the adjoining pillar – close by. Sir Walter seemed not to have thought of it before (or to have forgotten, if he had), but to judge merely from the wording that Swift himself wrote it. She is described as 'Mrs Hester Johnson, better known to the world by the name of Stella, under which she is celebrated in the writings of Dr Jonathan Swift, Dean of this cathedral.' 'This,' said Sir Walter, 'the Dean might say – any one else would have said more.'

[28] SWIFT'S EPITAPH; TRANSLATED BY W. B. YEATS.

Swift's epitaph on himself is the Latin inscription in St Patrick's, above his tomb. Yeats called it 'the greatest epitaph in history'.

> Swift has sailed into his rest;
> Savage indignation there
> Cannot lacerate his breast.
> Imitate him if you dare,
> World-besotted traveller; he
> Served human liberty.

A tourist admires the monument to Dean Swift in St Patrick's Cathedral, engraving from Walker's *Hibernian Magazine*, 1802

[29] THACKERAY ATTENDS MORNING SERVICE IN ST PATRICK'S;
FROM *AN IRISH SKETCHBOOK* BY W. M. THACKERAY.

William Makepeace Thackeray, who had not yet made his name as a novelist, wrote his Irish Sketchbook in 1842 as a sequel to a Paris Sketchbook. The gaunt ruin he found was soon afterwards to be restored to its present form by the munificence of Sir Benjamin Guinness, later Lord Ardilaun whose statue stands outside the entrance to the cathedral.

The service at Saint Patrick's is finely sung; and the shameless English custom of retreating after the anthem, is properly prevented by locking the gates, and having the music after the sermon. The interior of the cathedral itself, however, to an Englishman who has seen the neat and beautiful edifices of his own country, will be anything but an object of admiration. The greater part of the huge old building is suffered to remain in gaunt decay, and with its stalls of sham Gothic, and the tawdry old rags and gimcracks of the 'most illustrious order of Saint Patrick,' (whose pasteboard helmets, and calico banners, and lath swords, well characterize the humbug of chivalry which they are made to represent,) looks like a theatre behind the scenes. 'Paddy's Opera,' however, is a noble performance; and the Englishman may here listen to a half-hour sermon, and in the anthem to a bass singer whose voice is one of the finest ever heard.

Marsh's Library

[30] Swift's epitaph on Archbishop Marsh, 1716; from *All Graduates and Gentlemen* by Muriel McCarthy.

The beautiful library adjoining St Patrick's, which contains many of Swift's books, was founded in 1700 by Narcissus Marsh, Provost of Trinity College and later Archbishop of Armagh, to provide a free library for scholars and dispel the dismal ignorance he found among his own Trinity students. Though one of Swift's earliest patrons, he did not earn his affection. Swift wrote this spiteful character study three years before Marsh's death.

Marsh has the reputation of most profound and universal learning; this is the general opinion, neither can it be easily disproved. An old rusty iron-chest in a banker's shop, strongly lockt and wonderful heavy, is full of gold; this is the general opinion, neither can it be disproved, provided the key be lost, and what is in it be wedged so close that it will not by any motion discover the metal by the clinking. Doing good is his pleasure; and as no man consults another in his pleasures, neither does he in this . . . without all passions but fear, to which of all others he hath least temptation, having nothing to get or to lose; no posterity, relation or friend to be solicitous about; and placed by his station above the reach of fortune or envy . . . He is the first of human race, that with great advantages of learning, piety and station ever escaped being a man . . . He is so wise to value his own health more than other men's noses, so that the most honourable place at his table is much the worst, especially in summer . . . No man will be either glad or sorry at his death, except his successor.

The Liberties

[31] HOW THE LIBERTIES DEFEND THEIR BOUNDARIES;
FROM THE *RECOLLECTIONS* OF JOHN O'KEEFFE.

The Liberties had belonged originally to the Great Abbey of Thomas Court,
but after its suppression by Henry VIII the largest of them was granted to his
Chancellor, William Brabazon. His descendant, the Earl of Meath, settled
large numbers of Huguenot weavers there, and it quickly became Dublin's
most prosperous quarter, though not for long.

John O'Keeffe (1747–1835) was a Dublin actor and later an immensely
popular London playwright. His Recollections, published in his extreme old
age, give a delightfully rambling picture of his early Dublin life.

In what is called the Earl of Meath's Liberty, the Lord Mayor of Dublin
has no jurisdiction, this quarter of the town having a court of its own.
This Liberty consists of some of the largest, finest, and richest streets in
Dublin; for instance, Meath-street, Francis-street, and the Coombie. In
the latter was the Weavers' Hall: over the gate a pedestrian gilt statue,
as large as life, of George the Second. The Lord Mayor walked the
boundaries, his sword-bearer before him; but when arrived at the point
where the Liberty begins, he was met by a certain chosen number of
people, who stopped his progress, and in a kind of seeming scuffle took
the sword from the sword-bearer: if not thus prevented, and the Lord
Mayor permitted to go on, wherever he went, with his sword of office
borne before him, the power of his warrant would reach; but this ceremony is done without the least riot or ill-will, being part of the business
previously well prepared. All this affair took place in one day, the first
of August, every third year. To this grand triennial festival people
flocked to Dublin from all parts of Ireland, England, Scotland, and even
from the Continent: it was always looked to with great joy. The Regatta
at Venice was something in this way.

[32] A PLEA FOR THE WEAVERS OF THE LIBERTIES BY DEAN SWIFT;
FROM *A BIOGRAPHY OF DUBLIN* BY CHRISTINE LONGFORD.

Another of the Liberties formed part of Swift's little 'kingdom' at St Patrick's.
He wrote this poem for a benefit performance for the weavers who were
already suffering the ruin of their trade by foreign imports. He also (as
Letitia Pilkington shows on pp. 64–5) practised charity from his own pocket
to help them. After his death, their situation became increasingly desperate
and they took drastic steps (see next extract) to discourage the wearing of
foreign cloth.

> We'll dress in manufactures made at home,
> Equip our kings and generals at the Combe.
> We'll rig in Meath Street Egypt's haughty queen,
> And Antony shall court her in rateen.
> In blue shalloon shall Hannibal be clad
> And Scipio trail an Irish purple plaid.
> In drugget dressed, of thirteen pence a yard,
> See Philip's son amidst his Persian guard;
> And proud Roxana, fired with jealous rage,
> With fifty yards of crape shall sweep the stage.

[33] THE CUTTING WEAVERS TAKE THEIR REVENGE;
FROM *IRISH VARIETIES* BY J. D. HERBERT.

Another party of lawless myrmidons were allowed frequently to commit
the greatest enormities, with no further punishment than dispersion by
a magistrate and soldiers; . . . These delinquents were weavers out of
work, and they considered their want of employment proceeded from
the fashion of wearing India nankeens, muslins and French silks. For
the purpose of deterring persons from the wear of these articles of
dress, they assembled in numerous bodies, and with knives made for
the occasion, cut every foreign dress worn by man or woman, no matter

.of what rank, if they were walking, and, in some cases, have stopped carriages, and destroyed ladies' dresses, putting every one to the knife, and in terror and fear of their life; for they were so infuriate, that description faints in giving an adequate idea of the horror and alarm many suffered under this wild and savage-like operation. It was a fine field for the doctors: nervous fevers produced them an abundant harvest.

Another mode of revenge taken by the lads of the loom was seizing on some mercer, haberdasher, or tailor, who might have been the vendor or maker of these objectionable dresses; and when they got such a well-known character in their possession they hurried him along, to utter dismay or hope of escape of him or friends, until they had done with him. After dragging him through miry channels – for this practice was followed in muddy weather generally – they brought him perhaps to the Weaver's Square . . . in the Liberties of Dublin . . . There they stripped him naked; then with a brush, not camel's hair, they daubed him over with warm tar; then a bag of feathers was got, and everyone who could get at the victim stuck the feathers over him: then they led him in mock triumph through the Liberties, and, when saturated, let him get home if he was able . . .

[34] A CLERGYMAN SURVEYS THE LIBERTIES, 1790S; FROM *REPORT ON THE POPULATION OF IRELAND* BY JAMES WHITELAW, QUOTED IN CONSTANTIA MAXWELL'S *DUBLIN UNDER THE GEORGES*.

The Reverend James Whitelaw (1749–1813) was the rector of St Catherine's church in the Liberties, and spent his life working among the Dublin poor. He died of fever, caught from his parishioners, in 1813.

The streets [in this part of the City] are generally narrow; the houses crowded together; the rears or backyards of very small extent, and some without accommodation of any kind. Of these streets, a few are the residence of the upper class of shopkeepers or others engaged in trade; but a far greater proportion of them, with their numerous lanes and alleys, are occupied by working manufacturers, by petty shopkeepers, the labouring poor, and beggars, crowded together to a degree distressing to humanity. A single apartment in one of these truly wretched habitations, rates from one to two shillings per week, and to lighten this rent two, three, or even four families become joint tenants. As I was usually out at very early hours on the survey I have frequently surprised from ten to sixteen persons, of all ages and sexes, in a room not 15 feet square, stretched on a wad of filthy straw, swarming with vermin, and without any covering, save the wretched rags that constituted their wearing apparel.

This crowded population wherever it obtains is almost universally accompanied by a very serious evil – a degree of filth and stench inconceivable except by such as have visited these scenes of wretchedness. Into the backyard of each house, frequently not 10 feet deep, is flung from the windows of each apartment, the ordure and other filth of its numerous inhabitants; from which it is so seldom removed, that I have seen it nearly on a level with the windows of the first floor; and the moisture that, after heavy rains, oozes from this heap, having frequently no sewer to carry it off, runs into the street, by the entry leading to the staircase. One instance out of a thousand that might be given, will be sufficient. When I attempted in the summer of 1798 to take the population of a ruinous house in Joseph's Lane near Castle market, I was interrupted in my progress by an inundation of putrid blood, alive with maggots, which had from an adjacent slaughter yard burst the back door, and filled the hall to the depth of several inches. By the help of a plank and some stepping stones which I procured for the purpose (for the inhabitants without any concern waded through it) I reached the staircase. It had rained violently, and from the shattered state of the roof a torrent of water made its way through every floor, from the garret to the ground. The sallow looks and filth of the wretches who crowded round me indicated their situation, though they seemed insensible to the stench, which I could scarce sustain for a few minutes. In the garret I found the entire family of a poor working shoemaker, seven in number, lying in a fever, without a human being to administer to their wants. On observing that his apartment had not a door, he informed me that his landlord, finding him not able to pay the week's rent in consequence of his sickness, had the preceding Saturday taken it away, in order to force him to abandon the apartment. I counted in this style 37 persons; and computed, that its humane proprietor received out of an absolute ruin which should be taken down by the magistrate as a public nuisance, a profit rent of above £30 per annum, which he extracted every Saturday night with unfeeling severity. . . .

In July 1798 the entire side of a house 4 storeys high, in School-House Lane, fell from its foundation into an adjoining yard, where it destroyed an entire dairy of cows. I ascended the remaining ruin, through the usual approach of shattered stairs, stench and filth. The floors had all sunk on the side now unsupported, forming so many inclined planes; and I observed with astonishment, that the inhabitants, above 30 in number, who had escaped destruction by the circumstance of the wall falling outwards, had not deserted their apartments. I was informed, that it had remained some months in this situation, and that the humane landlord claimed, and actually received for it, the usual rent. . . .

[35] A TRINITY STUDENT ATTENDS A MEETING OF THE UNITED IRISHMEN IN THE TAILORS' HALL, 1791; FROM *IRELAND SIXTY YEARS AGO* BY J. E. WALSH.

John Walsh (1816–1865) was the Irish Attorney General and Master of the Rolls. His account of eighteenth-century Dublin, especially its underworld (pp. 290–93), was first published in 1849 and reprinted again and again. Here an anonymous student penetrates the so-called Back Lane Parliament set up by the United Irishmen, before they turned to revolution (see p. 41).

The three men described all became leaders in the Rebellion of 1798: Hamilton Rowan fled, Tandy was sent to prison, and Wolfe Tone cut his throat with a penknife to escape execution.

I entered college in the year 1791, a year rendered memorable by the institution of the society of the United Irishmen. They held their meetings in an obscure passage called Back-Lane, leading from Corn Market to Nicholas-street. The very aspect of the place seemed to render it adapted for cherishing a conspiracy. It was in the locality where the tailors, skinners, and curriers held their guilds, and was the region of the operative democracy. I one evening proceeded from college, and found out Back-lane, and having inquired for the place of meeting, a house was pointed out to me, that had been the hall in which the corporation of tailors held their assemblies. I walked in without hesitation – no one forbidding me – and found the society in full debate, the Hon Simon Butler in the chair. I saw there, for the first time, the men with the three names, which were now become so familiar to the people of Dublin – Theobald Wolfe Tone, James Napper Tandy, and Archibald Hamilton Rowan.

The first was a slight effeminate-looking man, with a hatchet face, a long aquiline nose, rather handsome and genteel-looking, with lank, straight hair combed down on his sickly red cheek, exhibiting a face the most insignificant and mindless that could be imagined. His mode of speaking was in correspondence with his face and person. It was polite and gentlemanly, but totally devoid of any thing like energy or vigour. I set him down as a worthy, good-natured, flimsy man, in whom there was no harm, and as the least likely person in the world to do mischief to the state.

Tandy was the very opposite looking character. He was the ugliest man I ever gazed on. He had a dark, yellow, truculent-looking countenance, a long drooping nose, rather sharpened at the point, and the muscles of his face formed two cords at each side of it. He had a remarkable hanging-down look, and an occasional twitching or convulsive motion of his nose and mouth, as if he was snapping at something on the side of him while he was speaking.

Not so Hamilton Rowan. I thought him not only the most handsome, but the largest man I had ever seen. Tone and Tandy looked like pigmies beside him. His ample and capacious forehead seemed the seat of thought and energy; while with such an external to make him feared, he had a courtesy of manner that excited love and confidence. He held in his hand a large stick, and was accompanied by a large dog.

I had not been long standing on the floor, looking at and absorbed in the persons about me, when I was perceived, and a whisper ran round the room. Some one went up to the president, then turned round, and pointed to me. The president immediately rose, and called out that there was a stranger in the room. Two members advanced, and taking me under the arm, led me up to the president's chair, and there I stood to await the penalty of my unauthorized intrusion. I underwent an examination; and it was evident, from the questions, that my entrance was not accredited, but that I was suspected as a government spy. The 'battalion of testimony,' as it was called, was already formed, and I was supposed to be one of the corps. I, however, gave a full and true account of myself, which was fortunately confirmed by a member who knew something about me, and was ultimately pronounced a harmless 'gib,' and admitted to the honour of the sitting.

[36] The arrest of Lord Edward FitzGerald
in Thomas Street; from *Ireland, its Scenery,
Character etc.* by Mr and Mrs S. C. Hall.

Anna Maria Hall, née Fielding, was born in Dublin in 1800, was taken to live in London aged fifteen, and became an immensely popular novelist and playwright especially for her stories and sketches of Irish society.

Lord Edward FitzGerald, described here, was the son of the Duke of Leinster (see pp. 41 and 191) and another of the leaders of the 1798

Rebellion. The mysterious theft of his dagger was explained long after-
wards in Sheridan Lefanu's memoirs Seventy Years of Irish Life (1893): his
mother, Emma Lefanu, had stolen it on a patriotic impulse as a child from
Major Swan's house in North Great George Street, and hidden it in her
feather mattress.

Many matters of melancholy interest are associated with 'the
Liberties' of Dublin. The records of Thomas-street, and the streets in
its immediate vicinity, might fill a volume. It was in this street that
the gallant and unhappy Lord Edward Fitzgerald was taken, on the
19th of May, 1798. Major Sirr (town-major of the city), having received
information that he was concealed in the house of a man named
Murphy, a feather-dealer, in Thomas-street, proceeded, with a sufficient force, to arrest him. He was accompanied by Mr Ryan and Mr
Swan, both officers of Yeomanry. The two burst into the small
bedroom in which Lord Edward was sleeping, partly dressed. He was
armed with a dagger, with which he mortally wounded Mr Ryan,
having stabbed him in fourteen places, and severely injured Mr Swan.
Mr Sirr entered while Mr Ryan and Lord Edward were struggling on
the floor, and fired a pistol at his lordship; the ball entered the shoulder, and a short time afterwards, on the 3rd June, caused his death in
the prison of Newgate. 'The dagger,' says Mr Moore, 'was given, by
Lord Clare, a day or two after the arrest, to Mr Brown, a gentleman
well known and still living in Dublin, who has by some accident lost
it. He describes it to me, however, as being about the length of a large
case-knife, with a common buck-handle, the blade, which was two-
edged, being of a waved shape.' Of the room in which this tragic scene
occurred, Mr McManus made a drawing, in 1838. He informs us that
no change has taken place in its furniture or character since 1798,
except that it has received a coat of whitewash – one part of it,
however, having been left untouched; this spot is of about a foot
square, nearly three feet from the ground. It is covered with large
drops of faded blood.

The arrest of Lord Edward FitzGerald in Thomas Street, 1798; cartoon by George Cruikshank, from W. H. Maxwell's *History of the Irish Rebellion*. Both Lord Edward and Major Sirr (firing) are buried in St Werburgh's church nearby

[37] ROBERT EMMET'S RISING IN THOMAS STREET; FROM *IRELAND IN '98* BY R. R. MADDEN.

The abortive Emmet rising of 1803 provided a tragic coda to the 1798 Rebellion. Emmet, aged twenty-four, was captured in his hiding-place at Harolds Cross a few weeks later, and executed outside St Catherine's church in Thomas Street (see next extract). His famous speech at his trial, 'Let no man write my epitaph', earned him a place in the pantheon of Irish revolutionary heroes.

On the morning of the appointed day, June 23, 1803, the Kildare men were seen directing their steps towards the capital. They had collected round one of the depots in Thomas Street in unusual crowds, when about five o'clock they were persuaded by their officers to return home. Here treachery began. It is highly probable that its full extent was never known to Emmet, who was of a trusting, sanguine nature, constitutionally opposed to suspecting his fellow-men, and so single-minded that he regarded others with whom he was acting as like himself. The defection of the Wicklow and Wexford followers would have deterred a less ardent spirit than Emmet's from proceeding. He never quailed under the disappointment, though he bitterly felt the pain of their disloyalty. Towards dusk he directed the distribution of pikes to the waiting crowds in Thomas Street, and proceeded to make the necessary arrangements for the contemplated attack. The different leaders received their instructions; the forces were assembled in their respective places. These were to act on the signal of a rocket, which Emmet was to send up when he considered the time had arrived for the commencement of hostilities; Emmet and two of his followers were to head the attack on the Castle. At eight o'clock they sallied out of the depot in Thomas Street, and were met by ringing cheers from the insurgents. The consternation excited by their presence was vivid: every avenue was thronged, every window had its inquisitive heads; shopkeepers ran to their doors and beheld with amazement a lawless band of armed insurgents in the midst of a peaceable city, an hour at least before dark. The scene at first might have appeared amusing to a careless spectator, but when a rocket ascended and burst over the heads of the people, the aspect of affairs underwent a wonderful change. The impulse of the moment was self-preservation; those who a few moments before seemed to look on with vacant wonder, now assumed a face of horror and fled with precipitation. The wish to escape was simultaneous, and the eagerness with which the people retreated impeded their own flight, as they crowded upon one another down alleys, courtways and lanes, while the screams of women and children were heartrending. 'To the Castle!' shouted the enthusiastic leader, drawing his sword, while his followers clustered at his heels. On they went, but on reaching the Markethouse his adherents visibly diminished. On looking round him, he found hardly fifty to sustain him in his reckless attempt to storm the citadel. Among those who were left, a thirst for outrage and revenge had destroyed all discipline and supplanted patriotism. He hastened from front to rear, from man to man, in vain endeavours to quell disorder. Their worst passions, inflamed by the whisky with which they had plied themselves, had brutalised them. 'Our cause is lost!' exclaimed Emmet, snatching a rocket which a man was about to send up, and trampling it under his foot; 'let our friends at a distance escape; comrades, provide for your own safety.'

[38] EMMET'S EXECUTION OUTSIDE ST CATHERINE'S CHURCH; FROM R. R. MADDEN'S *IRELAND IN '98*.

The scaffold on which the young martyr [Emmet] suffered was a mere temporary arrangement, consisting of a few boards laid across a number of empty barrels, that were placed for this purpose nearly in the middle of the street. Through this platform rose two posts, fifteen feet high, and a traverse beam was placed across them. Underneath the beam, about three feet from the platform, was a single narrow plank supported on two ledges, on which the prisoner was to stand at the moment of being launched into eternity. The platform was about six feet from the ground, and was ascended by a ladder.

When Emmet alighted from the carriage, and was led to the foot of the scaffold, his arms being tied, he was assisted to ascend by the executioner, but he mounted quickly and with apparent alacrity. He addressed a few words to the crowd in a firm, sonorous voice, avoiding any reference to political matters, or to the events with which his fate was connected. He merely said: 'My friends, I die in peace, and with sentiments of universal love and kindness towards all men.' He then shook hands with some friends who were near, presented his watch to the executioner, and removed his stock. The immediate preparations for execution were then carried into effect; he assisted in adjusting the rope round his neck, and was then placed on the plank underneath the beam, with the cap drawn over his face; but he contrived to raise his hand and partly remove the cap, and spoke a few words in a low tone to the executioner. The cap was replaced, and he stood with a handkerchief in his hand, the fall of which was to be the signal for the last act of the finisher of the law. After standing on the plank for a few seconds, the executioner asked, 'Are you ready, sir?' One of his friends who stood close by distinctly heard Robert Emmet say in reply, 'Not yet.' There was another momentary pause – no signal was given; again the executioner repeated the question, and the reply 'Not yet,' was given. The question was put a third time, and the same gentleman who gave the report, heard Emmet pronounce the word 'Not–'; but before he had time to utter another word, the executioner tilted one end of the plank off the ledge, and a human being, full of genius, patriotism, and truth, was dangling like a dog, writhing in the agonies of the most revolting and degrading of all deaths. . . .

The execution of Robert Emmet, 1803, a contemporary
Dublin painting

After hanging for a moment motionless, life terminated with one convulsive movement of the body. At the expiration of the usual time the remains were taken down, and extended on the scaffold. The head was struck from the body, grasped by the hair, and paraded along the front of the gallows by the hangman, proclaiming to the multitude, 'This is the head of a traitor!' Near the scaffold, where the blood had fallen on the pavement from between the planks of the platform, some dogs collected, lapping up the blood; more than one spectator loitered about, and, when the soldiers drove the dogs away, dipped their handkerchiefs in the blood. . . .

[39] A 'THIEVES' KITCHEN' IN THE LIBERTIES; FROM THE *AUTOBIOGRAPHY* OF WILLIAM CARLETON.

William Carleton (1794–1869), later famous for his stories and novels of Irish peasant life, arrived in Dublin in 1804 to seek his fortune, lost his job and his lodgings and, almost penniless, was directed to an unusual refuge for the night.

The man put threepence into my hand, and desiring me to follow him, went to the door of a cellar exactly over the way; at this he kicked and, on its being opened, told me I might pass the night there.

'I am putting you into very respectable company,' said he, 'so be sure and conduct yourself like a gentleman.'

The cellar was very spacious; I should think that the entrance into Dante's Inferno was paradise compared with it. I know and have known Dublin now for about half a century, better probably than any other man in it. I have lived in the Liberty and in every close and outlet in the City of the Panniers, driven by poverty to the most wretched of its localities, and I must confess that the scene which burst upon me that night stands beyond anything the highest flight of my imagination could have conceived. Burns must have witnessed something of the sort, or he could never have written the most graphic and animated of all his productions – 'The Jolly Beggars'.

When I got down to the cellar and looked about me, I was struck, but only for an instant, by the blazing fire which glowed in the grate. My eyes then ran over the scene about me, but how to describe it is the difficulty. It resembled nothing I ever saw before or since. The inmates were mostly in bed, both men and women, but still a good number of them were up, and indulging in liquors of every description, from strong whiskey downwards. The beds were mostly what are called 'shake-downs' – that is, simple straw, sometimes with a rag of sheet, sometimes with none. There were there the lame, the blind, the dumb, and all who suffered from actual and natural infirmity; but in addition to these, there was every variety of impostor about me – most of them stripped of their mechanical accessories of deceit.

If not seen, the character of those assembled and their conduct could not possibly be believed. This was half a century ago, when Dublin was swarming with street beggars and impostors of every possible description. This, I understood afterwards, was one of the cellars to which these persons resorted at night, and there they flung off all the restraints imposed on them during the course of the day. I learned afterwards that there were upwards of two dozen such nightly haunts in the suburban parts of the city. Crutches, wooden legs, artificial cancers, scrofulous necks, artificial wens, sore legs, and a vast variety of similar complaints were hung up on the walls of the cellars, and made me reflect upon the degree of perverted talent and ingenuity that must have been necessary to sustain such a mighty mass of imposture. The songs and the gestures were infamous, but if one thing puzzled me more than another, it was the fluency and originality of blackguardism as expressed in language. In fact, these people possessed an indecent slang, which constituted a kind of language known only to themselves, and was never spoken except at such orgies as I am describing. Several offered me seats and were very respectful, but I preferred standing, at least for a time, that I might have a better view of them. While I was in this position, a couple of young vagabonds – pickpockets, of course – came and stood beside me. Instinct told me their object, but as I knew the amount in my purse – one penny – I felt little apprehension of having my pockets picked. On entering the cellar I had to pay twopence for my bed, so that I had just one penny left.

How the night passed I need not say. Of course I never closed my eyes; but, so soon as the first glimpse of anything like light appeared, I left the place and went out on my solitary rambles through the city.

[40] AN AMERICAN DOCTOR IN THE LIBERTIES IN
1844; JAMES JOHNSON, QUOTED IN *DEAR, DIRTY
DUBLIN, A CITY IN DISTRESS* BY JOSEPH O'BRIEN.

Dublin – rent and split – worm-eaten, mouldering, patched and plastered – unsightly to the eye, unsavoury to the taste, and not very grateful to the olfactories – here there is but one step from magnificence to misery, from the splendid palace to the squalid hove. . . .

. . . [And on the Liberties] winds and rain have *liberty* to enter freely through the windows of half the houses the pigs have *liberty* to ramble about – the landlord has *liberty* to take possession of most of his tenements – the silk-weaver has *liberty* to starve or beg.

[41] A FRENCHWOMAN IN THE LIBERTIES IN THE 1880S,
AND A VISIT TO THE GUINNESS BREWERY; FROM *THREE
MONTHS IN IRELAND* BY MADAME DE BOVET.

Anne Marie de Bovet, daughter of a famous French general, made her name as a literary critic and travel-writer. Her Lettres d'Irlande *were first published in 1889.*

To see the abject squalor of Dublin in its very depths one has only to walk along by St Patrick's, and particularly the street which joins the two cathedrals – a street consisting of two rows of tumbledown, mouldy-looking houses, reeking of dirt, and oozing with the disgusting smell of accumulated filth of many generations, with old petticoats

hung up instead of curtains, and very often instead of glass in the dilapidated windows. On each ground floor, shops with overhanging roofs,
and resembling dirty cellars, expose for sale sides of rancid bacon,
bundles of candles and jars of treacle – a delicacy as much sought after
as soap is neglected – greens, cauliflowers, musty turnips and bad potatoes; while at every three doors is a tavern, which in the midst of these
hovels resembles a palace. Every other house is an old-clothes' shop,
where the sale of the above-mentioned rags is combined with money-
lending at large interest. Shoes that are taken out of pawn there on
Saturday night for Sunday mass are pledged again on Monday morning.
Business is as brisk there all Sunday as it is during the week. . . .

On the pavements, strewn with vegetable-refuse and other mess, a
permanent market is held. There are barrels of red herrings, pickled in
brine: flat baskets, in which are spread out the most disgusting bits of
meat that one can possibly imagine; stale cows' feet; overkept sheeps'
heads, bits of flabby pink veal, tripe, intestines, skins, and fat of every
animal eatable and otherwise – refuse that no well-trained dog would
touch. . . . But all these ragged and vermin-covered people are most
affable; there are none of those fierce looks, those looks of hatred with
which in other countries the poor welcome 'the rich' who happen to
have missed their way among them; on the contrary, they are very
pleased when ladies and gentlemen think it worth while to visit them.
They look at them with a curiosity which is neither low-bred nor inso-
lent, require very little encouragement to be made to talk, and willingly
shake hands with the good-natured stranger who will sacrifice his
gloves. Far from being ashamed of their rags, they are proud of being
looked at; pretty, fair, or redhaired girls, whose freshness has not yet
been spoilt by bad air, insufficient food, or drinking to excess, nudge
each other, laughing and blushing; cheeky children come and stare at
you, under your very nose, and vanish like a flock of sparrows if you
pretend to be angry; mothers smile at you gratefully if you glance
tenderly at the baby.

One should not leave the Liberties without visiting the immense industrial establishment which, on the confines of this miserable quarter, represents the fortune of Dublin. I mean the Guinness Brewery, where is manufactured the black beer called stout, or porter, which looks like bottled blacking, and in every part of the world where the English language is spoken is the rival of Bass and Co's pale ale. Founded in 1750, the Guinness Brewery has, during the last fifty years, grown to such proportions that in 1885 its business transactions were five times greater than in 1837. One can form some idea of what this is from the fact that three years ago the business was sold for six millions sterling to a company, Sir Edward Cecil Guinness, Bart, remaining Chairman of the Board. By way of a joke, people say that Dublin beer is black because it is made with the water of the Liffey. The truth is, that its colour as well as its peculiar taste is due to the malt having been first roasted. . . . To reduce [the barley] to malt it is soaked for two or three days in vats, then it is left in the air to sprout, after which it is dried and baked in an oven. The malt is then warehoused in air-tight rooms till the moment it is wanted. The brick building used for this purpose is the largest in Dublin, and can hold a million bushels. After being carefully winnowed, the malt is crushed by metal rollers, and then macerated with warm water. From this process comes an insipid and colourless must, removed by suction pumps into copper boilers that hold nearly twenty two thousand gallons, where it is boiled with hops which give a bitter taste to the malt liquor. . . . The mixture then passes through pipes into refrigerators, whence, once reduced to a proper temperature, it is again poured into vats, where it comes into contact with yeast. It is then that fermentation is produced, the result being the decomposition of the saccharine matter into alcohol. This operation, which lasts from three to four days, is overlooked by excise-men, and the sum received by the Treasury in this way comes to a daily amount of 1200*l*. The vats are twenty-seven in number, and together hold over a million gallons.

The visitor who has the curiosity to poke his nose through one of the openings made in the side may have a very good idea of the feelings the Duke of Clarence experienced when he was drowning in the butt of

Malmsey, with this difference, that if he fell headlong into this seething frothy mixture, he would be asphyxiated by the carbonic acid gas it gives off, before he could arrive at the surface. It would be a very pleasant way of committing suicide. Before one has experienced it one can form no idea of the strength of the fermenting fumes of stout, nor of the delicious perfume that emanates from it – absolutely different from that of any other spirituous liquor. After a vat is emptied the washers are obliged to wait four and twenty hours before they can enter it. One second of it is enough to turn you dizzy, and two to make you insensible. . . .

A bird's-eye view of the Guinness Brewery, St James Gate, 1880s

Kilmainham

[42] THE FOUNDING OF THE ROYAL HOSPITAL AT KILMAINHAM – CHARLES II'S LETTER TO JAMES, DUKE OF ORMONDE, 1679; FROM 'THE HOSPITALS AT KILMAINHAM' IN THE DUBLIN HISTORICAL RECORD, VOL. 20.

The first Duke of Ormonde, who ruled Ireland as Viceroy on and off from 1661 to 1684, was responsible for many of Dublin's greatest improvements: Kilmainham, Phoenix Park, King's Hospital (originally for old men and boys) and the layout of the quays.

Whereas many of the soldiers in our army in Ireland, who are grown aged, or otherwise unserviceable, are yet continued in our pay for want of some fitting provision for their livelihood and maintenance – Our will and pleasure, therefore, is, and we do hereby authorize and require you to cause deduction of sixpence in the pound to be from time to time made out of all the pay that from and after the 29th day of March last, shall grow due by the present, or any future establishment, to any person or persons whatsoever upon our military list in our said Kingdom.

And we do hereby give unto you full power and authority from time to time, to issue and employ the same towards the building and settling an hospital for such aged and maimed officers and soldiers as shall be dismissed out of our army as unserviceable men, and for making provision for their future maintenance, in such way and manner as you shall think fit.

[43] THE DUKE OF ORMONDE'S FAREWELL TOAST, 1685;
FROM *IRELAND UNDER THE STUARTS* BY RICHARD BAGWELL.

Ormonde, a devoted servant of the Stuarts, but staunchly Protestant, was dismissed as Viceroy almost immediately on James II's accession, to be replaced by his old adversary, Richard Talbot, Earl of Tyrconnel.

As soon as the bad news reached him, Ormonde called the Council together. All leave was stopped, officers were ordered to their quarters, and on the following day King James was proclaimed with great pomp, but with many gloomy forebodings among the Protestants of Dublin. The Lord Lieutenant's commission expired with Charles II, Lord Granard and Archbishop Boyle remaining Lords Justices. But Ormonde gave a dinner to all the officers then in Dublin, at the Royal Hospital, just built most appropriately upon the site once occupied by the Priory of St John and dedicated to the use of worn-out soldiers. Raising his glass, he said. 'Look here, gentlemen! They say at Court that I am now become an old coating fool; you see my hand doth not shake, nor does my heart fail, nor doubt but I will make some of them see their mistake,' and so drank the new King's health. He then left Ireland for the last time. On the road he chanced to see in the *Gazette* that his regiment of horse had been given to Richard Talbot without any notice to him. Many of those Protestants who were in a position to do so, followed their protector to England, many sought the colonies, and the shadow of coming change was over those that remained.

[44] EXTRACTS FROM THE RECORDS OF THE HOSPITAL AT
KILMAINHAM; FROM *THE DUBLIN HISTORICAL RECORD*, VOL. 20.

1693 Apr. 7 – Ordered that each soldier in the Hospital be allowed 2d every week for buying tobacco.
1700 Dec. 16 – Ordered – That it be an established rule, that if any soldier of the Hospital shall presume to marry, he be immediately turned out of the house and the Hospital clothes taken from him.

1703 Sep. 22 – The Governors are of the opinion that Sir Patrick Dun, Physician of the Hospital and Mr Peter Goodwin, the Providore, be directed to settle a particular table for more suitable diet for such soldiers, who by reason of their age or other infirmities or distempers, cannot eat the common food . . .

1706 Dec. 17 – For the better preservation and attendance of the soldiers, many having been lost for want of a surgeon being at hand to bleed them or apply other remedies, the Master appointed Robert Curtis, Surgeon's Mate, Resident Surgeon of the Hospital.

1710 Dec. 11 – The Governors taking into consideration the clothing of the decayed officers, and what particulars will be fit to be provided for them in order to their decent appearing at the Hospital as Commissioned Officers – Resolved – That each Officer be furnished with a scarlet coat, an Athlone hat laced with gold lace, and a pair of blue worsted stockings, to be paid out of the pay of each officer.

1769 Nov. 29 – It appearing that numbers of the soldiers (especially those who come from abroad) are violently afflicted with scorbutic disorders – being advised, we also approving of the same, that Lucan Spa Water may be of great service to them, and therefore of opinion that a car with proper vessels and a horse, should be immediately provided and maintained at the hospital for this sanitary purpose.

1802 Jan. 12   Ordered that on Christmas Day, St Patrick's Day and the King's Birthday, each man should receive a double allowance of rations and two quarts of ale in lieu of beer.

[45] JOHN WESLEY VISITS KILMAINHAM HOSPITAL IN 1749; FROM WESLEY HIS OWN BIOGRAPHER (EXTRACTS FROM HIS JOURNALS).

John Wesley, the famous evangelical preacher and founder of Methodism, visited Ireland more than twenty times between 1747 and 1768, but made little impact on the religious views of its citizens.

Thursday, 20. – I saw Dr Stephen's Hospital, far cleaner and sweeter than any I had seen in London, and the Royal Hospital for old soldiers,

standing on the top of an hill overlooking Phoenix Park. All the buildings are kept not only in good repair, but likewise exactly clean. The
hall is exceeding grand: the chapel far better finished than anything of
the kind in Dublin. O what is wanting to make these men happy? Only
the knowledge and the love of God.

[46] PARNELL IN KILMAINHAM JAIL; FROM
RECOLLECTIONS BY WILLIAM O'BRIEN.

*Kilmainham jail, built in the 1790s, was used for a succession of famous
political prisoners, including the leaders of the 1916 rising (see pp. 262).
Charles Stewart Parnell, leader of the Irish Parliamentary Party, was
arrested with other leading members of his party in 1881 for his part in the
Land League agitation. He was released a few months later after the
so-called Kilmainham Treaty with Gladstone. William Smith O'Brien, one
of Parnell's most militant supporters, was editor of the* Land League
Journal. *He later voted against Parnell in the great party split of 1891.*

The period of repose, in the hope of which I welcomed the cells of
Kilmainham, proved thus to be one of the most laboriously active
passages of a pretty active life. But it was sweetened by an exhilaration
of combat and a companionship with revered and trusty men, and, it
must be added, a rugged courtesy on the part of our captor, which leave
me scarcely a single memory of those six prison months that it is not a
personal luxury to recall. . . . Mr Forster's (*Secretary of State for Ireland*)
prison arrangements were unquestionably humane. All the prisoners
were allowed to mingle together freely in the prison yards during the
abundant hours of exercise; to smoke their pipes, to read their newspapers, to play at hand-ball, or, if their tastes were more sedentary, at
chess or dominoes, and to have their meals supplied by a friendly
restaurateur (or, as it happened, restaurateuse).

There was, indeed, one element of serpentlike calculation mixed
with Mr Forster's dovelike prison arrangements. The exultant remark

he let drop about the prodigal expenditure of the League funds by the Ladies' Land League lets out the secret. As the suspects were allowed to get in their meals from outside, the privilege cost the League funds £1 a week per suspect, and Forster had only to fill his jails with a sufficient number of prisoners to deplete the League exchequer by over £1000 a week, which was the figure the support of the prisoners had actually reached in the November of 1881. But there once more Mr Forster challenged an encounter with an antagonist against whom he was but poorly matched. Parnell at once saw the game, and with an unswerving instinct made his move. He passed the word through all the jails that the suspects, after a date named, would go back to prison fare, in order to spare the Land League funds the crushing burden of their support. Needless to say, he himself set the example. The food question was, indeed, with him at all times of a profound unconcern worthy of the traditional Irish contempt for 'the dirty belly.' It was the mechanically ingenious view of the prison fare question, as of most other things, that chiefly interested him. The prison fare included twice a week a lump of inferior beef per man, and Parnell conceived the project of pooling all our lumps of beef together in a common pot, from which, with the aid of broken bread and of the vegetables fished out of the prison soup of the previous day's dietary, he concocted a famous dish of Irish stew. He and Dr Kenny collaborated in producing this curious mess, over which, I am afraid, we grimaced more than over the unadorned prison food, but which was to the cooks a source of never-failing joy and pride . . .

It has been mentioned that six or eight of us were lodged together in 'a concentration camp,' of which Parnell's room was the dining-room and the club-window. It has often been a matter of bitter regret that I took no notes of our *noctes coenaeque* around the Chief's frugal table. At the time and for many a year after, anything I might put in writing was liable to seizure and official scrutiny, with the unfortunate result that my diaries were kept mostly in uneventful periods when they were least useful. Not, indeed, that Parnell was in the smallest degree a professor of table-talk. He would have been the last to understand Dr Johnson's passion for 'talking for victory.' He was much more truly an admirer of Biggar's immortal axiom of obstruction: 'Never talk except in Government time.' At table, as everywhere else, he was simple, genial, unpretentious. But he was in the habit of dropping pregnant sayings, for any record of which surer than my own memory I would now give much. . . .

There was no subject on which Parnell better loved to chat than America and the American Revolution. He would delight to trace Washington through his constant retreats and devices for avoiding battle, holding that to his willingness to decamp and play an inglorious waiting-game it was due that the insurrection was not promptly suppressed by the troops. 'Washington would be a highly unpopular leader in Ireland,' he would say, with a smile. For the United States of our day, bursting with youthful energy and rude strength, he had the admiration of one who was half American by blood and five-sixths in sympathy. He would always topple over Mr O'Kelly's calculations of disaster to England from France or Russia with the observation: 'Pooh! The United States are the only people that could smash England. They may even be the means of freeing Ireland without the smashing.' . . .

Parnell's superstitions have been frequently and unduly dwelt upon. They always seemed to me whimsicalities that amused him, rather than beliefs that had any real influence. His objection to the colour green was genuine, and often laughable; but arose, in my judgment, chiefly from a fear of arsenical poisoning. 'How could you expect a country to have luck that has green for its colour!' he once said. When I reminded him that green, as the National colour, dated no farther back than the United Irishmen, and that until then the Irish ensign was supposed to be blue, he responded smiling: 'It's just the same – blue is more than half green.' A lady worked for him, while he was in prison, a superb eider-down quilt, covered with green satin, with his monogram worked in gold bullion – a present worthy of a king. I am sure he must have sent a sweet and gracious acknowledgement, but the gorgeous quilt never rested on his bed. It was hidden away carefully underneath a press, where, I am afraid, the mice soon tarnished its glory. Lady devotees sent him innumerable other marks of homage worked in the dangerous colour embroidered smoking-caps, tea-coseys, and even bright green hosiery. The latter he insisted resolutely on destroying; the others he distributed freely among his brother-prisoners, until almost every man in the prison, except himself, had his green tasselled turban and green woollen vests. . . .

His terror of contagious disease was very real indeed. One evening, I happened to mention at dinner that I had got a note informing me that two of my sub-editor's children were down with scarlatina. 'My God! O'Brien,' he cried, almost in a panic, 'what did you do with the letter?' When I told him it was still in my pocket, he begged of me instantly to throw it into the fire. Seeing how genuine was his concern, I did so. 'Now,' said he, 'wash your hands.' This time I found it difficult to avoid smiling. He bounded from the dinner-table, and with his own hands emptied the water ewer into the basin on the wash-hand-stand. 'For God's sake, O'Brien, quick!' he cried, holding out the towel towards me, with an earnestness that set the whole company in a roar. He returned to his dinner in a state of supreme satisfaction. 'Buckshot,' he said, 'is not going to get rid of us so cheaply as that.'

Recreation time in Kilmainham gaol for Parnell and his followers, from *The Illustrated London News*, 1882

[47] JOHNNY CASSIDY VISITS KILMAINHAM JAIL WITH HIS
UNCLE; FROM PICTURES IN THE HALLWAY BY SEAN O'CASEY.

*Sean O'Casey (1880–1964) came from a lower-middle-class Protestant
Dublin family, which fell into acute poverty after his father's early death.
This episode comes from the second book of his six-volume autobiography,
which charts his sickly childhood, his work as a Dublin labourer, his involve-
ment in the trade-union struggles led by Larkin (see p. 245) and his final
emergence as the Abbey Theatre's most brilliant playwright since John
Synge.*

There it was. A great, sombre, silent stone building, sitting like a toad
watching the place doing its ragged middle-aged minuet. A city of cells.
A place where silence is a piercing wail; where discipline is an urgent
order from heaven; where a word of goodwill is as far away as the right
hand of God; where the wildest wind never blows a withered leaf over
the wall; where a black sky is as kind as a blue sky; where a hand-clasp
would be low treason; where a warder's vanished frown creates a carni-
val; where there's a place for everything, and everything in its improper
place; where a haphazard song can never be sung; where the bread of
life is always stale; where God is worshipped warily; and where loneli-
ness was a frightened, hunted thing.

His uncle pulled his coat open showing the Crimea medal shining
on his waistcoat, with two bars striding across the coloured ribbon.
They went through the iron gateway leading to the main door of the
jail, the ready way in and the tardy way out, a heavy thick iron gate set
deep, desperately deep, into solid stone, with a panel of five scorpions
wriggling round each other carved out of the stone that formed the
fanlight that gave no light to the poisoned city of Zion inside. As Johnny
and his uncle came near, the heavy thing swung open, and a warder
stood there, with the Crimea medal glittering on his breast, and a hand
stretched out to greet Tom, who seized it and held it for a long time.

– Come along in, Tom, me son, and your young friend, said the warder. You're welcome, he's welcome, you're both as welcome as the rooty call blowing for dinner.

They went inside to the courtyard, the heavy thing swung back again, and Johnny was installed as a freeman among the prisoners and captives.

They went into the central hall, and, standing on the flagged floor, gazed at the three tiers of cells, with narrow railed lobbies on the first and second floors, and a narrow steel stairway leading to each of them.

– It's a great sight, said the warder, to see the prisoners coming in, in single file, step be step, hands straight be their sides, over a hundhred of them, quiet an' meek, marching right, left, right, left, each turning into his own little shanty when he comes to it; with half a dozen warders standing on the alert, and the sound of the steel doors clanging to, like the sound of waves on a frozen sea, all shut up safely for the night, to read their Bible or stretch themselves down and count the days to come before the Governor dismisses them and wishes them godspeed. Here, me lad, he said, opening a cell door, have a decko at the nice little home we provide for them who can't keep their hands from pickin' an' stealin' . . . Go on in, me lad – no fear o' the door closing on them who are the friends of those sent by the Queen for the punishment of evildoers.

Johnny went a little way into the cell, with his heart beating. It was spick and span, the little stool scrubbed till it was shining like a dull diamond, and the floor spotless. A slop-pail stood to attention in a corner; over it a tiny shelf holding a piece of yellow soap and a black-covered Bible, showing that cleanliness was next to godliness; and a tiny grating to the side of the door, letting the air through to keep the cell fresh and wholesome; all, in the night, lighted up by a baby-tongued flicker of gas in a corner . . .

– Here's something to see, said the warder, showing a fairly-sized room, lighted with two arched windows, for this is the room where Parnell was kept when we had him prisoner here. A man, he went on, if ever there was one, a sowl man. The least little thing you done for him, it was always thank-you, thank-you, from him even when you opened the door before you locked him up for the night. A sowl man, I'm tellin' you, Tomas, an honour to do anything for him, he was that mannerly, even to us, mind you, that you'd fall over yourself in thryin' to please him; and never the icy glint in his eye, unless the name of some big bug in the opposite camp was mentioned; oh, be Jasus, then the flame in his eye 'ud freeze you, ay, man, an' shook hands when he was leaving, too; imagine that, Tom, shook hands with us that was busy holdin' him down, though no-one in this world, ay, or in the next either, could really hold Parnell down; for even in here he was more dangerous than he was roamin' about outside, a deal more dangerous, for, with Parnell a prisoner, the Irish 'ud stop at nothin', ay, an' well he knew it – an' one of us, too, Tom, me boy.

– How one of us? asked Uncle Tom.

– Why a protestant, man, makin' him fair an' equally one of ourselves. Not fit to do anything for themselves, the roman catholics must have a protestant to lead them. Looka at them now, an' Parnell gone! Gulpin' down the sacrament while they're tryin' to get at each other's throats; furiously tetherin' themselves to the roar o' ruin; twistin' into a tangle everything that poor Parnell had straightened out, with the hope of ever standing up against a single law that England likes to make gone for ever!

Dublin North of the River

Previous page:
The Old Customs House and Essex (Capel Street) Bridge, 1706,
by Joseph Tudor

Phoenix Park

[48] The Duke of Ormonde saves Phoenix Park from
Charles II's mistress, Lady Castlemaine, in 1663; from
Thomas Carte's *Life of James, Duke of Ormonde*.

*The creation of Phoenix Park, west of the city, was one of the Duke of
Ormonde's first acts after the Restoration. Thomas Carte, a Jacobite historian, wrote a momumental life of Ormonde based on Ormonde's own collection of documents. In Dr Johnson's view, however, he 'diffused the matter in
too many words'.*

The Countess of *Castlemaine*, whose understanding bore no proportion to her power, . . . had occasion of resentment against the Duke of
Ormonde, and at this time, as well as at all others, whenever an opportunity offered, did him all the ill offices that were in her power. She
had obtained of the King a warrant for the grant of the *Phoenix* park
and house near *Dublin*, which was the only place of retirement in the
summer season for a chief Governor; and the more necessary at that
time, when his Grace coming over, found the castle of *Dublin* so out
of repair, and in such a miserable condition, after the neglect of it
during the late usurpation, that it did not afford him sufficient accommodations. The Lord Lieutenant refused to pass this warrant, stopped
the Grant, and prevailed with his Majesty to enlarge the park by the
purchase of 450 acres of land adjoining in *Chapel Izod* of the Lord
Chancellor *Eustace*, and to fit up the house for the convenience of
himself and his successors in the government of *Ireland*. This incensed
the Lady *Castlemaine* so highly, that upon his Grace's return to
England, meeting him in one of the apartments about Court, she
without any manner of regard to the place or company, fell upon him
with a torrent of abusive language, loaded him with all the reproaches
that the rancour of her heart could suggest, or the folly of her tongue
could utter, and told him in fine, that she hoped to live to see him

hanged. The Duke heard all unmoved, and only made her this memorable reply; 'that he was not in so much haste to put an end to her days, for all he wished with regard to her was, that he might live to see her old.'

[49] THE PHOENIX BECOMES A PEOPLE'S PARK IN THE 1770S; FROM *DUBLIN OLD AND NEW* BY STEPHEN GWYNN.

This complaint from the Freeman's Journal *recalls the strict reign of Nathaniel Clements as Ranger of Phoenix Park. Clements designed and built the handsome classical Ranger's Lodge (1751) which later was expanded to become the Viceregal Lodge, and is now Aras an Uachtaran, the residence of the Irish President.*

Under the rule of Mr Clements every impropriety was rigorously expelled from that beautified spot. Ill-looking strollers of either sex could never get admittance at the gate except on public occasions. Cars and noddies [the cheapest form of shay] were refused passage. But now the gates are opened, wide to Tag, Rag and Bobtail. The Sabbath is abused by permitting a hurling match to be played there every Sunday evening, which is productive of blasphemous speaking, riot, drunkenness, broken heads and dislocated bones, among ten thousand of the lower class; and meanwhile the deer are hunted by detached parties of these vagrants and their dogs.

[50] A SHAM BATTLE IN PHOENIX PARK, IN THE 1820S; FROM CHARLES LEVER'S NOVEL, *JACK HINTON, THE GUARDSMAN*.

The Fifteen Acres – now playing-fields – opposite the Viceregal Lodge were the venue for military drill and manoeuvres in the eighteenth and nineteenth centuries, which provided an immensely popular spectacle for Dubliners. Here a manoeuvre gets out of hand.

*   *   *

Winding along the quays, we crossed an old and dilapidated bridge; and after traversing some narrow and ruinous-looking streets, we entered the Park, and at length reached the Fifteen Acres.

The carriages were drawn up in line; his Grace's led horses were ordered up, and staff-officers galloped right and left to announce the orders for the troops to stand to arms. . . . The manoeuvres of the day included a sham battle; and scarcely had his excellency passed down the line, when preparations for the engagement began. The heavy artillery was seen to limber up, and move slowly across the field, accompanied by a strong detachment of cavalry; columns of infantry were marched hither and thither with the most pressing and eager haste; orderly dragoons and staff-officers galloped to and fro like madmen; redfaced plethoric little colonels bawled out the word of command, till one feared they might burst a blood-vessel and already two companies of light infantry might be seen stealing cautiously along the skirts of the wood, with the apparently insidious design of attacking a brigade of guns . . .

In the midst of all this confusion, a new element of discord suddenly displayed itself. That loyal corps, the Cork militia, who were ordered up to attack close to where the Duke and his staff were standing, deemed that no better moment could be chosen to exhibit their attachment to church and state than when marching on to glory, struck up with all the discord of their band, the redoubled air of 'Protestant Boys.' The cheer burst from the ranks as the loyal strains filled the air; but scarcely had the loud burst subsided, when the Louth militia advanced with a quick step, their fifes playing 'Vinegar-hill.'

For a moment or two the rivalry created a perfect roar of laughter; but this very soon gave way, as the two regiments, instead of drawing up at a reasonable distance for the interchange of an amicable blank cartridge, rushed down upon each other with the fury of madmen. So sudden, so impetuous was the encounter, all effort to prevent it was impracticable. Muskets were clubbed or bayonets fixed, and in a moment really serious battle was engaged; the musicians on each side encouraging their party, as they racked their brains for party-tunes of the most bitter and taunting character; while cries of 'Down with King William!' 'To hell with the Pope!' rose alternately from either side.

[51] A DUEL IN THE PHOENIX; FROM THE RECOLLECTIONS OF AUBREY DE VERE.

Aubrey de Vere (1814–1903), Limerick landowner, poet and essayist, published his memoirs in 1897. Here he is recalling the Ireland of his grandfather's days.

In those days a duel was the most mirthful of pastimes, and in Dublin there still remains a tradition of two lawyers, – one the biggest, and the other the smallest, man in Irish society – who met in the Phoenix Park, just after sunrise, to indulge in that amusement. As they approached each other, the big man set his glass to his eye, and exclaimed: 'But where is my honourable opponent? For I really cannot see him.'

'What's that he's saying?' demanded the little man.

'I just remarked,' replied the big man, 'that I am so large that if you miss me, you are like the man who, when he took aim at the parish church, never succeeded in hitting the parish.'

'What is that big "Golumbus" of a man babbling about?' was his small antagonist's rejoinder. 'That I can't miss him and he cannot see me? Let his second get a bit of white chalk, and draw my exact size and shape on that huge carcass of his; and any bullet of mine that hits outside that white line shall not count.'

[52] QUEEN VICTORIA WRITES TO THE KING OF THE BELGIANS FROM THE VICE-REGAL LODGE; FROM THE COLLECTED LETTERS OF QUEEN VICTORIA, EDITED BY G. E. BUCKLE.

Queen Victoria paid her first visit to Ireland in 1849 when Ireland was still reeling from the great Famine, but her letters make no mention of it. On her third visit – in 1861 – stones were thrown at Prince Albert through the Kildare Street Club windows. She did not return for forty years.

LODGE, PHOENIX PARK, 6 August, 1849.

My dearest uncle, – Though this letter will only go tomorrow, I will begin it today and tell you that everything has gone off beautifully since we arrived in Ireland, and that our entrance into Dublin was really a magnificent thing. . . . We came in with ten steamers, and the whole harbour, wharf, and every surrounding place was *covered* with *thousands* and thousands of people, who received us with the greatest enthusiasm. We disembarked yesterday morning at ten o'clock, and took two hours to come here. The most perfect order was maintained in spite of the immense mass of people assembled, and a more good-humoured crowd I never saw, but noisy and excitable beyond belief, talking, jumping and shrieking, instead of cheering. There were numbers of troops out, and it really was a wonderful scene. This is a very pretty place and the house reminds me of dear Claremont. The view of the Wicklow mountains from the windows is very beautiful and the whole park is very extensive and full of fine trees.

We drove out yesterday afternoon and were followed by jaunting-cars and riders and people running and screaming, which would have *amused* you. In the evening we had a dinner party, and so we have tonight. This morning we visited the Bank, the Model School (where the Protestant and Catholic Archbishops received us), and the College; and this afternoon we went to the Military Hospital. Tomorrow we have a Levee, where 1700 are to be presented, and the next day a Review, and in the evening the Drawing-Room, when 900 ladies are to be presented.

George [the Duke of Cambridge] is here, and has a command here. He rode on one side of our carriage yesterday. You see more ragged and wretched people here than I ever saw anywhere else. *En revanche,* the women are really very handsome – quite in the lowest class – as well at Cork as here; such beautiful black eyes and hair and such fine colours and teeth.

I must now take my leave. Ever your most affectionate Niece, VICTO-RIA R.

[53] THOMAS CARLYLE CALLS AT THE VICE-REGAL LODGE, 1849; FROM *REMINISCENCES OF MY IRISH JOURNEY* BY THOMAS CARLYLE.

Unlike Queen Victoria, the great historian Thomas Carlyle came to Ireland especially to study the 'Irish problem' in the wake of the Famine, as a painful duty. His comments on Dublin were particularly dyspeptic – perhaps partly as the result of a bad sea-crossing and he showed little patience with Dublin social etiquette.

Of Thursday I can remember only a dim hurly-burly, and whirlpool of assiduous hospitable calls and proposals, till about 4 o'clock when a 'Sir Philip Crampton,' by no means the most notable of my callers, yet now the most noted in my memory, an aged, rather vain and not very deep-looking Doctor of Physic, came personally to 'drive me out,' – drive me to the Phoenix Park and Lord Lieutenant's, as it proved. *Vapid-inane* looking streets in this Dublin, along the quays and every-where; sad defect of waggons, real *business* vehicles or even gentle-man's carriages; nothing but an empty whirl of street cars, huckster carts and other such 'trashery.' Sir P's talk, of Twistleton mainly – Phoenix Park, gates, mostly in grass, monument a pyramid, I really don't remember in 'admonition' of what, – some victory perhaps? Frazer's Guide-Book would tell. Hay going on, in pikes, coils, perhaps swaths too; patches of potatoes even: a rather diminish wearisome look. House with wings (at right angles to the body of the building) with esplanade, two sentries, and utter solitude, looked decidedly dull. Sir Ph, some business inside, tho' Ldship *out*, leaves me till that end; I write my name, with date merely, not with address, in his

Lordship's *book* ('haven't the honor to know her Ladyship,') am conducted through empty galleries, into an empty room in the western (or is it *northern?*) wing, am there to wait. Tire soon of waiting; walk off leaving message.

[54] A CHILDHOOD MEMORY OF THE VICE-REGAL LODGE;
FROM *MY EARLY LIFE* BY WINSTON CHURCHILL.

When does one first begin to remember? When do the waving lights and shadows of dawning consciousness cast their print upon the mind of a child? My earliest memories are Ireland. I can recall scenes and events in Ireland quite well, and sometimes dimly, even people. Yet I was born on November 30, 1874, and I left Ireland early in the year 1879. My father had gone to Ireland as secretary to his father, the Duke of Marlborough, appointed Lord-Lieutenant by Mr Disraeli in 1876. We lived in a house called 'The Little Lodge,' about a stone's throw from the Viceregal. Here I spent nearly three years of childhood. . . .

My nurse, Mrs Everest, was nervous about the Fenians. I gathered these were wicked people and there was no end to what they would do if they had their way. On one occasion when I was out riding on my donkey, we thought we saw a long dark procession of Fenians approaching. I am sure now it must have been the Rifle Brigade out for a route march. But we were all very much alarmed, particularly the donkey, who expressed his anxiety by kicking. I was thrown off and had concussion of the brain. This was my first introduction to Irish politics!

In the Phoenix Park there was a great round clump of trees with a house inside it. In this house there lived a personage styled the Chief Secretary or the Under Secretary, I am not clear which. But at any rate from this house there came a man called Mr Burke. He gave me a drum. I cannot remember what he looked like, but I remember the drum. Two years afterwards when we were back in England, they told me he had been murdered by the Fenians in this same Phoenix Park we used to walk about in every day. Everyone round me seemed much upset about it, and I thought how lucky it was the Fenians had not got me when I fell off the donkey.

It was at 'The Little Lodge' I was first menaced with Education. The approach of a sinister figure described as 'the Governess' was announced. Her arrival was fixed for a certain day. In order to prepare for this day Mrs Everest produced a book called *Reading without Tears*. It certainly did not justify its title in my case. I was made aware that before the Governess arrived I must be able to read without tears. We toiled each day. My nurse pointed with a pen at the different letters. I thought it all very tiresome. Our preparations were by no means completed when the fateful hour struck and the Governess was due to arrive. I did what so many oppressed peoples have done in similar circumstances: I took to the woods. I hid in the extensive shrubberies – forests they seemed – which surrounded 'The Little Lodge.' Hours passed before I was retrieved and handed over to 'the Governess.' . . .

I revisited 'The Little Lodge' when lecturing on the Boer War in Dublin in the winter of 1900. I remembered well that. it was a long low white building with green shutters and verandahs, and that there was a lawn around it about as big as Trafalgar Square and entirely surrounded by forests. I thought it must have been at least a mile from the Viceregal. When I saw it again, I was astonished to find that the lawn was only about sixty yards across, that the forests were little more than bushes, and that it only took a minute to ride to it from the Viceregal where I was staying.

[55] THE PHOENIX PARK MURDERS; FROM *THE ILLUSTRATED LONDON NEWS*, 3 MAY 1882.

The murder of Lord Frederick Cavendish (Gladstone's nephew) and Thomas Burke by a Fenian splinter group, the Invincibles, caused widespread horror among Irish nationalists. Parnell (who had just been released from jail after

*making the so-called Kilmainham pact with Gladstone) offered his resigna-
tion, but Gladstone dissuaded him. Most of the Invincibles were caught, and
five were eventually executed.*

A twofold murder, perpetrated last Saturday evening in Phoenix Park,
Dublin, has furnished a new example of the atrocious wickedness of
that foul conspiracy of the enemies of civilised society – Nihilists or
Anarchists, or Fenians, by whatever name they may be called in Europe
or America, the same in Ireland, under cover of an agitation for different political objects – who are plotting everywhere to subvert all regular Government, for the purpose doubtless of Communistic plunder –
by evoking the terrorism of assassination . . .

Saturday last was the day upon which the new Lord Lieutenant of
Ireland, Earl Spencer, KG, succeeding to that great office upon the
retirement of Earl Cowper, arrived from England, and made his
public entry into Dublin, receiving a formal address from the Lord
Mayor and Corporation of that city, and loudly cheered by the people
as he rode on horseback through the streets. On arriving at the Castle
the new Viceroy . . . was conducted . . . to the Privy Council Chamber,
where the ceremony of swearing him in took place. Mr Burke, the
Under-Secretary, bore the sword of State, and afterwards Earl
Spencer took his seat at the council board, with his head covered, as
Lord Lieutenant. Lord Frederick Cavendish was then sworn as Chief
Secretary by the Clerk of the Council. A rocket from the Castle yard
announced the completion of the ceremony, and a salute of fifteen
guns was fired in the adjacent Phoenix Park. . . . The new Chief
Secretary, Lord Frederick Cavendish, remained in the offices of his
own department, engaged in business, till past seven o'clock, when
he set out for his lodge in Phoenix Park, which is about the centre of
that inclosure. His Lordship went on foot. He knew the way well, for
he had been there before when his brother, Lord Hartington, was
Chief Secretary. He had arrived from England but at noon of that
fatal day.

The Phoenix Park murders – a sketch of the scene outside the Vice-regal Lodge; from *The Illustrated London News*, May 1882

Mr Burke, the Under-Secretary, left the Castle on a car some minutes later, and overtook Lord F. Cavendish about the Park gate. The Under-Secretary then got off the car, which he dismissed, and the Under-Secretary and Chief-Secretary walked together on the left-hand path. It is presumed that Lord Cavendish was going merely to look in at his own house, for he and the Under-Secretary were to dine with Earl Spencer at the Viceregal Lodge. About two hundred yards from the Phoenix Column, they were murderously attacked. It was then nearly half-past seven o'clock, but it was still broad daylight. The attack was so sudden and silent that it scarcely attracted any notice. A common hackney car appears to have driven up and four fellows jumped off it, the driver remaining in his seat. Lord Frederick Cavendish was on the outside of the path, and Mr Burke was next the grass. The assailants rushed upon them with daggers, and a fierce struggle for life took place. But the murderers killed their victims in a few moments, and then drove off by a side road in the direction of Chapelizod, and rapidly disappeared.

The Rotunda

[56] A Charity breakfast for Dr Mosse's
Lying-in Hospital, 1751; from *The Autobiography
and Correspondence of Mrs Delany*.

*Bartholomew Mosse (1712–1759) was one of Dublin's most remarkable
benefactors. After studying surgery and midwifery in Europe, he returned
to Ireland to found the first free lying-in hospital in the British Isles.
Originally it was sited in George's Lane, but in 1748 he leased five acres of
waste ground north of Gardiner's Mall (the future O'Connell Street) and
began to build a magnificent new hospital to the designs of Richard
Cassells. At the same time he laid out a walled pleasure garden with
refreshment rooms whose entrance fee would help support the hospital.
The hospital, its tower topped with a golden cradle, was finally completed
in 1757 A Rotunda or concert room (now an exhibition hall) was added
soon after, giving the hospital its modern name. Mosse planned several
other great philanthropic projects for Dublin, but died, worn out and in
debt, aged only 45. His successor, Sir Fielding Ould, was celebrated in the
following Dublin rhyme:*

> *Sir Fielding Ould is made a knight.*
> *He should have been a Lord by right,*
> *For then the ladies' cry would be,*
> *'O Lord, good Lord, deliver me!'*

Went to Dr Moss's *gratis breakfast*, Mrs F. Hamilton with us . . . Dr
Moss, you must know, is the chief manager and operator of the Lying-in
Hospital, and has gardens laid out for the entertainment of company in
the manner of Vauxhall and Ranalagh; and in order to gather together
subscribers for the next season he gave a *gratis breakfast* and a fine
concert of music in a large room which was not opened before, and is
in the gardens The music allured us, and we went, D.D. [Dr Delaney]

with us, at about half an hour after eleven, the concert to begin at 12. When we came, with some difficulty we squeezed into the room, which they say is 60 feet long, and got up to the breakfast-table, which had been well pillaged; but the fragments of cakes, bread and butter, silver coffee-pots, and tea-kettles without number, and all sorts of spring flowers strewed on the table, shewed it had been set out plentifully and elegantly. The company, indeed, looked as if their principal design of coming was for a breakfast. When they had satisfied their hunger the remains were taken away, and such a torrent of rude mob (for they deserved no better name) *crowded in* that I and my company *crowded out* as fast as we could, glad we escaped in whole skins, and resolving never more to add to the throng of a *gratis* entertainment. We got away with all speed, without hearing a note of the music.

Dr Mosse's Lying-In Hospital and the Rotunda, aquatint by S. F. and H. Brocas from *Coloured Views in Dublin, 1820*

[57] A CLERGYMAN APPLAUDS DR MOSSE'S HOSPITAL,
1777; FROM A *PHILOSOPHICAL SURVEY OF THE SOUTH
OF IRELAND* BY THE REVD THOMAS CAMPBELL.

*Thomas Campbell (1738–1795) was a rather sententious clergyman from the
North of Ireland. A friend of Dr Johnson, he was the author of several 'philosophical' travel books in the Johnsonian manner.*

In my last, I mentioned to you Mosse's Hospital; which, I think,
deserves particular notice, whether we consider it as a specimen of
architecture, or, as an example to prove, that every principle of our
nature may be rendered subservient to the interests of humanity.

As a building, it is magnificent, and, being the most faultless I ever
beheld, is a lasting monument of the abilities of Mr Castels, who was
also the designer of the duke of Leinster's, and the Parliament House. In
other respects, the structure must do eternal honour to the founder, Dr
Mosse, a physician of this city; who, by the mere effort of his own
genius, in defiance of avowed opposition, and contempt of popular
clamour, erected this stately fabric, for the purpose of relieving lying-
in-women; the first charity of the kind in these kingdoms, and in which,
above 10,000 poor females have been delivered within twenty years.
His only resources were lotteries, and the emoluments arising from the
concerts and gardens. The benevolence of the public was at length
awakened; the king gave stability to the institution by a charter, and
parliament bestowed a bounty on the widow of him, who had devoted
his life to the service of his fellow-creatures.

The present master of this hospital, is a Doctor Jebb, a gentleman of
fine parts; whose acquaintance, I am sure, you would be pleased with.
He tells me, that except some beds given, and endowed by private
donors, the fund for support of this charity, is raised from musical
entertainments, and from subscriptions to a right of walking in the
gardens at all times. They have lately built a large circular room, called
the Rotunda, of an area, as I guess, about a third of that of Ranelagh, but

without any pillar in the centre. Here they have an organ and orchestra for concerts, in the wet evenings of summer, and for balls in winter. So that, upon the whole, this is the Vauxhall, Ranelagh, and Pantheon of Dublin.

Nay, it is something more than all these, it is a polite place of public resort on Sunday evenings. Whether this entertainment be strictly defensible, in a religious point of view, I shall not determine; but, if the goodness of the end may in any instance be pleaded in justification of the means, I think it may in this. However, it seems rather a matter of wonder, that London, so fond of amusement, and so ready to adopt new fashions of dissipation, has not struck out something similar . . . On these nights, the rotunda and gardens are prodigiously crowded, and the price of admission being only sixpence, every body goes.

[58] THE IRISH VOLUNTEERS ASSEMBLE IN THE ROTUNDA IN 1778; FROM *THE RISE AND FALL OF THE IRISH NATION* BY SIR JONAH BARRINGTON.

The Volunteer movement had sprung up in the late 1770s, ostensibly to provide a defence for Ireland against France while the British had their hands full fighting the American colonists. In fact they soon became a proto-Nationalist movement of their own, taking their ideas from the Americans and demanding free trade and legislative independence. Eventually their more moderate leaders, notably the Earl of Charlemont (see next extract), became alarmed, fearing a head-on clash with the English government, and persuaded their regiments to disband – much to Barrington's disapproval.

The Royal Exchange of Dublin was first selected for the meeting of the volunteer delegates. Whoever has seen the metropolis of Ireland, must admire the external architecture of that building; but, as it was constructed solely for mercantile purposes, it would have been inadequate to the accommodation of a very large deliberative assembly. It was therefore determined that the Rotunda (being the finest room in Ireland) was best adapted for the meeting of the National Convention. This was, and continues to be, the great assembly-room of Dublin, and it consists of a circular salon of very large dimensions, connected with numerous and very spacious chambers, and terminates Sackville Street, the finest of the Irish metropolis. It is surmounted by a dome, exceeding in diameter the Irish House of Commons, and was perfectly adapted to the accommodation of a popular assembly. . . .

The firing of twenty-one cannon announced the first movement of the delegates from the royal Exchange to the Rotunda; a troop of the Rathdown cavalry, commanded by colonel Edwards, of Old-court, county of Wicklow, commenced the procession; the Liberty brigade of artillery, commanded by Napper Tandy, with a band, succeeded. A company of the barristers' grenadiers, headed by colonel Pedder, with a national standard for Ireland, borne by a captain of grenadiers, and surrounded by a company of the finest men of the regiment came after, their muskets slung, and bright battle-axes borne on their shoulders. A battalion of infantry, with a band, followed, and then the delegates, two and two, with side arms, carrying banners with motto and in their respective uniforms – broad green ribands were worn across their shoulders. Another band followed playing the special national air alluded to. The chaplains of the different regiments, in their cassocks, marched each with his respective corps, giving solemnity to the procession, and as invoking the blessing of heaven on the surrounding multitude. Several standards and colours were borne by the different corps of horse and foot; and another brigade of artillery, commanded by councillor Calbeck, with labels on the cannons' mouths, was escorted by the barristers' corps in scarlet and gold (the full dress uniform of the king's guards); the motto on their buttons being 'Vox populi supreme lex est.'

The procession itself was interesting, but the surrounding scene was still more affecting. Their line of march, from the Exchange to the Rotunda, was through the most spacious streets and quays of the city, open on both sides to the river . . . an immense body of spectators, crowding every window and housetop; . . . every countenance spoke zeal, every eye expressed solicitude, and every action proclaimed triumph: green ribands and handkerchiefs were waved from every window by the enthusiasm of its fair occupants; crowds seemed to move on the house-tops; ribands were flung on the delegates as they passed. . . . Those who did not see or who did not recollect that splendid day, must have the mortification of reflecting, that (under all its circumstances) no man did before, and no man ever will, 'behold its like again.'—

The entrance of the delegates into the Rotunda was most interesting and awful. Each doffed his helmet or his hat, as if he felt the influence of that sacred place where he was about to sacrifice at the Shrine of Freedom.

Charlemont House
(now the Municipal Art Gallery)

[59] LORD CHARLEMONT FURNISHES HIS NEW LIBRARY AT HIS TOWN HOUSE, 1784; FROM *THE PLEASING HOURS* BY CYNTHIA O'CONNOR.

James Caulfield (1728–1799), first Earl of Charlemont, was a noted aesthete who had travelled extensively in Europe and Asia, before returning to live in Ireland as 'an indispensable duty'. He built a magnificent town house for himself in the 1760s and 70s north of the Rotunda gardens, at the same time creating superb pleasure gardens at his Marino estate at Clontarf (see pp. 227–8) drawing extensively on designs from his friend, Sir William Chambers. The plans for the library itself were commissioned from Chambers' pupil, James Gandon, in 1776. Charlemont's library is said to have been one of the finest in Europe and to have given the hitherto boorish Ascendancy a new taste for reading. He himself emerged as the political leader of the Irish Volunteer movement in the 1780s (see extract 58).

My dear Chambers,

There is yet one thing remaining with regard to the Library apartment – I mean the best method of lighting it – the Great Room, will, I imagine, be sufficiently illuminated by the Lights which are to stand on the Chimneypiece and by candles placed on the Tables, but with regard to the Ante Chamber I think that nothing could be more proper than girandoles of two candles each fix'd in the center of the two long panels at each side of the room. A design, however, which corresponds with the other ornaments of this beautiful room, will be necessary and such a one I beg you wou'd immediately send me – I should imagine that an Amazonian shield, cross'd by branches of Laurel and Palm might make a pretty ornament and might serve for the basis from whence the branches for candles might spring.

Whenever it may best suit your convenience I shou'd be much obliged to you if you wou'd choose for me among the many vases of plaister, which are so common in the Statuary's shops such as you may think proper to be put up on the upper shelf in the Library. They must be bronzed and not exceed twenty eight inches in height.

[60] A JUDGEMENT ON LORD CHARLEMONT BY EDMUND BURKE; FROM FRANCIS HARDY'S *MEMOIRS OF THE EARL OF CHARLEMONT*.

Every foreigner, of taste congenial to his own, and every Englishman of rank and talents, visited Lord Charlemont during their occasional residence in Dublin. . . . Mr Burke once said to me of this accomplished nobleman: 'Lord Charlemont is a man of such polished manners, of a mind so truly adorned, and disposed to the adoption of whatever is excellent and praiseworthy, that, to see and converse with him, would alone induce me, or might induce anyone who relished such qualities, to pay a visit to Dublin.'

Portrait of an aesthete, James Caulfield, 1st Earl of Charlemont, painted by Pompeo Batoni, 1756

Belvedere House

[61] After the hell-fire sermon at Belvedere College; from *Portrait of the Artist as a Young Man* by James Joyce.

Belvedere College in Great Denmark Street was originally the town house of the Earls of Belvedere and one of the last great houses to be built north of the Liffey. By 1841 it had already become a Jesuit College. James Joyce attended the school briefly in the 1890s, and later used the terrifying hell-fire sermon given during a religious retreat as the climax of his autobiographical novel.

He came down the aisle of the chapel, his legs shaking and the scalp of his head trembling as though it had been touched by ghostly fingers. He passed up the staircase and into the corridor along the walls of which the overcoats and waterproofs hung like gibbeted malefactors, headless and dripping and shapeless. And at every step he feared that he had already died, that his soul had been wrenched forth of the sheath of his body, that he was plunging headlong through space.

He could not grip the floor with his feet and sat heavily at his desk, opening one of his books at random and poring over it. Every word for him! It was true, God was almighty. God could call him now, call him as he sat at his desk, before he had time to be conscious of the summons. God had called him. Yes? What? Yes? His flesh shrank together as it felt the approach of the ravenous tongues of flames, dried up as it felt about it the swirl of stifling air. He had died. Yes. He was judged. A wave of fire swept through his body: the first. Again a wave. His brain began to glow. Another. His brain was simmering and bubbling within the cracking tenement of the skull. Flames burst forth from his skull like a corolla, shrieking like voices:

—Hell! Hell! Hell! Hell! Hell!—

—Voices spokes near him:—

—On hell.—

—I suppose he rubbed it into you well.—

—You bet he did. He put us all into a blue funk.—

—That's what you fellows want: and plenty of it to make you work.—

He leaned back weakly in his desk. He had not died. God had spared him still. He was still in the familiar world of the school. Mr Tate and Vincent Heron stood at the window, talking, jesting, gazing out at the bleak rain, moving their heads.

—I wish it would clear up. I had arranged to go for a spin on the bike with some fellows out by Malahide. But the roads must be kneedeep.—

—It might clear up, sir.—

The voices that he knew so well; the common words, the quiet of the classroom when the voices paused and the silence was filled by the sound of softly browsing cattle as the other boys munched their lunches tranquilly lulled his aching soul.

O'Connell Street
(called Sackville Street until 1922)

*Shelley came to Dublin aged nineteen with his young wife Harriet and took
rooms in Sackville (now O'Connell) Street which had become the main
Dublin thoroughfare after the building of Carlisle (O'Connell) Bridge in the
1790s. His attempt to awaken Dubliners to their wrongs by his 'address to the
Irish people' ('printed at the lowest possible cost of 5d') met with little
success, despite his hopes.*

I have already sent 400 of my Irish pamphlets into the world, and they
have excited a sensation of wonder in Dublin. Eleven hundred yet
remain for distribution. Copies have been sent to sixty public-houses.
No prosecution is yet attempted. I do not see how it can be. Congratulate
me, my friend, for everything proceeds well. I could not expect more
rapid success. The persons with whom I have got acquainted approve of
my principles. . . .

Expectation is on the tip-toe. I send a man out every day to distrib-
ute copies, with instructions how and where to give them. His account
corresponds with the multitudes of people who possess them. I stand at
the balcony of our window and watch till I see a man who looks likely I
throw a book to him.

[63] George IV makes a royal progress down
Sackville (O'Connell) Street in 1821; from the
journal of Colonel William Blacker, in Constantia
Maxwell's *History of Trinity College*.

William Blacker was a landowner from Co Armagh who served as Vice-treasurer of Ireland from 1817 to 1829. His account shows Dubliners still far from revolutionary nine years after Shelley's visit. George IV was the first king to visit his subjects in 400 years.

Dublin now presented a singularly animated scene . . . preparations were busily carried on for His Majesty's grand entry into the city. At the head of Sackville St was erected an edifice in wood intended to represent a triumphal arch. This was the Temple Bar of Dublin where the Lord Mayor and civic authorities were to receive the sovereign and go through the antiquated farce of handing him a bunch of keys and getting them back again. . . . Scaffolding was erected in front of many of the houses especially in Sackville St and being generally filled with 'elegantly draped females' as the newspapers say . . . The neighbouring counties sent forth their peasantry in their Sunday clothes and the entire of Sackville St (except what was clear) – was a mass of [frieze?] and jolly faces. . . . The whole scene was most amusing. 'Arrah, then Paddy dear will he have a crown of gold upon his head?' 'To be sure he will, Judy.' 'Will you take your elbow out of me ribs. Stan' quiet can't ye and not be rouling about in that fashion.' 'Take care of ye pockets,' etc. . . .

A mighty shout came rolling on heralding his Majesty's approach and after a pause of a few minutes while the Lord Mayor was going through the aforesaid farce of the keys, the royal barouche penetrated the mass of laurels.

I have his Majesty's bloated person at this moment in my eye as he stood up in the barouche dressed in scarlet and holding in his hand his hat decorated with an immense bunch of Shamrock which he took care should not escape the notice of the nobility as he repeatedly pointed to it with his finger . . . At length the royal barouche rolled slowly on followed by Lord Talbot and the civic authorities – the Lord Mayor and the 'Lord knows who.'

George IV makes a royal progress down Sackville Street
(now O'Connell Street), August 1821

[64] THE MAGNIFICENT NEW DUBLIN POST OFFICE AND
THE POSTAL SERVICES OF THE TIME; DESCRIBED BY WILLIAM
CURRY IN HIS *NEW PICTURE OF DUBLIN, 1820.*

The first stone of this magnificent edifice was laid by his Excellency
Earl Whitworth, on the 12th of August, 1815. With the exception of the
Board-room, which is rather an elegant apartment, and in which there
is a white marble bust of Earl Whitworth, there is no object worthy the
notice of the Tourist in the interior. The departure of the coaches from
the office, would by some be deemed rather an interesting exhibition.
Ten or twelve mail-coaches leave Dublin every evening for different
parts of Ireland. They are provided with a double guard well armed; the
cattle and accommodations are excellent, and the drivers, in general,
sober, correct, and intelligent. They all assemble at the General Post
Office every evening, a little before seven o'clock, and having received

the bags, each in their turn, set out for their different destinations. This nightly exhibition always attracts a crowd of spectators, when the sound of the horns, the prancing of the horses, and the last adieus of friends, form altogether a very interesting and animated picture.

As a public convenience of the highest utility, the Post-Office, in its present improved state, must be considered as one of the most useful and important establishments in any country. . . .

The introduction of Mail Coaches has been attended with the greatest advantage to the general interests of Ireland and has greatly improved the system of the Post-office. Previous to their introduction, the state of the roads was such, that it commonly took five or six days to perform a journey from Dublin to Cork; and it is said that persons, in those days, deemed it a matter of more serious importance to undertake a long journey through Ireland, than many do at present to undertake a voyage to America. The first mail-coaches commenced running from Dublin to Cork and Belfast on the 5th of July, 1790. A regular improvement in the state of the Irish roads has continued from that time to the present, and they are now allowed to be amongst the best in Europe.

The most admirable regularity and despatch are apparent in all the proceedings of this office. Houses are appointed for receiving letters in various parts of the city, where boxes are open till four o'clock in the evening, after which the letter-carriers, (of whom there are sixty-five for the Irish and twenty for the English departments,) go about for another hour, with a bell, to collect letters, with which a penny each are paid. At the General Post Office, inland letters are received until six o'clock, but a small sum must be paid with any put in after that hour. English letters are received at any hour. A Penny Post is the medium of conveyance from the several parts of the city with each other. From sixty receiving-houses the letters are delivered four times a day with such celerity and exactness that two persons living at opposite extremities of the city may write four letters and receive three answers every day, for the trifling expense of three pence.

[See also the section, 'Dublin in revolution']

The Custom House

[65] Building the new Custom House in 1781 – political problems; from *The Life of James Gandon* by T. J. Mulvaney.

As this letter from John Beresford to Gandon, the architect, makes clear, the plan for a new customs house east of Sackville Street aroused ferocious opposition. John Beresford (1750–1805), Commissioner of Revenue, was one of the most powerful men in Ireland, and had already pioneered many Dublin improvements as head of the Wide Streets Commission.

James Gandon (1743–1825), his choice for architect of the Custom House, was a brilliant pupil of Sir William Chambers. He turned down an invitation to become the official architect in St Petersburg to come to Dublin, and settled permanently in Ireland.

Dublin, 15th January, 1781

Sir, – I have the pleasure to inform you, that I have at length obtained an order from Government for the building of a new Custom House, with all possible expedition, and I have proceeded so far as to send to take possession of a large lot in the lower situation. I expect to accomplish this in the course of this week, and the sooner afterwards we can settle our plans the better. This business must be kept a profound secret, as long as we can, to prevent clamour, until we have everything secured.

Our first step will be, to wall in the ground as soon as we shall get possession of it. This will discover us, and the clamour will then be made that there will not be sufficient room for shipping: to answer which, it will be right to have our plans for the new docks ready, to shew the people how well they will be accommodated.

I therefore request you will turn your thoughts immediately to that subject, and, as I hope we may hereafter claim you as our own, that you attend to us in the first instance, as the business is of a delicate nature, and must be managed still with dexterity, having the city [*Corporation*] of Dublin, and a great number of the merchants, together with what is considered as the most desperate of the mob, to contend with, on this side of the water; and also some persons of high interest and weight on your side, who will make use of every exertion to prevent us.

However, a Custom House must now be built, so we shall now expect you; and I must beg to know when you think you can come over? . . .

I am, Sir,
Your humble Servant,
JOHN BERESFORD.

[66] BUILDING THE CUSTOM HOUSE – CONSTRUCTIONAL PROBLEMS; GANDON'S ACCOUNT FROM *THE LIFE OF JAMES GANDON* BY T. J. MULVANEY.

The labourers had scarce got down two feet below the surface when they came to water, which four men emptied with scoops as they continued to extend the line of trenches, which were carried on in short lengths, and, for convenience, of different depths. It became necessary to make dams across parts of them with sods, and to empty the water from the lower to the higher dam, until it was at last sent off in a drain prepared for that purpose, our pumps not being then ready. The ground was opened first at the north and continued round to the east front; then to the south end, where a boiling spring with sand appeared at about four-feet below the surface, which filled up as fast as it was cast out. It extended for a considerable distance. Inch and half-sheeting piles, about seven feet long, were driven down with a maul, to keep up the bank, and sods were fitted in layers between it and the piles, which prevented the sand from being washed out. When the trenches were thus prepared and cleared out, the rough masons then proceeded to carry on the first bench or course with all possible expedition with the black stone, and immediately filling in with earth, in order to give less water to the pumps. In the meantime another length, and of the same depth, was got ready, and an additional number of masons set to work. In this manner the whole was continued until all was brought up to the level of the ground.

[Having drained and levelled his site with enormous difficulties, Gandon directed his builders to lay a foundation of a huge timber grating covered with 'four inch fir planks'. Here is his humorous account of some unwanted Dublin advice:]

The novelty of this operation drew many visitors to the works, and a very whimsical opinion, delivered with suitable gravity, was very near giving some interruption to the progress of the works. Amongst the visiters were several of the 'faculty,' and one of these gentlemen, who had increased his fortune more by speculating in building than in gallipots, assumed vast knowledge and consequence on the occasion, and, of course, was by many much attended to. He gave his opinions freely and without a fee! He surveyed the grating, and inquired of the master bricklayer for what purpose such large balks of timber were laying down? On being informed, he observed with great sagacity, 'that it would answer no durable purpose, as fir was an improper timber to lay in salt water, an immediate decay being brought on by its destruction of the turpentine!' This he averred, from his own knowledge, to be the fact . . .

James Gandon's Custom House, aquatint by James Malton, 1797

[67] THE *DUBLIN EVENING POST* REPORTS THE EFFECT OF THE NEW
CUSTOM HOUSE ON NORTH DUBLIN RENTS, 1790; FROM *JAMES
GANDON – VITRUVIUS HIBERNICUS* BY EDWARD MCPARLAND.

Since the building of the New Custom-House, more especially since
the idea of a new bridge went abroad, a new town has risen and is still
rising in the North East vicinity of the city.

. . . The Gardiner estate on the north side of the river, the greater
part of which was within the last twenty years an universal cabbage
garden, is now covered with superb streets. Elegant mansions seem to
vegetate and propogate there, like the former produce of the soil: and
building ground which formerly was given by Lord Mountjoy (Luke
Gardiner) at 4s. 6d. per foot, is now eagerly caught at 10s.

The Quays

*The family home of Edmund Burke (see p. 143) was on Arran Quay – built
in the early 1700s, but still subject to flooding in the 1740s, as this letter to
Burke's schoolfriend, Dick Shackleton, shows.*

I have not seen such a flood in the Liffey as is now for some years; and our
cellars as well as all on the quay, are full of water; and I, like a good child,
spent most of the morning sailing on it in a tub; and I believe I should be at
it till now, had not the water grown too deep, and an accident befallen me,
which was this. After having made two or three pretty successful voyages
into the Ocean of our street kitchen, I had a mind to try my fortune in the
Back Sea; but to be short, as soon as I entered it, I perceived at a distance
two bottles in a terrible condition; who making signals of distress I made
what sail I could to their relief. But lo! my ballast leaning starboard sunk me
to the bottom, so I was thrown ashore at a great distance from where I
foundered, and having changed clothes (my courage, as you may guess,
being pretty well cooled) I sat down to write to my dear Dick.

*The Four Courts – James Gandon's second great masterpiece on the Dublin
Quays – was, like his Custom House, a subject of furious political debate and
took twenty years to complete.*

I next walked to the *Four Courts*, and surveyed the building from the
opposite bank of the Liffey, . . . I was astonished at the elegance of its

exterior, exhibiting all the embellishments which architectural and sculptural science can bestow. In order to take a view of the interior of the building I then crossed the narrow stream of the Liffey, over a bridge which the prototype of was at Westminster. As if making my approach to an Athenian Temple I ascended a lofty range of stone steps. I was soon ushered by an Irish Cicerone into a splendid circular hall, nearly seventy feet in diameter, from which the four courts of justice radiate at equal distances. My eye dwelt with pride and admiration on fluted shafts and Corinthian Capitals. I enumerated the emblematical devices which adorn this hall; the signing of the great Charter of our common liberties by King John at Runnymede, and those of the city of Dublin by King James, with crowds of feudal knights and barons bold, armed at all points. I looked higher towards the roof of the building and numbered eight statues as if supporting the dome. There was Liberty and Eloquence, Prudence and Justice, Wisdom and Law, with Punishment and lastly Mercy bringing up the rear. Roving thus from ornament to ornament from the intersecting black and white marble squares of the hall . . . up to the cupola where the emulous plaisterer had exerted all his skill; I began to fancy myself in one of these Fairy palaces which some ingenious romance-writers have described. But by some accident in coming out; the talisman was broke . . . the visionary fabric melted into air. I found myself as much surprised as many other simple knights-errant have been when they awakened from a similar trance. My olfactory nozzle (vulgarly called the nose) was assailed by the horrid stench which arises from the Liffey, (the cloaca maxima of Dublin;) my auditory nerves were assaulted with the clamorous importunities of a crowd of beggars; and my organs of sight turned away with disgust from every edifice and object within the horizon.

View of the Four Courts looking down the Liffey, aquatint by S. F. and
H. Brocas from *Coloured Views in Dublin, 1820*

[70] A SOUP KITCHEN ON THE QUAYS, 1847; FROM 'AN OPEN LETTER TO LORD JOHN RUSSELL' BY JOHN MITCHEL, QUOTED IN M. J. McMANUS'S *IRISH CAVALCADE*.

Dublin escaped the worst horrors of the Great Famine, but not the ruin of many of its small tradesmen and an influx of refugees. John Mitchel (1815–1875), a Protestant lawyer, was originally a supporter of Daniel O'Connell (see pp. 130, 161, 195), but had left him eventually to found and edit the Republican newspaper, The United Irishman, which declared 'holy war' on the English government. He was arrested in 1848, and transported for 'treason felony' to Tasmania. He escaped to America in 1853, and his Jail Journal (published in 1854) became a classic.

On the Easter Monday of last year Dublin saw one of the most igno-minious Easter festivals – one of the ghastliest galas ever exhibited under the sun – the solemn inauguration of the Irish nation in its new career of national pauperism.

There, in the esplanade before the Royal Barracks, was erected the national model soup-kitchen, gaily bedizened, laurelled and bannered, and fair to see; and, in and out, and all around, sauntered parties of our super-cilious second-hand 'better classes' of the Castle offices, fed on superior rations at the people's expense, and bevies of fair dames, and military offic-ers, braided with public braid, and padded with public padding.

And there, too, were the pale and piteous ranks of model-paupers, broken tradesmen, ruined farmers, destitute semp-stresses, ranged at a respectful distance till the genteel persons had duly inspected the arrangements – and then marched by policemen to the place allotted them, where they were to feed on the meagre diet with chained spoons – to show the 'gentry' how pauper spirit can be broken, and pauper appe-tite can gulp down its bitter bread and bitterer shame and wrath together; and all this time the genteel persons chatted and simpered as pleasantly as if the clothes they wore, and the carriages they drove in, were their own – as if Royal Barracks, Castle and soup-kitchen were to last for ever.

St Mary's Pro-Cathedral

[71] Death of the Liberator: Daniel O'Connell's
body is brought home to Dublin for burial, May
1847; from *The Illustrated London News*.

*Daniel O'Connell (see p. 161 and 195) died in Geneva aged seventy-
one, on his way to Rome. Here the funeral rites are performed over
his body in the Marlborough Street Chapel – the future Pro-Cathedral,
Dublin's main Catholic church. The imposing classical portico,
modelled on the Temple of Theseus in Athens, had originally been
intended for Sackville Street [O'Connell Street] but ended up tucked
away in Marlborough Street – possibly in deference to Protestant
sensibilities?*

As the steamer neared the Custom House, opposite to which it was
arranged that the debarkation of the Remains should take place, the
quays presented from end to end one vast mass of human beings; yet,
save occasionally a low wail which broke from the multitude, not a
sound issued from amongst them. It was all sad and respectful silence.
The arrangements for the reception of the Remains were very complete.
An open bier, without canopy, drawn by six black horses, was in attendance, with mutes and wand-bearers, under the superintendence of the
undertaker, Mr Lawlor, of Henry-street. The Members of the Associated
Trades were drawn up in procession order, each Member bearing a
wand tied with love ribbon.

Preparations were now made for the debarkation. The side curtains
of the Chapel were thrown up, exposing to public view the coffin
within, surrounded by its lighted tapers. And then, of that vast crowd
not one remained standing where room was left to kneel. The scene
was solemn and impressive beyond description; many on board the
vessel, as well as on the quays, were moved to tears. . . .

The coffin was next placed on the bier, and the procession
having formed, the Remains, preceded by the Trades, headed by

Thomas Reynolds, Esq, the City Marshal, and followed by sons, relatives, and friends, moved through the dense crowd along the quay, and up Marlborough-street, to the chapel. The great gate was opened, and displayed a partial view of the interior, with its numerous lights and dark drapery. . . . The coffin was then borne into the chapel, and surrounded by the acolytes bearing torches, whilst a Sub-Deacon in a white surplice and soutan, held the lofty crucifix at the foot . . .

At the conclusion of the ceremonial, the officiating Clergy and the choir retired to the vestry, leaving the Remains lying in state. The tapers round the catafalque were lit, and the anxious people were allowed to enter the church, and view its splendid arrangement, until eleven o'clock, when the doors were closed.

THE OBSEQUIES IN THE CHAPEL

On Wednesday, the funeral rites of the Catholic Church were solemnized over the Remains . . . The rain fell in torrents; but, for more than two hours before the commencement of the solemnities, every approach to the Chapel was crowded with Priests, and gentry, to be admitted by tickets.

The front gallery was set apart for the immediate friends and relatives of the illustrious deceased. In it were seated the four sons of the Liberator – Maurice, John, Morgan, and Daniel – with many other relatives, and several of the ladies of the family. . . . In front of it was suspended the O'Connell arms, with the supporters, motto, and crest, beautifully executed in the form of a hatchment. On the sides and ends of the upper dais of the catafalque, the arms of the family were emblazoned. Over the front door they were also on stained glass, on a white ground, diapered with shamrocks, and surrounded with a border of the same national emblem. In the corners of this stained glass were the Irish Harp, and the initials D.O.C. in ornamental letters of golden hue. In front of the organ-loft, and round the catafalque, were suspended scrolls, on which were written in Latin the inscriptions adopted at the Obsequies in Rome. . . .

The Office commenced a little after eleven. The nine lessons of the Nocturns were read by nine of the prelates present. Peculiarly mournful was the low deep chant of the solemn office for the dead. The joyous notes of the organ were hushed. Nothing was heard but the saddest tones of the human voice, and ever and anon the tolling of the death bell. The Grand High Mass, at which Dr Whelan acted as celebrant, and the Venerable Metropolitan presided, commenced as soon as the Office had terminated.

The Funeral Oration was preached by Dr Miley. It will be found reported entire, in the *Weekly Freeman's Journal* for Saturday last.

The Absolution, a ceremony but rarely celebrated, and which raised O'Connell to the dignity of a Prince in the Catholic church of his native land, was then performed. The five senior Bishops left the sacristy in black copes, followed the Master of the Ceremonies to the catafalque, and took their positions at the respective corners, the celebrant remaining at the head. Each in turn then gave the usual absolution prescribed in the Roman pontifical. And thus ended the Obsequies.

Daniel O'Connell's body lies in state in Marlborough Street Chapel
(later the Pro-Cathedral); from *The Illustrated London News*, 1847

Dublin Moves South-East

Previous page:

'They will follow me wherever I go' – the Duke of Leinster builds a palatial mansion south of the Liffey, 1754

Trinity College

The original recommendation for the founding of a university in Dublin had been made in a papal bull in the fourteenth century, but the need only became acute in English eyes after the Reformation, to provide Protestant ministers for Ireland. The site chosen was that of a ruined monastery built originally by the King of Leinster, Dermot Mac Murchadha and by then the property of the Dublin mayor and corporation. The first Provost of Trinity was the Lord Chancellor of Ireland, Adam Loftus.

Whereas by your letters and the rest of our Council, joined with you, directed to our Council here, we perceive that the Mayor and the citizens of Dublin are very well disposed to grant the site of the Abbey of All Hallows, belonging to the city . . . to serve for a college for learning, whereby knowledge and utility might be increased by the instruction of our people there, whereof many have usually heretofore used to travel into France, Italy, and Spain, to get learning in such foreign universities, where they have been infected with popery and other ill qualities, and so become evil subjects. . . . We do by these our letters, warrant and authorise you our Deputy and our Chancellor, in our name, to erect and make a foundation and corporation of a college for learning in the place aforementioned, taking order that the college may be erected and established in such manner, and with such good orders and statutes, as some other of our colleges here in England in our universities are. . . .

[73] CATHOLIC FEARS AT THE FOUNDING OF TRINITY
– A PETITION TO THE POPE FROM IRISH CATHOLICS
IN EXILE, 1595; FROM CONSTANTIA MAXWELL'S
IRISH HISTORY FROM CONTEMPORARY SOURCES.

Though Ireland was once such a school of religion and learning that
many came from neighbouring nations to learn, and from it went out
many to spread special knowledge and faith abroad, this glory had gradually decayed, whether by frequent and fierce invasions of foreign
nations (i.e. Northmen) or because of the constant civil wars among
the chiefs, or by other concurrent causes. At all events the English
(who) became masters of Ireland, though they corrected there some
things inconsistent with the Christian religion, yet afterwards deliber-
ately contrived to keep the natives in the gloom of barbaric ignorance,
so as thus to retain them like slaves in abject obedience. Whence it
happened that the Irish, though full of genuine love of the Catholic
faith, were not educated enough to detect and repel that corruption of
religion which for some decades of years the English have sought by
fraud and force to introduce into Ireland. This policy of keeping the
Irish in ignorance dates from the days when the Catholic faith flour-
ished both in England and Ireland, but now, a year or two since, a new
policy has been adopted, whereby England, devoted to heresy, may
draw Ireland into the same snare, and bind it closer to itself. This is the
building of a certain ample and splendid college beside Dublin, in
which the Irish youth shall be taught heresy by English teachers. From
this college a great danger threatens the Irish.

[74] SEVENTEENTH-CENTURY STUDENT OFFENCES
LISTED IN THE BOOK OF CENSURES; FROM *TRINITY
COLLEGE, DUBLIN* BY W. MACNEILE DIXON.

Aug 4, 1617. – Gower and Tolles punished with the rod for going into the
country and lodging in the town all night. Gower censured for his

negligence in his studies, which was by the Examiners of the Midsummer Term discovered and complained of Patrick Smith removed from the College for non-proficiency and incapacity of learning.

Nov 21, 1617. - Mr Taylor, Senior Fellow and Dean, severely censured and punished for a wound committed upon the person of Gower, a Scholar of the House.

June 2, 1619. – Thomas Cuff and Jos. Travers for abusing M. Middop's servant, and for their irreverent and savage carriage in the presence of Sir John King, to make three public acknowledgments of their faults at three several times in the Hall; to forbear going out into town for six months except to hear sermons, and for six months not to keep company with each other. Cuff for wounding with a knife the scullion of the kitchen to lose his privilege of adult age, and to rest subject to the rod until he graduates.

Sept 5, 1619. – Rowland Eustace, for his drunkenness and other misde-meanours, was punished with a public acknowledgment of his fault in the Hall at dinner, to be performed for three days together on his knees, from the beginning of dinner to the end; . . . Beere, Temple (son of the Provost), and Paget were sharply corrected for departing from the Sermon (at Christ Church) to go a-walking, and for consenting to the plucking of cherries from a tree of dean Wheeler's garden hanging on the wall.

From Bedell's Register:

1628, July 29. – Six natives, Dominus Kerdiffe, Ds Conway, Ds Baker, Ds Davis, Ds Kerdiffe, Jun, and Burton, admonished for being often absent from Irish prayers.

1629, Aug 19. – The natives to lose their weekly allowance if they are absent from prayers on the Lord's Day.

1629, Aug 29. – Sir Springham said to keep a hawk. Rowley for drunkenness and knocking Strank's head against the seat of the Chapel, to have no further maintenance from the house.

Booth, for taking a pig of Sir Samuel Smith's, and that openly in the day time before many, and causing it to be dressed in town, inviting Mr

Rollon and Sir Conway (who knew not of it), was condemned to be whipped openly in the Hall, and to pay for the pig.

[75] THE FATE OF THE COLLEGE UNDER JAMES II –
EXTRACTS FROM TRINITY COLLEGE REGISTER; FROM
TRINITY COLLEGE, DUBLIN BY W. MACNEILE DIXON.

James II, the Catholic King, made a triumphal entry into Dublin on Palm Sunday, March 1689. Although he originally declared religious tolerance, the Trinity dons' fears were soon justified. The College became a barracks and prison, and by October, Mass was being said in the College chapel. But the College was largely saved from destruction by its new Catholic Provost, Dr Michael Moore.

Feb 19, 1688/9 – It was agreed on by the Vice-Provost and Senior Fellows that two hundred pounds of the College money should be sent into England for the support of those Fellows that should be forc't to fly thither. At the same time the dangers of staying in the College seemed so great that it was judged reasonable that all those who thought fit to withdraw themselves from the College for their better security might have free liberty to do so.

Feb 25, 1688/9 – All the Horse, Foot and Dragoons were drawn out and posted at several places in the town, from whence they sent parties, who searcht the Protestant houses for arms, whilst others were employed in breaking open stables and taking away all their horses. Two Companies of Foot, commanded by Talbot, one of the Captains in the Royal Regiment of Foot Guards, came into the College, searcht all places, and took away those few fusils, swords, and pistols that they found. At the same time a party of Dragoons broke upon the College stables, and took away all the horses. The Foot continued in the College all night; the next day they were drawn off. . . .

March 1, 1688/9 – Dr Browne, Mr Downes, Mr Barton, Mr Ashe, and Mr Smyth, embark't for England; soon after followed Mr Scroggs, Mr Leader, Mr Lloyd, Mr Sayers, and Mr Hasset. Mr Patrickson soon after died; and (of ye Fellows) only Dr Acton, Mr Thewles, Mr Hall, and Mr Allen, continued in the College.

March 2, 1688/9 – King James landed in Ireland; and upon the 24th of the same month, being Palm Sunday, he came to Dublin. The College, with the Vice-Chancellor, waited upon him, and Mr Thewles made a speech, which he seemed to receive kindly, and promis'd 'em his favour and protection . . .

Sept 6. – The College was seized on for a Garrison by the King's order, and Sir John Fitzgerald took possession of it. Upon Wednesday the 11th, it was made a prison for Protestants of the City, of whom a great number were confined to the upper part of the Hall. Upon the 16th the Scholars were all turned out by souldiers, and ordered to carry nothing with 'em but their books. But Mr Thewles and some others were not permitted to take their books with 'em. Lenan, one of the Scholars of the House, was sick of the small-pox, and died, as it was supposed, by removing. At the same time the King sent an order to apprehend six of the Fellows and Masters, and commit 'em to the main guard, and all this without any provocation or crime as much as pretended; but the Bishop of Meath, our Vice-Chancellor, interceded with the King, and procured the last order to be stopt.

Sept 28. – The Chappel-plate and the Mace were seized on and taken away. The plate was sent to the Custom-house by Colonel Lutterel's order; but it was preserved by Mr Collins, one of the Commissioners of the Revenue.

Oct 21. – Several persons, by order of the Government, seized upon the Chappel and broke open the Library. The Chappel was sprinkled and new consecrated, and Mass was said in it; but afterwards being turned into a storehouse for powder, it escaped all further damage. The Library and Gardens and the Provost's lodgings were committed to the care of one Macarty, a Priest and Chaplain to ye King, who preserved 'em from the violence of the souldiers, but the Chambers and all other things belonging to ye College were miserably defaced and ruined.

[76] INVENTORY OF A COLLEGIAN'S CHAMBER; FROM *THE POEMS OF JOHN WINSTANLEY*.

John Winstanley (1676–1750), Dublin poet and satirist, attended Trinity College briefly at the turn of the century.

> Imprimis, there's a *table* blotted;
> A tattered *Hanging* all bespotted;
> A *Bed* of Flocks as one may rank it
> Reduc'd to Rag and half a Blanket;
> A Tinder-box as People tell us;
> A Broken-winded pair of Bellows.
> A pair of *Tongs*, bought from a Broker
> A Fender, and a rusty Poker.
> A *Penny-pot* and *basin*, this .
> Design'd for Water, that for Piss
> A *Trencher*, and a *College-bottle*
> Riding on *Locke* or *Aristotle*
> A smutty *Ballad*, musty *Libel*
> A *Burger's dissius*, and a *Bible*;
> A *Prayer-book*, he seldom handles;
> Item a Pound of *Farthing-candles*;
> A rusty Fork, a blunted *Whittle*
> To cut his *table*, and his *Vittle*
> There is likewise a pair of *Breeches*
> But patch'd, and fallen in the stitches.
> Item, a *Surplice*, not unmeeting
> Either for *chappel*, or for *sheeting*,
> Hung up in study very little,
> Plastered with Cobwebs, Ink and Spittle
> With lofty *Prospect*, all so pleasing
> And Sky-Light window without Glazing
> Item, if I'm not mistaken

A *mousetrap*, with a Bit of Bacon
A *Candlestick*, without a Snuffer
Whereby his Fingers often suffer;
And *Chairs* a couple (I forgot 'em)
But each of them without a *Bottom*
A *Battle Standish, Pen* unmended,
His inventory thus is ended.

Interior of Trinity College Library, aquatint by James Malton, from
Picturesque Views of Dublin, 1794

[77] EDMUND BURKE IS ADMITTED TO TRINITY,
1744; FROM *THE EARLY LIFE AND CORRESPONDENCE
OF EDMUND BURKE* BY ARTHUR SAMUELS.

*Edmund Burke (1729–1797), the famous philosopher and statesman,
entered Trinity aged just fifteen, and proved a precocious scholar. He
later helped to found the College Debating Society, ancestor of the
'Hist'. His statue stands outside Trinity, beside that of his less*

successful fellow-student, Oliver Goldsmith. Here he is writing to his
friend, Dick Shackleton, whose father's school in Ballitore he had
attended as a boy.

Without further prologue I shall acquaint you with my adventures since
I left you, which though perhaps not so entertaining nor so full of
surprising events as those of Don Quixote, Josey etc. may serve to let
you know that Dick Chidley and I arrived pretty safe at this City rather
of the latest, for the ρασχελλει watchman had the impudence to inform
the town how bad travellers we were by saying, 'Past twelve o'clock'! I
was however let in, went to bed, slept, and was sent in company with
Jack Baily immediately after breakfast next morning (i.e. Monday
morning) to Dr Pellasier, Fellow of Trinity College, near Dublin, a
gentleman (since it falls my way to give his conjectural character)
accounted one of the most learned in the University, an exceedingly
good humoured, cleanly, civil fellow (NB I judge by outward appearances). We were admitted into his rooms, and he has three very grand
ones. He and Jack Baily had a good deal of chat and a couple of men
were setting up a barometer in his room – so he could not for a while
examine me. At last he brought out Francis's Horace, Dauphine's Virgil
and Homer, with I don't know whose notes; he made me construe
Scriberis Vario &c *Eheu fugaces, Postume* &c and in Virgil I began the
103rd line of the Sixth Aeneid, and in Homer with the 227th line of the
Third Iliad, and the 406th of the Sixth and he was pleased to say (what
I would not say after him unless to a particular friend) that I was a good
Scholar, understood the Authors very well, and seemed to take pleasure
in them (yet by the bye, I don't know how he could tell that) and that I
was more fit for the College than three parts of my class; but he told me
I must be examined again by the Senior Lecturer. He was sent for but
was not at home, therefore Dr Pellasier told me I must have the trouble
of calling again. He was going out and introduced me (according to
custom I believe) to the Provost, who is an old sickly looking man. To
be short, this morning I was examined very strictly with another young

lad by Mr Aubins or Robbins (I don't know which) the Senior Lecturer, in the Odes, Sermons and Epistles of Horace, and am admitted. . . .

Tell Master Pearce for his comfort that I was examined in *As in praes* and give my service to all the girls, and inform Nanny Morris that I have thought of her once or twice, and that if she has a mind for a coach and six let her tell what coloured horses she will have, and it shall be sent her by the first opportunity, but in the mean time give her a box, and place it to account, and this shall be sufficient warrant for so doing, and it is almost night, and I must write to the Master, so I must conclude without more ado, all-a-one-now.

NED BURKE.

[78] A VISIT TO THE TRINITY COLLEGE CELLARS; FROM THE *RECOLLECTIONS* OF JOHN O'KEEFFE, 1750S.

It was a custom with the students to lend their cellar-books to a friend. These books, consisting of seven leaves, were passports to the college cellar. One of them being lent to me, I brought with me two companions, and, on hearing the bell ring at nine o'clock, the notice that the cellar is open, we went. It was on the left hand of the first court, and stretched under the great dining-hall, in low arches, extending very far, and containing large butts of ale regularly arranged. Close by the entrance, on the left hand, was a little box, like a kind of pulpit, and there sat the college butler, as he was termed. I delivered to him the little book he with few words, quiet and proper in his manner, gave his orders to his attendants, and we were led to a large table, of which there were many in the cellar. On our table was a great iron candlestick with three legs, and in it a wax candle, as thick as my wrist, which spread a brilliant light through the vaulted gloom. A silver cup or vase, with two handles, was placed before us; this was full of the college ale, called Lemon October: the cup held about three quarts. A wicker basket was brought full of small loaves, called by them Manchets; but such ale or such bread, I never tasted before or since, except in this college cellar.

The tinkling bell continued ringing until half-past nine, the signal when the cellar doors are closed. While we were enjoying this, indeed, delicious regale, we observed numbers of the servants of the collegians giving the little books to the butler up in his box, for them to receive ale, and take it to their masters . . .

I thought it whimsical to see the students, some sixteen years of age or so, thrust their heads through windows, and cry 'Boy!' when a little old man would get up from a bench in the court or hall, and shuffle up to him, answering, 'Yes, Sir.' These old men, constantly in waiting, are called Boys.

[79] A VISIT TO THE ANATOMY HOUSE IN THE 1770S;
FROM *A PHILOSOPHICAL SURVEY OF THE SOUTH OF
IRELAND* BY THE REVD THOMAS CAMPBELL.

The gentlemen of Ireland are full as tall as those of England, the difference then, between them and the commonality can only proceed from the difference of food. The following case may, perhaps, tend to illustrate this matter, which, however, I only give upon uncertain authority. In the Anatomy-house of Trinity College, Dublin, is a human skeleton, of between seven and eight feet high. They told me, it belonged to one Magrath, an orphan, in this county, somewhere near Cloyne. The child fell into the hands of the famous Berkeley, then bishop of that see. This subtile doctor, who denied the existence of matter, was as inquisitive in his physical researches, as he was whimsical in his metaphysical speculations. When I tell you, that he had well nigh put an end to his own existence, by experimenting what are the sensations of a person dying on the gallows, you will be more ready to forgive him for his treatment to the poor foundling, whose story I am now to finish.

The bishop had a strange fancy to know whether it was not in the power of art to increase the human stature. And this unhappy orphan appeared to him a fit subject for trial. He made his essay according to his preconceived theory, whatever it might be, and the consequence was, that he became seven feet high in his sixteenth year. He was carried through various parts of Europe for the last years of his life, and exhibited as the prodigious *Irish giant*. But so disproportioned were his organs, that he contracted an universal imbecility both of body and mind, and died of old age at twenty. His underjaw was monstrous, yet the skull did not exceed the common size.

In the same place, I saw the skeleton of one Clark, a native of this city, whom they call the *ossified man*. Early in life his joints stiffened, his locomotive powers were lost, and his very jaws grew together. They were obliged, for his sustenance, to pour liquids into his mouth by a hole perforated through his teeth. He lived in this state for several years, leaning against a wall, till at length the very organs of life were converted into bone. Account for this, Doctor, if you can.

[80] The Trinity students lose their
Parliamentary privileges in the 1790s; from
Ireland Sixty Years Ago by J. E. Walsh.

The Irish House of Commons was a rotunda, the most ill-contrived in point of convenience that ever was built. Round it was a narrow circular gallery for spectators. . . . Admission to this place was obtained by a member's order only, except by students of the University, who were always admitted.

The student's passport was his gown. He rapped at the wicket, and the porter looked through a grating; the applicant held up his gown, and the door was opened, admitted him, and again closed. This was a privilege often abused. The students' gowns were lent put indiscriminately to friends and acquaintances, and the gallery appeared sometimes half full of gownsmen, not half of whom were members of the University. When I first entered College, I was very fond of using this privilege. It was a proud thing for a 'gib' [*Trinity term for a freshman*] to present himself to a crowd round the door, hear many a cry, 'Make way for the gentleman of the College!' pass the avenue made for him, find the door expand to the 'open sesame' of his gown, and himself admitted alone to the great council of the nation, while the suppliant crowd were excluded. . . .

This proud distinction the gownsmen, however, soon forfeited. Lord Fitzwilliam had been sent over as a popular Viceroy, and on his sudden recall a strong feeling of disappointment prevailed. On a night when the subject was brought before the House, our gallery was full, and I remember well the inexpressible excitement that seemed to actuate us all. At length it broke out. Grattan rose to deprecate the measure as one calculated to cause the greatest disturbance in Ireland, by what was considered the perfidy of the Government, first exciting the high hopes of the people by promised measures of liberal policy, and then dashing them by the sudden removal of the man who had been sent over expressly to accomplish them. At the conclusion of Grattan's inflammatory speech, the enthusiasm in the gallery was no longer capable of restraint. We rose as one man, shouting and cheering with the boisterous tumult of a popular meeting. When this subsided Foster's peculiar voice was heard through his nose, ordering the students' gallery to be cleared, and a serjeant-at-arms with a posse of messengers entered among us. We were pushed out in a heap, without the slightest ceremony, and were never again suffered to enter as privileged persons.

The Speaker had counted on the loyalty and propriety of the students of the University, and this display of what he considered riot and sedition at once changed his estimate of their character. Many a penitent memorial was presented, and solemn promises were made of better manners in future, but Foster was inexorable. No student ever after found his gown a passport to the House, till the Union removed the Parliament, and extinguished the hope of recovering the lost privilege for ever. Groups of us were constantly seen in the passages, waiting to intercept the Speaker, or entreating, with uplifted hands, a passage to the gallery; but stern Charon passed in at the door, leaving us, like ghosts on the banks of the Styx, casting wistful and unavailing looks on the Elysium on the opposite side of the house.

[81] STUDENT JAPES IN THE EARLY 1820S – AND AN ECCENTRIC
VICE-PROVOST; FROM *CHARLES O'MALLEY* BY CHARLES LEVER.

*Charles O'Malley is the most autobiographical of Lever's novels – he
went to Trinity in 1822, and lived very much the wild life recorded here.
Dr Jacky Barrett (1753–1821) was Professor of Oriental languages,
famous for his scholarship and his eccentricity. He lived in a garret in
Library Square.*

They voted morning chapels a bore, Greek lectures a humbug, examinations
a farce, and pronounced the Statute Book with its attendant train of fines and
punishment an 'unclean thing' . . We rose about eleven and breakfasted;
after which succeeded fencing, sparring, billiards or tennis in the Park; about
three, got on horseback and cantered in the Phoenix or about the squares till
visiting time; after which made our calls, and then dressed for dinner, which
we never thought of taking at Commons, but had it from Morrison's, we both
being reported sick in the Dean's list, and thereby exempt from the routine
fare of the Fellows' table. In the evening our occupations became still more
pressing; there were balls, suppers, whist parties, rows at the theatre, shin-
dies in the street, devilled drum-sticks at Hayes', select oyster parties at the
Carlingford; in fact every kind of method of remaining up all night, and
appearing both pale and penitent the following morning. . . .

Dr Barrett was, at the time I speak of, close upon seventy years of
age, scarcely five feet in height, and even that diminutive stature less-
ened by a stoop. His face was thin, pointed, and russet-coloured; his
nose so aquiline as nearly to meet his projecting chin, and his small
grey eyes, red and bleary, peered beneath his well-worn cap with a
glance of mingled fear, and suspicion. His dress was a suit of the rusti-
est black, threadbare, and patched in several places, while a pair of
large brown leather slippers, far too big for his feet, imparted a sliding
motion to his walk, that added an air of indescribable meanness to his
appearance; a gown that had been worn for twenty years . . . covered
his rusty habiliments, and completed the equipments of a figure that it

was somewhat difficult for the young student to recognize as the Vice-Provost of the University. Such was he in externals. Within, a greater or more profound scholar never graced the walls of the college; a distinguished Grecian, learned in all the refinements of a hundred dialects; a deep Orientalist, cunning in all the varieties of Eastern languages, and able to reason with a moonshee, or chat with a Persian ambassador. With a mind that never ceased acquiring, he possessed a memory ridiculous for its retentiveness even of trifles; no character in history, no event in chronology, was unknown to him, and he was referred to by his

A Trinity student reels back to college after a night's dissipation; engraving from Walker's *Hibernian Magazine*, 1774

contemporaries for information in doubtful and disputed cases, as men consult a lexicon or dictionary. With an intellect thus stored with deep and far-sought knowledge, in the affairs of the world he was a child. Without the walls of the college, for above forty years, he had not ventured half as many times, and knew absolutely nothing of the busy, active world that fussed and fumed so near him; his farthest excursion was the Bank of Ireland, to which he made occasional visits to fund the ample income of his office, and add to the wealth which already had acquired for him a well-merited repute of being the richest man in College.

[82] A TALL STORY ABOUT DR BARRETT; FROM THE DUBLIN-PENNY JOURNAL, 1840.

SIMPLICITY OF CHARACTER

Dr Barrett having on a certain occasion detected a student walking in the Fellows' Garden, Trinity College, Dublin, asked him how he had obtained admission. 'I jumped over the library, sir,' said the student. 'D'ye see me now, sir? you are telling me an infernal lie, sir!' exclaimed the Vice-Provost. 'Lie, sir!' echoed the student; 'I'll do it again!' and forthwith proceeded to button his coat, in apparent preparation for the feat; when the worthy doctor, seizing his arm, prevented him, exclaiming with horror, 'Stop, stop – you'll break your bones if you attempt it!'

[83] PROVOST MAHAFFY REMEMBERED; FROM IT ISN'T THIS TIME OF YEAR AT ALL BY OLIVER ST JOHN GOGARTY.

Sir John Pentland Mahaffy (1839–1918) was Professor of Ancient History at Trinity for more than thirty years, and a legendary scholar and conversationalist. Passed over for the Provostship of Trinity in 1904, for political reasons, he finally became Provost on the eve of the First World War. His books ranged from a study of Kant's philosophy to Greek antiquities, Egyptian papyri and Irish history. As founder of the first Irish Georgian

Society, he also helped carry out a massive survey of Dublin's historic build-ings between 1908 and 1914.

Mahaffy was the greatest don I ever met. The examination for fellowship, which leaves its successful candidates text-drunk and good for nothing but to draw the salary that goes with what is a lifelong appointment, and take a few pupils, had not the least effect on him. He had taken it in his stride as a matter of course. He had taken much more in his stride: long before Egyptology had become a subject for research workers, Mahaffy had written a book on the subject which after all these years has not been found wanting. He had a perfect musical ear, and that, they tell me, is a thing that appears only once in a century . . .

He was as omniscient as the scholarship and science of his day permitted. Now people grow tired of omniscience.

It is related how one night the dons of the college conspired to get the great man on some subject on which he was not an authority and so could not talk. After a consultation they selected Chinese music as the subject that they would bring up, as it were, accidentally at dinner. They discoursed on Chinese music, traced its origin and its effect, and expounded the difference in the Chinese conception of music and the European attitude. Mahaffy said not a word. The dons, inwardly delighted, kicked each other under the table. When they had exhausted the subject, Mahaffy said, 'Gentlemen, you have fallen into two errors that I myself nearly fell into, and you know how I hate to do anything foolish, when I wrote the article which you have been discussing; for the *Encyclopaedia Britannica* twenty years ago.'

Parliament House, College Green

Chichester House was purchased as the first Parliament House on College Green to replace the old Assembly Hall at the Castle. It was demolished and replaced by Edward Lovett Pearce's splendid Parliament House – now the Bank of Ireland – in 1728.

The first Parliament held in Ireland after the Restoration was opened at Chichester House, on the 8th of May, 1661. In the House of Peers, the Lords having taken their places, John Bramhall, the Protestant Primate of Ireland, seated on the woolsack, delivered the King's commission constituting him Speaker; the Lords Justices, Sir Maurice Eustace, Roger Boyle, Earl of Orrery, and Charles Coote, Earl of Mountrath, took their seats in chairs set on an elevation under the cloth of state, – Lord Baltinglas bearing the sword, Viscount Montgomery carrying the cap of maintenance, and the Earl of Kildare holding the robe. The House of Commons was composed almost exclusively of settlers and officials. The Speaker, Sir Audley Mervyn, in his official address to the Lords Justices, observed: – 'I may warrantably say, since Ireland was happy under an English Government, there was never so choice a collection of Protestant fruit that ever grew within the walls of the Commons' House. Your Lordships have piped in your summons to this Parliament, and the Irish have danced. How many have voted for and signed to the returns of Protestant elections? So that we may hope for, as we pray, that Japhet may be persuaded to dwell in the tent of Shem.' Among the members of the House of Commons were Sir William Temple, Sir James Ware, Sir William Petty, and Dr Dudley Loftus.

This Parliament continued, with various prorogations, to sit till the 8th of August, 1666, when it was dissolved. In the previous year it had

passed the Acts of Settlement and Explanation, placing the Cromwellian
adventurers in the possession of the lands of the Irish adherents of the
Stuarts, to the extent of seven millions eight hundred thousand acres.
'A measure of such sweeping and appalling oppression,' observed an
English writer, 'is, perhaps, without parallel in the history of civilized
nations.'

[85] A DIATRIBE AGAINST PARLIAMENTARY CORRUPTION
IN THE 1730S; ANONYMOUS, FROM SIR JOHN
GILBERT'S *HISTORY OF THE PARLIAMENT HOUSE*.

Ye paltry underlings of state;
Ye senators who love to prate;
Ye rascals of inferior note,
Who, for a dinner, sell a vote;
Ye pack of pensionary peers,
Whose fingers itch for poets' ears;
Yet bishops, far removed from saints,
Why all this rage? why these complaints?
Why against printers all this noise?
This summoning of blackguard boys?
Why so sagacious in your guesses?
Your F's, and T's, and R's and S's!
Take my advice; to make you safe,
I know a shorter way by half.
The point is plain: – remove the cause;
Defend your liberties and laws;
Be sometimes to your country true;
Have once the public good in view;
Bravely despise champagne at court,
And choose to dine at home with port;
Let prelates, by their good behaviour,
Convince us they believe a Saviour;

Nor sell what they so dearly bought –
This country – now their own – for nought.

[86] BENJAMIN FRANKLIN ADMIRES THE IRISH PARLIAMENT;
FROM A LETTER TO THOMAS GUSHING, IN SIR JOHN
GILBERT'S *THE HISTORY OF THE PARLIAMENT HOUSE.*

*Benjamin Franklin (1706–1790) visited Dublin in 1771 when he was
based in London trying to negotiate political and trading rights for the
American Colonies, and took a close interest in the Irish Parliament
which had already extracted concessions from the English
administration.*

Their Parliament makes a most respectable figure, with a number of
very good speakers in both parties and able men of business. . . . I
supposed I must have gone to the gallery, when the Speaker [Pery]
having been spoken to by some of the members, stood up and acquainted
the members that there was in town an American gentleman of character, a member or delegate of some of the Parliaments of that country,
who was desirous of being present at the debates of this House; that
there was a standing rule of the House for admitting members of the
English Parliament; that he did suppose the House would consider the
American Assemblies as English Parliaments, but this being the first
instance, he had chosen not to give any order without receiving their
directions. On the question, the whole House gave a loud unanimous
Aye, when two members came to me without the bar where I was
standing, led me in and placed me very honorably. This, I am the more
particular in to you, as I esteemed it a mark of respect for our country
and a piece of politeness, in which I hope our Parliament will not fall
behind theirs whenever an occasion shall offer. Ireland is itself a poor
country, and Dublin a magnificent city; but the appearances of general
extreme poverty among the lower people are amazing. They live in
wretched hovels of mud and straw, are clothed in rags, and subsist

chiefly on potatoes. Our New England farmers, of the poorest sort, in regard to the enjoyment of all the comforts of life are princes when compared to them.

The Speaker enters the Irish House of Commons, 1780s,
from a painting by Francis Wheatley

[87] HENRY GRATTAN HAILS THE NEW IRISH 'NATION' IN 1782;
FROM SIR JONAH BARRINGTON'S *RISE AND FALL OF THE IRISH NATION*.

Henry Grattan (1746–1820), statesman and orator, gave his name to the Irish Parliament which wrested an apparent measure of independence from England in the wake of the American Revolution. This famous speech was the high point of his career, and he was voted £50,000 by a grateful Parliament. But he retired ill and disillusioned with Irish Ascendancy politics in 1797.

It is not unworthy of remark, that in describing the events of that important evening, the structure of the Irish House of Commons at the period of these debates was particularly adapted to convey to the people an impression of dignity and of splendour in their legislative assembly. The interior of the Commons' House was a rotunda of great architectural magnificence; an immense gallery, supported by Tuscan pillars, surrounded the inner base of a grand and lofty dome. In that gallery, on every important debate, nearly 700 auditors heard the sentiments and learned the characters of their Irish representatives; the gallery was never cleared on a division; the rising generation acquired a love of eloquence and of liberty; the principles of a just and proud ambition; the details of public business; and the rudiments of constitutional legislation.

After the speech of Mr Hutchinson, which, in fact, decided nothing, a low confidential whisper ran through the House, and every member seemed to court the sentiments of his neighbour, without venturing to express his own; at length Mr Grattan, slowly rising from his seat, commenced the most luminous, brilliant, and effective oration ever delivered in the Irish Parliament.

'I am now,' said he, 'to address a free people: ages have passed away, and this is the first moment in which you could be distinguished by that appellation. – I found Ireland on her knees, I watched over her with an eternal solicitude; I have traced her progress from injuries to arms, and from arms to liberty. Spirit of Swift! spirit of Molyneux! your genius has prevailed! Ireland is now a nation! in that new character I hail her! and, bowing to her august presence, I say, "Esto perpetua!" She is no longer a wretched colony, returning thanks to her Governor for his rapine, and to her King for his oppression; nor is she now a squabbling, fretful sectary, perplexing her little wits, and firing her furious statutes with bigotry, sophistry, disabilities, and death, to transmit to posterity insignificance and war.'

Henry Grattan addresses the Irish House of Commons, 1782, a
contemporary engraving

[88] GRATTAN RETURNS TO PARLIAMENT TO VOTE AGAINST THE
UNION; FROM *THE LIFE AND TIMES OF HENRY GRATTAN BY HIS SON.*

*In the wake of the Rebellion of 1798, William Pitt, the English Prime Minister,
resolved to abolish Ireland's legislative independence and transfer Irish
representation to Westminster. The Act of Union was finally pushed through
the Irish Parliament after a massive handout of bribes and patronage. This
dramatic episode in the struggle is related first by Grattan's wife, then by his
son. Grattan's statue still stands, with mute appeal, outside the old
Parliament House.*

At the close of 1799 he returned from the Isle of Wight, and retired to Tinnehinch, almost broken-hearted – not only hopeless, but helpless; enfeebled in body and depressed in spirits, but in mind still unsubdued. Immediately on his arrival, a deputation from his friends waited on him to request that he would re-enter Parliament; but he was obliged to decline the offer in consequence of the state of his health. Soon after they informed him that a seat was vacant, Mr Gahan, one of the members for the town of Wicklow having died, and Mr William Tighe, the patron of the borough, would not be averse that he should be returned for it. Mr Arthur Moore, a most zealous and sincere friend of Mr Grattan, was very zealous on the occasion, and pressed him strongly to comply. . . . Mr Moore at length succeeded, and arranged that Mr Grattan should be put in nomination.

The Sheriff being friendly, he allowed the election to be held after 12 o'clock on the night of the 15th. Mr Tighe got the officer to sign the return, and set off immediately on horseback with it. He arrived in Dublin about five in the morning, when we heard a loud knocking at the door. Mr Grattan had been very ill, and was then in bed, and turning round, he exclaimed, 'Oh, here they come, why will they not let me die in peace?' The question of Union had become dreadful to him; he could not bear the idea or listen to the subject, or speak of it with any degree of patience; he grew quite wild, and it almost drove him frantic.

I shall never forget the scene that followed. I told him he must get up immediately, and go down to the House: so we got him out of bed, and dressed him. I helped him down stairs; then he went into the parlour and loaded his pistols, and I saw him put them in his pocket, for he apprehended he might be attacked by the Union party, and assassinated. We wrapped a blanket round him, and put him in a sedan chair, and when he left the door I stood there, uncertain whether I should ever see him again. Afterwards, Mr M'Can came to see me and said that I need not be alarmed, as Mr Grattan's friends had determined to come forward in case he was attacked, and if necessary take his place in the event of any personal quarrel. When I heard that, I thanked him for his kindness, but told him, 'My husband cannot die better than in defence of his country' . . .

At seven o'clock in the morning Mr Egan had risen to speak, when Mr Grattan entered the House. He was so debilitated that he was scarcely able to walk, and was supported by Mr W. B. Ponsonby and Mr Arthur Moore. The House and the galleries were seized with breathless emotion; and a thrilling sensation, a low murmur, pervaded the whole assembly, when they beheld a thin, weak and emaciated figure, worn down by sickness of mind and body, scarcely able to sustain himself; the man who had been the founder of Ireland's independence in 1782 was now coming forward, feeble, helpless, and apparently in his last moments, to defend or to fall with his country.

His friends crowded round him, anxious to assist him, – Bowes Daly, in particular, seeing that Mr Grattan had on his hat, he told him it was contrary to the rules of the House. Mr Grattan calmly replied, 'Do not mind me, I know what to do.' He was dressed in the Volunteer uniform, blue, with red cuffs and collar. He had placed his cocked hat square to the front, and kept it on till he advanced half way up the floor; he then stopped and looked round the House with a steady and fearless eye, as if he wished to let them know that, though exhausted, he was yet prepared to give battle . . .

Grattan concluded his speech against the Act of Union in the following words:

'The constitution may be *for a time* so lost; the character of the country cannot be so lost; the Ministers of the Crown will, or may perhaps at length, find that it is not so easy to put down forever an ancient and respectable nation, by abilities, however great, and by power and by corruption, however irresistible. . . . Identification is a solid and imperial maxim, necessary for the preservation of freedom – necessary for that of empire; but without union of hearts identification is extinction, is dishonour, is conquest.

'Yet I do not give up the country; I see her in a swoon, but she is not dead. Though in her tomb she lies helpless and motionless, still there is on her lips a spirit of life, and on her cheek a glow of beauty.

> Thou art not conquered; beauty's ensign yet
> Is crimson on thy lips and in thy cheeks,
> And death's pale flag is not advanced there.'

[89] THE LAST HOURS OF THE IRISH HOUSE OF COMMONS; FROM *THE RISE AND FALL OF THE IRISH NATION* BY SIR JONAH BARRINGTON.

The Speaker rose slowly from that chair which had been the proud source of his honours and of his high character; for a moment he resumed his seat, but the strength of his mind sustained him in his duty, though his struggle was apparent. With that dignity which never failed to signalize his official actions, he held up the Bill for a moment in silence; he looked steadily around him on the last agony of the expiring Parliament. He at length repeated, in an emphatic tone, 'as many as are of opinion that THIS BILL do pass say aye.' The affirmative was languid but indisputable, another momentary pause ensued, again his lips seemed to decline their office: at length, with an eye averted from the object which he hated, he proclaimed with a subdued voice, '*the AYES have it.*' The fatal sentence was now pronounced, for an instant he stood statue-like; then indignantly, and with disgust, flung the Bill upon the table, and sunk into his chair with an exhausted spirit. An independent country was thus degraded into a province, Ireland as a nation, was EXTINGUISHED.

[90] THE LAST HOURS OF THE IRISH HOUSE OF LORDS IN 1799; FROM THOMAS DE QUINCEY'S *AUTOBIOGRAPHIC SKETCHES*.

Thomas de Quincey (1785–1859) poet, essayist and author of the famous Confessions of an Opium Eater, *was a schoolboy of fifteen, and staying with his friend, Lord Altamont, the young heir of the Marquis of Sligo, when he witnessed this scene.*

It was about the middle of the day, and a great mob filled the whole space about the two Houses. As Lord Altamont's coach drew up to the

steps of that splendid edifice, we heard a prodigious hissing and hooting; and I was really agitated to think that Lord Altamont, whom I loved
and respected, would probably have to make his way through a tempest
of public wrath – a situation more terrific to him than to others from
his embarrassed walking. I found, however, that I might have spared
my anxiety; the subject of commotion was, simply, that Major Sirr, or
Major Swan, I forget which (both being so celebrated in those days for
their energy as leaders of the police), had detected a person in the act
of mistaking some other man's pocket-handkerchief for his own – a
most natural mistake, I should fancy, where people stood crowded
together so thickly. . . .

We entered; and, by way of seeing everything, we went even to the
robing-room. The man who presented his robes to Lord Altamont
seemed to me, of all whom I saw on that day, the one who wore the face
of the deepest depression. But, whether this indicated the loss of a
lucrative situation, or was really disinterested sorrow, growing out of a
patriotic trouble at the knowledge that he was now officiating for the
last time, I could not guess. The House of Lords, decorated (if I remember) with hangings representing the battle of the Boyne, was nearly
empty when we entered. . . .

Gradually the House filled: beautiful women sat intermingled
amongst the peers. . . . Next came a stir within the House, and an uproar
resounding from without, which announced the arrival of His Excellency.
Entering the House, he also, like the other peers, wheeled round to the
throne, and made to that mysterious seat a profound homage. Then
commenced the public business, in which, if I recollect, the Chancellor
played the most conspicuous part – that Chancellor (Lord Clare) of
whom it was affirmed in those days, by a political opponent, that he
might swim in the innocent blood which he had caused to be shed. . . .

At which point in the order of succession came the royal assent to
the Union Bill, I cannot distinctly recollect. But one thing I *do* recollect
– that no audible expression, no buzz, nor murmur, nor *susurrus* even,
testified the feelings which, doubtless, lay rankling in many bosoms.

Setting apart all public or patriotic considerations, even then I said to myself, as I surveyed the whole assemblage of ermined peers, 'How is it, and by what unaccountable magic, that William Pitt can have prevailed on all these hereditary legislators and heads of patrician houses to renounce so easily, with nothing worth the name of a struggle, and no reward worth the name of an indemnification, the very brightest jewel in their coronets? This morning they all rose from their couches Peers of Parliament, individual pillars of the realm, indispensable parties to every law that could pass. Tomorrow they will be nobody men of straw – *terrae filii*. What madness has persuaded them to part with their birthright, and to cashier themselves and their children for ever into mere titular Lords?'

Perhaps there might be a little pause – a silence like that which follows an earthquake; . . . All was or looked courtly, and free from vulgar emotion. One person only I remarked whose features were suddenly illuminated by a smile, a sarcastic smile, as I read it; which, however, might be all a fancy. It was Lord Castlereagh; who, at the moment when the irrevocable words were pronounced, looked with a penetrating glance amongst a party of ladies. . . . After this I had no leisure to be interested in anything which followed. 'You are all,' thought I to myself, 'a pack of vagabonds henceforward, and interlopers, with actually no more right to be here than myself. I am an intruder, so are you.' Apparently they thought so themselves; for, soon after this solemn *fiat* of Jove had gone forth, their lordships, having no farther title to their robes (for which I could not help wishing that a party of Jewish old-clothesmen would at this moment have appeared, and made a loud bidding), made what haste they could to lay them aside for ever. The House dispersed much more rapidly than it had assembled. Major Sirr was found outside, just where we left him, laying. down the law (as before) about pocket-handkerchiefs to old and young practitioners; and all parties adjourned to find what consolation they might get in the great evening event of dinner.

[91] AN EPITAPH FOR THE PARLIAMENT HOUSE;
FROM *THE STORY OF DUBLIN* BY D. A. CHART.

After the Act of Union of 1801, the Parliament House had been sold and the House of Commons converted to a bank.

> Here, where old Freedom was wont to wait
> Her darling Grattan nightly at the gate,
> Now little clerks in hall and colonnade
> Tot the poor items of provincial trade;
> Lo! round the walls that Bushe and Plunket shook,
> The teller's desk, the runner's pocket-book.

[92] DANIEL O'CONNELL SALUTES THE PARLIAMENT HOUSE, 1844;
FROM *THE LIFE OF DANIEL O'CONNELL* BY MICHAEL MACDONAGH.

Daniel O'Connell, the Liberator, who dominated the Irish political scene in the early nineteenth century, has already won Catholic emancipation, and here he is freed after his arrest for his campaign to repeal the Union – in a triumphal procession through Dublin, he salutes the symbol of Ireland's eighteenth-century Parliament.

The electric telegraph was not yet at work. William Ford, one of the solicitors for the traversers, hurried to Dublin with the news. At Crewe he put his head out of the carriage window, and shouted: 'O'Connell is out!' 'Was it here the gentleman got out?' asked a stolid Saxon railway porter. On the evening of the 5th September thousands thronged the pier at Kingstown, Dublin, awaiting the arrival of the Mail steamer *Medusa* from Holyhead, which was expected to convey the issue of the proceedings before the House of Lords. Ford was on board, and as the vessel approached the pier, he shouted in a loud voice: 'O'Connell is free.' The news was received with wild uproar. The engine of the train which brought Ford from Kingstown to Dublin bore flags, on which were inscribed: 'Triumph of law and justice – the judgment reversed,' and 'O'Connell is free,' telling the glad tidings to thousands along the route. Clamorous shouts of joy were again raised as the train steamed into the terminus at Westland Row. In the crowd outside were several horsemen, who immediately spurred to Richmond Prison to be first with the intelligence. A messenger of the Repeal Association, named Edmond O'Hagarty, won in the race. He dashed, panting, up the corridor leading to O'Connell's apartments, exclaiming, 'I'm first! I'm first!' 'What is it all about?' said Barrett, who was walking in the corridor. 'Only that you are free!' said the man. 'Hurrah! I'm first! Where's the Liberator? I'm first!' He rushed wildly into the drawing-room, where O'Connell, wearing his green Mullaghmast cap, was sitting between his daughter and daughter-in-law, with, as was his wont, their hands clasped in his. 'I'm first!' roared O'Hagarty. 'You're free, Liberator. Thanks be to God for that same! I'm first!' 'Dah! it isn't true – it can't be true,' said O'Connell. All doubt was set at rest by the appearance of Ford, pale, with tears in his eyes, and blowing from his exertions. 'On the merits,' were the first words used by the aged attorney, as he flung his arms round O'Connell's neck. 'On the merits,' he repeated. 'No technicalities at all – nothing but the merits.' Then, as the news spread among the prisoners and their friends, there was much shaking hands, embracing, and weeping. Even the governor of the prison, Mr Purdon, was so excited by the news that he fainted; and the deputy governor, an Englishman, rushed out of the room to hide his emotion. O'Connell was deeply impressed. 'The hand of man is not in this,' said he reverently to FitzPatrick. 'It is the response given by Providence to the prayers of the faithful, steadfast people of Ireland.' But the trials had cost the treasury of the Repeal Association the enormous sum of £50,000.

The next day the order for the release of the prisoners arrived from London. The jail doors were flung open, and the citizens poured in to congratulate O'Connell. For hours he stood in the garden, while thousands of men, women, and children filed past and shook him by the hand. . . .

Daniel O'Connell in his triumphal car salutes the
Parliament House after his release from Richmond Gaol;
from *The Illustrated London News*, 1844

Then came the triumphant departure of the 'martyrs' from the peni-
tentiary. Outside were assembled the trades of Dublin, with bands and
banners; the equipages of the Lord Mayor and Corporation, the
committee of the Repeal Association, and thousands of well-to-do citizens. At the gate stood a triumphal chariot, consisting of three plat-
forms, rising one above the other, gorgeous in purple velvet and gold
fringe, and drawn by six splendid dapple greys. This cumbrous fantasti-
cal vehicle had been made specially for the occasion. At two o'clock the
prison was thrown open. Out came O'Connell, led by the hand of
William Smith O'Brien, MP, and followed by his fellow-prisoners.
O'Connell mounted the very topmost stage of the chariot, accompanied by his son Daniel and his chaplain, the Rev Dr Miley, and, standing to his full height in his ample cloak, took off his green velvet
Mullaghmast cap, and waved it again and again around his head, amid
a prolonged roar of applause. At his feet, on the second platform, sat an
old harper in ancient Irish garb, playing patriotic airs. On the third platform of the car were O'Connell's young grandchildren in green velvet

tunics and caps with white feathers. The other liberated prisoners drove in open carriages, the eccentric Tom Steel, 'Head Pacificator of Ireland,' being distinguished by an immense green bough – the emblem of peace – which he bore in his hands. In a vehicle by themselves were the attornies of the traversers, carrying a copy of the indictment made up in a huge volume, like the file of a newspaper. The procession was six miles long, and in it marched 200,000 men. It proceeded slowly into the city, winding its way through the principal streets, packed with people, to the residence of O'Connell in Merrion Square. Opposite the Parliament House in College Green the chariot stopped. O'Connell, removing his cap, pointed with his finger to the noble edifice, which he hoped to re-animate with the soul of national life; and, turning slowly round, gazed silently into the faces of the people. It was a dramatic episode – that silent gesture, eloquent of the national hopes and aspirations – and thunderous cheers greeted it.

St Stephen's Green

The history of Stephen's Green goes back to the time of the Crusaders, who, it was said, brought the fell disease of leprosy from the East. On the site of the Green a lazar hospital and church were erected, and placed under the care of monks, who ministered to the souls and bodies of those afflicted. In the Reformation days hospital, church, and monks were swept away, and the Green remained a public common, the haunt of wild birds, especially snipe, which were attracted by the marshy nature of the land, and multiplied exceedingly.

In 1663 we find the burgesses of the City beginning to awake to the fact that such a large area as sixty acres might be turned to better advantage than feeding snipe. The Green was therefore parcelled out in lots, and seven years later (1670) the further step was taken of enclosing a certain portion by a thick hedge, outside which ran the deep ditch alluded to. Inside the hedge a wide walk was made between two rows of lime trees. Later on a high wall was added, when we must suppose the hedge was removed. The wall does not appear in Malton's engraving [here reproduced in the plates]; but we have the ditch. Malton visited Dublin in 1775, quite a hundred years after the first steps were taken to make the Green habitable. It was then, as we can see by the print, a fashionable promenade, especially on Sundays after church, when a gay company could be seen walking in the Beaux' Walk on the north side, which was more 'the mode' than the French Walk on the west side, or Leeson Walk on the south.

[94] Bishop Clayton's wife receives on Stephen's Green, 1731; from *The Autobiography and Correspondence of Mrs Delany.*

Robert Clayton, Bishop of Cork, and his rich wife were among the most fashionable people in the Dublin of Mrs Delany's day (their portrait hangs in the Irish National Gallery). Their house on the south side of St Stephen's Green was designed by Richard Cassells, and now, much altered, forms part of Iveagh House, the Irish Foreign Office, still a venue for grand receptions.

You must know, madam, yesterday being Wednesday, Mrs Clayton opened her apartment and admitted all her acquaintance. I will describe to you how they are disposed and furnished. First there is a very good hall well filled with servants, then a room of eighteen foot square, wainscoted with oak, the panels all carved, and the doors and chimney finished with very fine high carving, the ceiling stucco, the window-curtains and chairs yellow Genoa damask, portraits and landscapes, very well done, round the room, marble tables between the windows, and looking-glasses with gilt frames. The next room is twenty-eight foot long and twenty-two broad, and is as finely adorned as damask, pictures, and busts can make it, besides the floor being entirely covered with the finest Persian carpet that ever was seen. The bedchamber is large and handsome, all furnished with the same damask. There was abundance of good and agreeable company; they went away about half an hour after ten, and so delighted with their reception, that Mrs Clayton has promised to admit her friends every Wednesday. I preside at the commerce table. I must leave off, my letter wanted to go to the post.

[95] LORD ORRERY WRITES TO CONGRATULATE BISHOP CLAYTON ON HIS NEW HOUSE AND RETAILS THE DUBLIN GOSSIP; FROM *THE ORRERY PAPERS*, EDITED BY THE COUNTESS OF CORK AND ORRERY.

Lord Orrery (1707–1762) was a great grandson of the great Earl of Cork (see p. 59). A dilettante of art and letters, he moved in the same circles as Swift, Pope and Dr Johnson, and wrote a life of Swift. His enormous correspondence is a mine of eighteenth-century Dublin gossip. The open ground he advises Bishop Clayton to acquire for his stables eventually became Iveagh Gardens, landscaped by Ninian Niven for Lord Iveagh in the 1860s with fantastic rockeries and fountains and now a secret garden for Dubliners.

Dublin, December 11th, 1736.

MY LORD, – This comes to congratulate your Lord^p upon your new House in Stevens-Green. *Felices quorum iam maria surgunt!* Mr Percival was so Kind as to go with me there yesterday: and Signor Cassells honoured us with his Company; but as your Lord^{ps} Commands did not extend so far as to order me to break my Neck or my Limbs, I ventur'd no further than the Hall Door, from whence my Prospect was much confin'd, except when I look'd upwards to the Sky. Your Palace, my Lord, appears finely upon Paper, and to shew You that the whole pleases me, I even admire your Coal Cellars. Your great Room will probably bring the Earl of Burlington over to this Kingdom, and do not wonder, my Lord, if Marcellus quits his Nitch and flings himself at Miss Donallan's Feet as soon as ever 'Verdi prati' reach his ears, but however your Hearing or Sight may be delighted, I am in some Fear that your Smell will not be regal'd from your Stables unless you stock your Garden as soon as possible with Roses, Lilies, and All the Flowers that are celebrated in Song. This inconvenience might be prevented if your Lord^p can purchase a little more Ground behind your House: but so that the Stable has a beautiful Cornish, Signor Cassells does not seem to care where it stands . . .

Mrs Rochfort has gathered new Beauties by her Marriage. She charms more as a Wife than she did as a Maid: . . . Nelly Grove's Eyes shine like Diamonds sett in Jett, and the Chetwoods are as charming, tho' not as brisk as. in a Parliament Winter. Lady Ross defies the circling Years, and as Antaeus gather'd Strength from the Ground, She gathers Charms from Age, so does likewise her Grandmother the gay Lady Dunn. This, my Lord, is the State of Beauty in this Metropolis, and yet in this fortunate Situation do I languish for Corke, which your Lordship's Family made me so happy in, that I can relish no other Place.

[96] THE POET GERARD MANLEY HOPKINS ARRIVES AT THE JESUIT UNIVERSITY COLLEGE (NEWMAN HOUSE) ON STEPHEN'S GREEN, 1884; FROM *LETTERS OF GERARD MANLEY HOPKINS TO ROBERT BRIDGES*.

The Jesuit University [which later developed into University College, Dublin] was housed in another great eighteenth-century house on the southwest side of Stephen's Green designed by Cassells, and ironically owned by a notorious priest-baiter, Richard 'Burn-Chapel' Whaley. It was acquired by Cardinal Newman in the 1850s, who also helped design the curious neo-Byzantine chapel next door. The gentle poet-priest Gerard Manley Hopkins was sent to teach classics in 1884, but never took to Dublin life. His bedroom is still preserved as during his time there, as is James Joyce's classroom [see next extract]

University College, 85 & 86, Stephens Green, Dublin.
March 7, 1884

My dearest Bridges, – Remark the above address: it is a new departure or a new arrival and at all events a new abode. I dare say you know nothing of it, but the fact is that, though unworthy of and unfit for the post, I have been elected Fellow of the Royal University of Ireland in the department of classics. I have a salary of £400 a year, but when I first contemplated the six examinations I have yearly to conduct, five of them running, and to the Matriculation there came up last year 750 candidates, I thought that Stephen's Green (the biggest square in Europe) paved with gold would not pay for it. . . .

The house we are in, the College, is a sort of ruin and for purposes of study very nearly naked. And I have more money to buy books than room to put them in.

I have been warmly welcomed and most kindly treated. But Dublin itself is a joyless place and I think in my heart as smoky as London is: I had fancied it quite different. The Phoenix Park is fine, but inconveniently far off. There are a few fine buildings. . . .

My examinations are over till the next attack of the plague. My lectures, to call them by that grand name, are begun: *vae unum abiit et vae alterum venit*. I was I cannot tell when in such health and spirits as on my return from Cadwalader and all his goats but 331 accounts of the First Punic War with trimmings, have sweated me down to nearer my lees and usual alluvial low water mudflats, groans, despair, and yearnings.

[97] STEPHEN DEDALUS CALLS ON THE DEAN OF STUDIES
AT THE JESUIT UNIVERSITY COLLEGE; FROM *PORTRAIT
OF THE ARTIST AS A YOUNG MAN* BY JAMES JOYCE.

James Joyce (1882–1941) attended the Jesuit University College from 1899 to 1902, specializing in languages but sharpening his wits with discussions of Thomas Aquinas' aesthetics, as in this extract. A bust of Joyce opposite Newman House in Stephen's Green commemorates his student days.

But the trees in Stephen's Green were fragrant of rain and the rainsodden earth gave forth its mortal odour, a faint incense rising upward through the mould from many hearts. The soul of the gallant venal city which his elders had told him of had shrunk with time to a faint mortal odour rising from the earth and he knew that in a moment when he entered the sombre college he would be conscious of a corruption other than that of Buck Egan and Burnchapel Whaley.

It was too late to go upstairs to the French class. He crossed the hall and took the corridor to the left which led to the physics theatre. The corridor was dark and silent but not unwatchful. Why did he feel that it was not unwatchful? Was it because he had heard that in Buck Whaley's time there was a secret staircase there? Or was the Jesuit house extra-territorial and was he walking among aliens? The Ireland of Tone and of Parnell seemed to have receded in space.

He opened the door of the theatre and halted in the chilly grey light that struggled through the dusty windows. A figure was crouching before the large grate and by its leanness and greyness he knew that it was the dean of studies lighting the fire. Stephen closed the door quietly and approached the fireplace.

– Good morning, sir! Can I help you? –

The priest looked up quickly and said:

– One moment now, Mr Dedalus, and you will see. There is an art in lighting a fire. We have the liberal arts and we have the useful arts. This is one of the useful arts.–

– I will try to learn it – said Stephen.

– Not too much coal – said the dean – working briskly at his task – that is one of the secrets. –

He produced four candle butts from the side pockets of his soutane and placed them deftly among the coals and twisted papers. Stephen watched him in silence. Kneeling thus on the flagstone to kindle the fire and busied with the disposition of his wisps of paper and candle butts he seemed more than ever a humble server making ready the place of sacrifice in an empty temple, a levite of the Lord. . . .

The dean rested back on his hunkers and watched the sticks catch. Stephen, to fill the silence, said:

– I am sure I could not light a fire. –

– You are an artist, are you not, Mr Dedalus? – said the dean, glancing up and blinking his pale eyes. – The object of the artist is the creation of the beautiful. What the beautiful is is another question. –

He rubbed his hands slowly and drily over the difficulty.

– Can you solve that question now? – he asked.

– Aquinas – answered Stephen – says *pulcra sunt quae visa placent*. –

– This fire before us – said the dean – will be pleasing to the eye. Will it therefore be beautiful? –

– In so far as it is apprehended by the sight, which I suppose means here esthetic intellection, it will be beautiful. But Aquinas also says *Bonum est in quod tendit appetitus*. In so far as it satisfies the animal craving for warmth fire is a good. In hell, however, it is an evil. –

– Quite so – said the dean – you have certainly hit the nail on the head. –

[98] W. M. THACKERAY TAKES A GRILLED HERRING
AT THE SHELBOURNE HOTEL AND EXPLORES THE
GREEN; FROM HIS *IRISH SKETCHBOOK*, 1843.

The Shelbourne Hotel – most enduring of Dublin institutions – was originally housed in three modest brick houses on the east side of Stephen's Green. By the 1830s it had already become Dublin's most fashionable hotel.

This then is the chief city of the aliens. – The hotel to which I had been directed is a respectable old edifice, much frequented by families from the country, and where the solitary traveller may likewise find society: for he may either use the 'Shelburne' as an hotel or a boarding-house, in which latter case he is comfortably accommodated at the very moderate daily charge of six-and-eightpence. For this charge a copious breakfast is provided for him in the coffee-room, a perpetual luncheon is likewise there spread, a plentiful dinner is ready at six o'clock: after which there is a drawing-room and a rubber of whist, with *tay* and coffee and cakes in plenty to satisfy the largest appetite. The hotel is majestically conducted by clerks and other officers; the landlord himself does not appear, after the honest, comfortable English fashion, but lives in a private mansion hard by, where his name may be read inscribed on a brass-plate, like that of any other private gentleman.

A woman melodiously crying 'Dublin Bay herrings' passed just as we came up to the door, and as that fish is famous throughout Europe, I seized the earliest opportunity and ordered a broiled one for breakfast. It merits all its reputation: and in this respect I should think the Bay of Dublin is far superior to its rival of Naples. Are there any herrings in Naples Bay? Dolphins there may be: and Mount Vesuvius, to be sure, is bigger than even the Hill of Howth; but a dolphin is better in a sonnet than at a breakfast, and what poet is there that, at certain periods of the day, would hesitate in his choice between the two? . . .

The papers being read, it became my duty to discover the town; and a handsomer town, with fewer people in it, it is impossible to see on a summer's day. In the whole wide square of Stephen's Green, I think there were not more than two nurserymaids to keep company with the statue of George I., who rides on horseback in the middle of the garden, the horse having his foot up to trot, as if he wanted to go out of town too. Small troops of dirty children (too poor and dirty to have lodgings at Kingstown) were squatting here and there upon the sunshiny steps, the only clients at the thresholds of the professional gentlemen whose names figure on brass-plates on the doors. A stand of lazy carmen, a policeman or two with clinking bootheels, a couple of moaning beggars leaning against the rails and calling upon the Lord, and a fellow with a toy and book stall, where the lives of St Patrick, Robert Emmet, and Lord Edward Fitzgerald may be bought for double their value, were all the population of the Green.

Thackeray's sketch of his bedroom window at the Shelbourne, 'enjoying itself in the sunshine' with the help of the Chambermaid's broom

Having a couple of letters of introduction to leave, I had the pleasure to find the blinds down at one house, and the window in papers at another; and at each place the knock was answered in that leisurely way, by one of those dingy female lieutenants who have no need to tell you that families are out of town. So the solitude became very painful, and I thought I would go back and talk to the waiter at the 'Shelburne,' the only man in the whole kingdom that I knew, who had been accommodated with a queer little room, and dressing-room on the ground floor, looking towards the Green: a black-faced, good-humoured chambermaid had promised to perform a deal of scouring which was evidently necessary, (a fact she might have observed for six months back, only she is no doubt of an absent turn,) and when I came back from the walk, I saw the little room was evidently enjoying itself in the sunshine, for it had opened its window, and was taking a breath of fresh air, as it looked out upon the Green.

[99] GEORGE MOORE STAYS AT THE SHELBOURNE AND
SALUTES THE SPRING IN STEPHEN'S GREEN; FROM *AVE*,
VOLUME I OF HIS TRILOGY, *HAIL AND FAREWELL*.

*George Moore (1852–1933), novelist, returned to Ireland in 1900 to play (he
believed) the leading role in the Irish Literary Renaissance with W. B. Yeats
– a vision whose failure he used later with brilliant comic effect against
himself and his friends in Hail and Farewell. His lyrical celebration of the
Green in this extract contrasts with his biting view of Dublin in two earlier
books, Parnell and his Island (see p. 185) and A Drama in Muslin. The
'neighbour in Mayo' he refers to rather grandly here is the first Lord Ardilaun,
who in 1880 had had the Green landscaped at his own expense and presented
to the people of Dublin.*

But it is difficult to be angry with Ireland on a May morning when the
sun is shining, and through clouds slightly more broken than yesterday's, but full of the same gentle, encouraging light – dim, ashen clouds
out of which a white edging rose slowly, calling attention to the bright
blue, the robe that perhaps noon would wear. All about the square the
old brick houses stood sunning themselves, and I could see a chimney-
stack steeped in rich shadow, touched with light, and beyond it, and
under it, upon an illuminated wall, the direct outline of a gable; and at
the end of the streets the mountains appeared, veiled in haze, delicate
and refined as *The Countess Cathleen*.

A town wandering between mountain and sea, I said as I stood
before my glass shaving, forgetful of Edward [*Martyn, his cousin*], for
below me was Stephen's Green, and it took me back to the beginning of
my childhood, to one day when I stole away, and inspired by an uncon-
trollable desire to break the monotony of infancy, stripped myself of my
clothes, and ran naked in front of my nurse or governess, screaming
with delight at the embarrassment I was causing her. She could not
take me home along the streets naked, and I had thrown my clothes out
of reach into a hawthorn – cap and jacket, shirt and trousers. Since

those days the Green had been turned into an ornamental park by a neighbour of mine in Mayo, and given to the public; and telling the hall-porter that if Mr Yeats called he would find me in the Green, I went out thinking how little the soul of man changes. It declares itself in the beginning, and remains with us to the end. Was this visit to Ireland any thing more than a desire to break the monotony of my life by stripping myself of my clothes and running ahead a naked Gael, screaming Brian Boru? . . .

The first thing I saw on entering the Green was a girl loosening her hair to the wind, and following her down a sunny alley, I found myself suddenly by a brimming lake curving like some wonderful caligraphy round a thickly planted headland, the shadows of some great elms reflected in the water, and the long, young leaves of the willow sweeping the surface. The span of a stone bridge hastened my steps, and leaning over the parapet I stood enchanted by the view of rough shores thickly wooded, and high rocks down which the water came foaming to linger in a quiet pool. . . . A nurse-maid rushes forward, a boy is led away screaming; and wondering what the cause of his grief might be, I went in quest of new interests, finding one in an equestrian statue that ornamented the centre of the Green. There were parterres of flowers about it, and in the shadow people of all ages sat half asleep, half awake, enjoying the spring morning like myself; perhaps more than I did, they being less conscious of their enjoyment.

I wandered on, now enchanted by the going and coming of the sun, one moment implanting a delicious warmth between my shoulderblades, and at the next leaving me cold, forgetful of Yeats until I saw him in his black cloak striding in a green alley . . .

'Mr W. B. Yeats presents Mr George Moore to the Queen
of the Fairies'; a cartoon by Max Beerbohm celebrates
Moore's recruitment to the Celtic Revival, early 1900s

[100] A NIGHTLY DRAMA FOR DUBLINERS; FROM
THE SHELBOURNE BY ELIZABETH BOWEN.

Elizabeth Bowen (1899–1973), novelist and historian, spent much of her
early childhood living in Dublin, where her father worked as a lawyer, and
described it later in her fragment of autobiography, Seven Winters *(see p.*
298).

Only a fool would glorify Dublin's climate: rain often slashed at finery,
gales rocked carriages. Seldom, however, did the dirtiest night dislodge
all onlookers from their vantage point across the road from the
Shelbourne; and on more springlike evenings large crowds gathered.
The departure in splendour, from the hotel, of guests bound for a ball
or Drawing-room was one of the spectacles of Dublin, a drama played
to an audience of oldtimers, critical, but well mannered. Nor were the
rights of this audience ever denied. Very early, people took up their
places – some climbed the Stephen's Green railings, to see better. All
eyes, expectant, were fixed on the Shelbourne's door – which, frequently
opening, exposed to view the bright-lighted hall, ivory pillars, and crimson carpet. The actors in this drama were grouped ideally – tier upon
tier up the steps of the noble staircase would be seated the ladies and
gentlemen waiting for their carriages. They wore the impersonality of
extreme grandeur – ladies' plumes nodded, satins gleamed, jewels shot
out rays; the black-and-white of the gentlemen was immaculate. One
after another, round rolled the carriages – each, as it stopped, for a
moment, blocking the view. Each time, a name was called: a couple or
a party rose from the stairs, advanced down the carpet, emerged from
the porch, drove off. The crowd looking on had come to be connoisseurs: each equipage drew an inspecting glance; the profiles inside its
windows were closely scanned.

That ceremony, satisfying to all, was repeated night after night for
unnumbered winters – being briefly renewed each August, when Horse
Show Week brought its own special round of festivities. The Eighties

and the Nineties, the Edwardian decade, and the few years left to run out before the cataclysm of 1914, swim together into a rosy haze.

[101] GEORGE MOORE DINES AT ELY HOUSE; FROM *AS I WAS GOING DOWN SACKVILLE STREET* BY OLIVER ST JOHN GOGARTY.

George Moore, during his decade in Dublin (1900–1911), lived at No. 4, Upper Ely Place, south of Stephen's Green, where his mannerisms and quarrels with his neighbours were mercilessly noted by Oliver Gogarty who lived opposite at No. 5. Sir Thornley Stoker, the owner of Ely House, was the brother of Bram Stoker, the creator of Dracula. Augustine Birrell was the Irish Secretary of State and a noted conversationalist.

Gogarty (1878–1957), Dublin poet, wit and surgeon (later cruelly immortalized as 'Buck Mulligan' in Joyce's novel, Ulysses), published this first volume of memoirs in 1937. They were considered highly scandalous and brought him a libel action; he eventually left Dublin to live in America.

Ely Place, Dublin. Like its namesake in London, it is a cul-de-sac. From St Stephen's Green, Hume Street runs into it at right angles, and Ely House, the residence of the long-dead Marquis, looks down Hume Street to the west. The prevailing wind, which is western, blows the dust of Hume Street against the great house, seven windows wide, and makes it unsafe to keep them open. Ely House is one of the few remaining palaces of the spacious Eighteenth Century which exist in Dublin without having fallen long ago into decay: old houses which were dedicated to mythological persons. Belvedere House to Venus, Ely House to Hercules. The Farnese Hercules stands like a pillar at the foot of the great stairs, which are balustraded by representations in gilt bronze of the wild beasts such as the Nemean Lion which fell to his club and whose hide he holds for ever on his left arm.

Sir Thornley Stoker, the famous surgeon, lives in Ely Place, and in the Eighteenth Century, which he never really leaves; hence the house is filled with period furniture, of which he is a collector and connoisseur. Chippendale, Adams, and old silver candelabra, match the silver jambs of the doors, and are contemporary with the silver linings of the great fireplaces, under their mantels of Siena and statuary marble.

A figure with hair silver as a dandelion in summer, pink porcelain face, sloping shoulders and peg-topped trousers in a suit of navy blue, came strolling down Ely Place from its garden end. He carried a Malacca cane with an ivory top shaped like an egg; he strolled leisurely, as became a novelist, a personage and a man of independent means. When he reached the long railings of Ely House he drew his stick across them as he went, causing a noise which he calculated would reach and irritate the somewhat strange and irascible owner. He passed on.

'Be sure you come punctually,' said Sir Thornley to me, 'it's a sign of bad manners to be late for dinner. Augustine Birrell is dining with us; but it's not for that reason that I ask you to be punctual, but for the general principle.'

The great dining-room was lit with candles, which of course were waxen.

'Nobody ever heard of paraffin candles at the time that this house was built; you see how much better the stucco designs appear on the blank walls in this mellow light. This is Mr Birrell; now I think we can all be seated. There is no use waiting any longer, and one has to consider the soup more than a tardy guest. Take your places, gentlemen.'

We had just finished the soup when the door of Domingo mahogany swung silently, reflecting the light. The butler said, 'Mr George Moore.'

Sir Thornley Stoker only half rose and turned sideways, holding his napkin like an apron in his lap.

'Sit down, Moore,' he said testily, 'sit down. We couldn't wait for you any longer.'

Moore went over to his empty chair, balanced it on its hind legs, admired what Sir Thornley would call 'the excellent skin' of its glossy Chippendale wood, and turning from his scrutiny, with a look of inquiry towards his host, asked: 'A cancer, Sir Thornley, or a gallstone?' referring to Sir Thornley's habit of buying after a big operation 'a museum piece.'

Moore resented the presence of Birrell. He had decided for the evening not to have read *Obiter Dicta* or, at the worst, if anyone mentioned it, to be unaware of its relation to Mr Birrell, or of Mr Birrell's relation to it.

Sir Thornley asked: 'The shoulder or the belly of this salmon, Moore? I'm chining the salmon. I killed this fish in the Slaney   King Harmon's water – and I think we'll find it a palatable fish. Shall I help you to the shoulder?'

'No, I think the fin, Sir Thornley.'

'Now, Moore, don't be peevish. You are the last that should pretend to be careless about your food. I've just been reading your long letter in the *Irish Times* on the grey mullet. Nobody ever heard of a fin.'

'On the contrary, the Chineses – as my friend here insists on calling them – find sharks' fins delicious.'

These antics fail to draw Birrell, so Moore addresses his remarks to me. Then Birrell says, 'How is your brother Bram, Sir Thornley?'

'Haven't seen him for some time.'

'Is he living in Herbert Street, or is he in London at all these days?'

'He is engaged on scientific research somewhere,' said Sir Thornley.

'Not on the habits of Dracula?' said Birrell, with a laugh.

At this stage the mahogany door burst open, and a nude and elderly lady came in with a cry, 'I like a little intelligent conversation!' She ran round the table. We all stood up. She was followed by two female attendants, who seized whatever napery was available, and sheltering her with this and their own bodies, led her forth, screaming, from the room.

Our consternation held us in the positions we had suddenly taken. Birrell looked like a popular figure in Madame Tussaud's, Sir Thornley, with his knuckles on the table, inclined his head as if saying a silent grace. At last he broke silence with: 'Gentlemen, pray sit down.'

Nobody liked to begin a conversation, because the farther it was off the subject, the more purposefully self-conscious it would seem. Sir Thornley recovered himself and spoke:

'Gentlemen, under my mahogany, I hope you will keep this incident, mortifying as it is to me, from any rumour of scandal in this most gossipy town. And now, Moore, I conjure you most particularly, as you are the only one who causes me grave misgivings.'

'But it was charming, Sir Thornley. I demand an encore.'

Sir Thornley rose, went over to Moore's chair, and pointing his beard into Moore's ear, hissed something. Then, taking the novelist by the shoulder, he pushed him to the door and into the hall, and out into the street. We heard the door banging and the yapping of her Ladyship's Pomeranian dog.

Sir Thornley insisted on his guests drinking more wine. The dinner dragged on, Sir Thornley asking questions without waiting for answers, from each of us in turn. I was counting the minutes towards the end of this melancholy feast. After some minutes the butler leant over and said something to Sir Thornley.

'Did you admit that scoundrel?' said Sir Thornley harshly.

'He says, sir, it's a matter of life and death.'

'Will you, pray, excuse me, gentlemen? I have to leave the room for a moment.'

We could hear the inarticulate sound of voices, and suddenly two loud screams. It transpired that George, on his way home, had been bitten by a mad dog and was in danger of hydrophobia. Sir Thornley had enlarged the two slight scratches on Moore's right calf and was screwing caustic into the wound. The yells increased, and through the door, which Sir Thornley had forgotten to close, we could hear him saying, 'I don't care whether you're in a dinner-jacket or not.

You'll have to send to your house for my honorarium, which is five guineas, before you leave this hall.' Moore produced a wallet of flexible green leather and handed Sir Thornley a five-pound note, with 'I'll send the silver in the morning by my cook.' The butler opened the door, to let out George Moore, and to let in a little Pomeranian dog. . . .

[102] W. B. Yeats recites at Lady Ardilaun's tea-party; from *Bricks and Flowers* by Katherine Everett.

Lady Ardilaun was the widow of the Lord Ardilaun, whose munificence had restored St Patrick's Cathedral and transformed Stephen's Green into a beautiful public garden, and was herself a generous patron of the arts, especially of the Abbey Theatre. Katherine Everett, who acted as her secretary and companion during the First World War, published this delightful autobiography in 1949.

The Ardilauns had owned three large houses: one in Carlton House Terrace, one called Ashford near Galway, with extensive shooting and, of course, St Anne's, four miles from Dublin, but I think no one of these places gave Olive as much pleasure as her small house overlooking St Stephen's Green. She was touchingly delighted when connoisseurs admired her rooms, for she had never before enjoyed informed appreciation of her great possessions. . . .

Sometimes to entertain our guests we had musical afternoons, or actors from the Abbey, and very good they were. I remember Sara Allgood's charming voice as she enacted funny scenes with that perfect absence of self-consciousness characteristic of the Irish players. Another time Olive thought it might result in a wonderful experience if she ventured to ask W. B. Yeats to address us and to recite some of his own poems; this he consented to do. A very mixed gathering awaited him: soldiers from the Phoenix Park, some Castle people and other Dublin friends, and an old and deaf peer from the country. Talk was general when Yeats arrived late, and when he was announced he remained standing in the doorway, voices being hushed while everyone looked at his sombre figure. Then, as he did not move, Olive came forward to greet him with charming kindliness, asking if he would prefer to have tea before we were to have the pleasure of hearing his verses.

'I'll speak now,' he answered.

There was some confusion getting everyone to sit down, but at last Yeats stood alone in silence in the centre of an expectant circle, his lock of black hair falling over his forehead and his eyes on the floor. After a pause which made for discomfort, though I suppose it lasted for less than two minutes, he looked past us all as if seeing some distant vision and said, 'I speak of the moon.'

He spoke a lot about the moon in a slow, chanting voice, sometimes as if she were a siren to allure and destroy, again as a medium of strange magic, or as a cold menace, and nobody understood any of it.

When he had stopped as abruptly as he began, Olive said, 'Perhaps, Mr Yeats, you would recite "The Lake Isle of Innisfree" for us.' But he seemed not to have heard and announced, 'A verse to the moon.'

This verse had only four lines, which he half said, half sung, and then he bowed and backed towards the door, saying he wouldn't stay for tea.

When he was gone and chattering began again with varied comments, an officer was heard saying in a clear, clipped voice, 'Quite batty, I suppose, poor fellow,' and the deaf peer rumbled:

'Couldn't catch it all, but there's no moon tonight.'

[103] A GLIMPSE OF YEATS AND MAUD GONNE ON STEPHEN'S GREEN; FROM *MY IRELAND* BY KATE O'BRIEN.

Kate O'Brien (1897–1974), novelist and playwright, was a student at University College during the First World War. She later lived and worked

mainly in London and Spain, but returned to Ireland in the 1950s. Her most
famous novel, That Lady, was banned in Spain.

[Yeats] lived then in Maud Gonne's house in Stephen's Green – she
being in prison in England. We students saw him often as he strode
about. I remember following him one cold night between the chains
and the railings of the Green, along the East side and the North, past
the Shelbourne lights and under the bare trees until he strode across
the tramlines and into his club near Grafton Street. One followed and
watched him with avid concern; as later, when she came back from
jail, one followed Maud Gonne [*see p. 240*] over the same courses.
And curiously, though both impressed, and solemnised the foolish
young passion of intrusiveness – an inescapable passion, for both
were myths to us, and he had made them – curiously each failed to
illumine in their flesh the immortal two of the poet's creation. . . .
Maud Gonne indeed strode through our common crowd as if on
forgetful travel down from some absurd and glorious Valhalla; dark
veils flying, rain beating foolishly against the prow-like face, and her
two wolfhounds profiling as low as to the curve of her great draped
knees. And after the first disappointment it hardly mattered that the
figure was too much, too mythical – that the whiff of saga, of simplic-
ity was a warning. That, after all, was a question of personal taste, of
nerves. What mattered was that the poet could not be discovered in
the proud and picturesque figure one pursued so cheekily from street
lamp to street lamp. Yeats looked magnificent. He was tall and heavy
and he strode head in air, and chanting or talking to himself. The head
was heavy, the heavy hair fell back from it; the ribbon fluttered from
the eye-glasses, the fur-collared coat flapped open; the wide-awake
hat was sometimes on the back of his head, sometimes swinging in
his hand; he always carried books and papers; he always walked as if
through empty space.

[104] BRENDAN BEHAN'S MOTHER REMEMBERS YEATS;
FROM *BRENDAN BEHAN'S ISLAND* BY BRENDAN BEHAN.

Kathleen Behan (1889–1984), mother of the great Dublin talker and writer, was a remarkable character in her own right. Brought up in a Dublin orphanage, she married twice, reared a family of six sons on republican principles, and ran messages to the GPO during the Rising of 1916. Her autobiography, Mother of all the Behans, *dictated to her fifth son, Brian, was published when she was ninety-five.*

My mother was a maid in the house owned by Madame Maud Gonne MacBride, and she knew Yeats quite well. . . . He used to visit that house which was in St Stephen's Green, and he used to call her 'Kitty' which she disliked for her name is Kathleen. He arranged his entrances to the house so infallibly that he was there just as she'd be coming up the stairs with a tray of tea and cakes and sandwiches for the visitors, and he'd stop and talk to her for a couple of minutes. I think it was probably an inverted form of snobbery to show the guests that he'd as leave talk to the housemaid as to a lord. But this didn't excuse my mother from Maud Gonne's tongue when she scolded her for having the tea cold.

My mother also told me that at lunch, where she often served Yeats, he was absolutely impervious to what he ate, as he didn't know what he was eating half the time. He absent-mindedly would put sugar in the soup and salt in the coffee and all sorts of peculiar things like that. The one dislike that he had in the way of food was parsnips. Once he was served parsnips by some mistake and he remarked: 'This is a very peculiar pudding.'

I was in the 'Deux Magots' in Paris one time and an American that I was introduced to asked me if I had known James Joyce. I said that I hadn't had that honour, but I told him that my mother had often served a meal to W. B. Yeats in Maud Gonne's house on Stephen's Green and that the poet turned up his nose to the parsnips. 'He didn't like parsnips?' said the American reaching for his notebook, 'You're sure this is factual?'

'It is to be hoped,' I replied, 'that you are not calling my mother a liar?'

'No, no, of course not,' he said, 'but she might have been mistaken – it might have been carrots,' he added hastily.

'You must think I'm a right fool to have a mother that can't tell a carrot from a parsnip,' I said nastily.

'No, no, of course – I mean I'm sure she could but it is very important. . . .' He wrote in the book: *Parsnips – attitude of Yeats to*. 'And you say he didn't like Stephen's greens either – now, what kind of vegetables are they?'

'Kildare Street

[105] THE KILDARE STREET CLUB; FROM *PARNELL*
AND HIS ISLAND BY GEORGE MOORE.

Moore wrote Parnell and His Island, *a biting attack on all aspects of Irish life, in 1886, when the Irish Land War was at its height. The O'Shea brothers, who sculpted the stonework of the club's windows, evidently shared his view of the club members – witness the monkeys playing billiards around the base of one of the capitals in Kildare Street. The club has moved to St Stephen's Green and the building is now shared between the Alliance Française and the manuscript section of the National Library.*

The Kildare Street Club is one of the most important institutions Dublin. It represents in the most complete acceptation of the word the rent party in Ireland; better still, it represents all that is respectable, that is to say, those who are gifted with an oyster-like capacity for understanding this one thing: that they should continue to get fat in the bed in which they were born. This club is a sort of oyster-bed into which all the eldest sons of the landed gentry fall as a matter of course. There they remain spending their days, drinking sherry and cursing Gladstone in a sort of dialect, a dead language which the larva-like stupidity of the club has preserved. The green banners of the League are passing, the cries of a new Ireland awaken the dormant air, the oysters rush to their window – they stand there open-mouthed, real panto-mime oysters, and from the corner of Frederick Street a group of young girls watch them in silent admiration.

Leinster House, engraved by James Malton, 1792

Leinster House

[106] A description of Leinster House; from *A Picturesque and Descriptive View of Dublin* by James Malton.

Leinster House [originally Kildare House] had been built by Richard Cassels for the 1st Duke of Leinster in the 1740s, the first great magnate to settle south of the river. James Malton, one of a noted family of artists, first published his famous aquatints of Dublin in 1797 'desirous to make a display of its beauty to the world' and they ran to numerous editions.

Leinster House, the town residence of his Grace the Duke of Leinster, is the most stately private edifice in the city, pleasantly situated at the south-east extremity of the town, commanding prospects few places can exhibit, and possessing advantages few city fabrics can obtain, by extent of ground both in front and rear; in front, laid out in a spacious courtyard;

the ground in the rear, made a beautiful lawn, with a handsome shrubbery on each side, screening the adjacent houses from view; enjoying, in
the tumult of a noisy metropolis, all the retirement of the country. A
dwarf wall, which divides the lawn from the street, extends almost the
entire side of a handsome square, called Merrion-square. . . . The greater
part of the building is of native stone [quarried at Ardbraccan, in the
county of Meath], but the west front, and all the ornamental parts
throughout, are of Portland. South of the building are commodious
offices and stables. The inside of this mansion in every respect corresponds with the grandeur of its external appearance.

The hall is lofty, rising two stories, ornamented with three-quarter
columns of the Doric order, and an enriched entablature; the ceiling is
adorned with stucco ornaments, on coloured grounds; and the whole is
embellished with many rich and tasty ornaments. To the right of the hall
are the family private apartments; the whole convenient, beautifully
ornamented, and elegantly furnished: overlooking the lawn is the great
dining parlour, and adjoining it, at the north end, is an elegant long room,
the whole depth of the house, twenty-four feet wide, called the supper
room, adorned with sixteen fluted Ionic columns, supporting a rich ceiling. Over the supper room is the picture gallery, of the same dimensions,
containing many fine paintings by the first masters. . . . From the windows
of the attic story, to the east, are most delightful prospects over the Bay of
Dublin, which, for three miles, is divided by that great work, the South
Wall, with a beautiful light-house at the termination: the sea, for a considerable extent, bounds the horizon, and every vessel coming in or going
out of the bay must pass in distinct view.

[107] A BALLOON ASCENT FROM LEINSTER HOUSE LAWN, 1785;
FROM SIR JOHN GILBERT'S *THE HISTORY OF THE CITY OF DUBLIN*.

*Richard Crosbie (1755–1800) was the first Irishman to make a balloon
ascent. A huge burly man from Co Wicklow, he was described by a contemporary as a mechanical genius, and had worked out his own system of*

ballooning after reading of Montgolfier's success. His ballooning dress is reported elsewhere as being 'a robe of white silk, lined with white fur, his waistcoat and breeches in one, of white satin quilted, . . . morocco boots and a . . . cap of leopardskin'.

At half-past two P.M. Mr Crosbie ascended with an elegant balloon from the Duke of Leinster's lawn, after being twice forced to descend; but, on throwing out more of his ballast, he surmounted all obstacles. The current of the wind, which carried him at first at due east, soon after seemed inclined to bear him north-east, and pointed his voyage towards White-haven. When the balloon was seventeen minutes in view, it immersed in a cloud, but in four minutes after, its appearance again was testified by the numerous plaudits of the multitude. It now continued in sight, by the aid of achromatic glasses, thirty-two minutes from its ascent, when it was entirely lost to the view; some rockets were then sent off, and the troops of Volunteers, who attended, discharged their last volleys. Mr Crosbie had about 300 lbs weight of ballast, but discharged half a hundred in his first rise of ascension. At upwards of fourteen leagues from the Irish shore, he found himself within clear sight of both lands of the sister kingdoms, at which time, he says, it is impossible to give the human imagination any adequate idea of the unspeakable beauties which the scenery of the sea, bounded by both lands, presented. 'It was such,' said he, 'as should make me risk a life to enjoy again.' He rose, at one time, so high that the mercury in the barometer sunk entirely into its globe, and he was constrained to put on his oil-cloth cloak, but unluckily found his bottle of cordial broke, and could obtain no refreshment. The upper current of air was different from the lower, and the cold so intense that his ink was frozen. . . . He now entered a black cloud, and encountered a prepulsion of wind, with lightning and thunder, which brought him rapidly towards the surface of the water. Here the balloon made a circuit, but, falling lower, the water entered his car, and he lost his notes of observation; but recollecting that his watch was at the bottom of the car, he groped for it, and

Richard Crosbie and his balloon ascent from Leinster House drawn
1785; a contemporary engraving

put it into his pocket. All his endeavours to throw out ballast were of no
avail; the intemperance of the weather plunged him into the ocean. He
now thought of his cork waistcoat, and by much difficulty having put it
on, . . . he went before the wind as regularly as a sailing vessel. In this
situation, he found himself inclined to eat a morsel of fowl. When at
the distance of another league, he discovered some vessels crowding
after him; but as his progress outstripped all their endeavours, he
lengthened the space of the balloon from the car, which gave a conse-
quent check to the rapidity of his sailing, when the Dunleary barge
came up, and fired a gun. One of the sailors jumped into his car, and
made it fast to the barge, on which the aeronaut came out with the
same composure and fortitude of mind which marked the whole
complexion of his adventure. . . .

The barge now steered for Dunleary, and towed the balloon after it.
About ten o'clock they landed. On the morning of the 20th Mr Crosbie
had the honour of receiving the congratulations and breakfasting with

their Graces the Duke and Duchess of Rutland, at Mr Lee's elegant
lodge at Dunleary. He was afterwards conducted to town. . . .

[108] A SPY REPORTS ON LORD EDWARD FITZGERALD IN 1798;
FROM SIR JOHN GILBERT'S *HISTORY OF THE CITY OF DUBLIN*.

Lord Edward Fitzgerald, the Duke of Leinster's son, had become a leader
of the revolutionary united Irishmen. The informer in this government
report is the brother-in-law of Wolfe Tone, Thomas Reynolds, who had
infiltrated the directory of the United Irishmen. The day after this letter,
almost all the other leaders of the 1798 Rebellion were arrested, on his
information, at Oliver Bond's house on the Quays.

About 4 o'clock on Sunday, the 11th of March, I called at Leinster
House upon Lord Edward Fitzgerald. I had a printed paper in my
hand, which I had picked up somewhere, purporting to be directions
or orders, signed by Counsellor Saurin, to the Lawyers' corps. These
required them, in case of riot or alarm, to repair to Smithfield, and
such as had not ball-cartridge were to get them at his house, and such
as were going out of town, and did not think their arms safe, were to
deposit them with him; and there was a little paper inside, which
mentioned that their orders were to be kept secret. Lord Edward
Fitzgerald, upon reading this paper, seemed greatly agitated: he said
he thought Government intended to arrest him, and he wished he
could get to France, to hasten the invasion, which he could do by his
intimacy with Talleyrand Perigord, one of the French Ministers. He
said he would not approve of a general invasion at first, but that the
French had some very fine fast-sailing frigates, and that he would put
on board them as many English and Irish officers as he could procure
to come over from France, and as many men as were capable of drill-
ing, and stores and ammunitions of different kinds, and run them into
some port in this country; he said he thought Wexford might do: that
it would be unsuspected, and if they succeeded they could establish a

rallying point until other helps should come. Lord Edward, after this conversation, walked up and down the room in a very agitated manner: 'No,' said he, 'it is impossible; Government cannot be informed of it; they never have been able to know where the Provincial meet.' Shortly after this the servant came, and asked was he ready for dinner. I went away; – he wanted me to stay [to] dinner, but I would not.

[109] LADY SARAH NAPIER DESCRIBES LORD EDWARD FITZ-
GERALD'S ESCAPE FROM LEINSTER HOUSE, MARCH 1798; FROM
SIR JOHN GILBERT'S *THE HISTORY OF THE CITY OF DUBLIN*.

Lady Sarah Napier was the sister of the dowager Duchess of Leinster, and mother of three (later) famous sons, Charles, George and Henry Napier.

The separate warrant went by a messenger, attended by Sheriff Carlton, and a party of soldiers, commanded by a Major O'Kelly, into Leinster House. The servants ran up to Lady Edward, who was ill with the gathering in her breast, and told her; she said directly, 'there is no help, send them up:' they asked very civilly for her papers and Edward's, and she gave them all. Her apparent distress moved Major O'Kelly to tears; and their whole conduct was proper. They left her, and soon returned (Major Boyle having been with two dragoons to Frescati, and taken such papers as were in their sitting-room, and not found Edward) to search Leinster House for him, and came up with great good nature, to say, 'Madam, we wish to tell you our search is in vain, Lord Edward has escaped.'

(Lord Edward was captured eleven weeks later in Thomas Street – see p. 77.)

[110] THE 'GREENING' OF LEINSTER HOUSE (DÁIL EIREANN),
1930; FROM *IN SEARCH OF IRELAND* BY H. V. MORTON.

*The Free State Parliament rejected Daniel O'Connell's dream of restoring an
Irish Parliament to the old Parliament House on College Green (see p. 152),
in favour of Leinster House, partly for reasons of security – a decision which
might have gratified Lord Edward FitzGerald!*

The Poet came on the following day to say that he would show me the
most interesting sight in Dublin:

'We are,' he explained, 'going to see Dáil Eireann which, as you may
know, is the Parliament of the Free State.'

The Dáil meets in a large eighteenth-century house, formerly the
residence of the Dukes of Leinster. In front of it is a statue of Queen
Victoria, which, while not complimentary, is not so bad as the one that
sits so heavily on Manchester.

'That,' explained the Poet, pointing to the statue, 'is known with
Justice as "Ireland's Revenge".'

The entrance to the Dáil is like that to any big London club. Members
enter smoking pipes and cigarettes, collect their letters from a porter's
box on the right, and go on through Grosvenor Square galleries and up
wide ducal stairways to the 'House'.

The Free State Parliament meets in the old lecture theatre of the
Royal Dublin Society, which was founded in 1731 for the purpose of
promoting useful arts and sciences. The gallery has recently been
altered and fitted wih protective railings to prevent the accidental fall
of spectators or other objects on the deputies' heads, but the floor of
the theatre has been fitted with shining mahogany seats, which rise in
tiers in a horseshoe round the Speaker's chair. The House is dignified.
Beneath the gallery are old prints of Dublin in Hogarth frames.

One's first impression is that immense pains have been taken to
introduce as much green into the landscape as possible. Members hold
green question papers. When they turn them in unison it is as if a

breeze has blown through a forest! The files are green. The note-books are bound in green. Now and then messengers tiptoe down through the seats to deliver emerald green telegrams. At the top of the steps and at the doors stand the most competent-looking chuckers-out seen in public since the heyday of the old music-hall. I would give a man of average physique two seconds to maintain a real row in the Dáil!

Merrion Square

[111] DANIEL O'CONNELL AT HOME IN MERRION SQUARE;
FROM *SKETCHES OF THE IRISH BAR* BY W. H. CURRAN.

*Daniel O'Connell bought No. 58 (formerly No. 30) on the east side of Merrion
Square in 1809 – much to his frugal wife Mary's dismay – 'Where on earth
will you be able to get a thousand guineas . . .?' – and lived there on and off
until his death in 1847.*

If any one of you, my English readers, being a stranger in Dublin, should
chance as you return upon a winter's morning from one of the 'small
and early' parties of that raking metropolis – that is to say, between the
hours of five and six o'clock – to pass along the south side of Merrion
Square, you will not fail to observe that among those splendid mansions
there is one evidently tenanted by a person whose habits differ materi-
ally from those of his fashionable neighbours. The half-open parlour
shutters and the light within, announce that some one dwells there
whose time is too precious to permit him to regulate his rising with the
sun. Should your curiosity tempt you to ascend the steps, and, under
cover of the dark, to reconnoitre the interior, you will see a tall, able-
bodied man standing at a desk, and immersed in solitary occupation.
Upon the wall in front of him hangs a crucifix. From this and from the
calm attitude of the person within, and from a certain monastic rotundity about the neck and shoulders, your first impression will be that he
must be some pious dignitary of the Church of Rome, absorbed in his
matin devotions. But . . . no sooner can the eye take in the other furniture of the apartment, the bookcases clogged with tomes in plain calf-
skin bindings, the blue-covered octavos that lie on the table and the
floor, the reams of manuscript in oblong folds and begirt with crimson
tape, than it becomes evident that the party meditating amidst such
objects must be thinking far more of the law.than the prophets. He is
unquestionably a barrister, but, apparently, of that homely, chamber-

keeping, plodding cast, who labour hard to make up by assiduity what they want in wit. . . . Should you happen in the course of the same day to stroll down to the hall of the Four Courts you will not be a little surprised to find the object of your pity miraculously transformed from the severe recluse of the morning into one of the most bustling, important, and joyous personages in that busy scene.

[112] DR WILLIAM WILDE STANDS TRIAL; FROM *THE*
LIFE OF OSCAR WILDE BY FRANK HARRIS.

Oscar Wilde's father, Dr William Wilde, was a well-known surgeon and anti-
quary who lived at No. 1 Merrion Square. In 1864 he became the central
figure in a cause célèbre – one of his patients, a Miss Mary Travers, accused
him of rape in the course of a trial for libel, Isaac Butt appearing as her
lawyer.

Frank Harris (1856–1931) writer and journalist, and himself a compul-
sive philanderer, makes the most of the scene.

The excitement in the court was becoming breathless. It was felt that the details were cumulative; the doctor was besieging the fortress in proper form. The story of embracings, reconciliations and loans all prepared the public for the great scene.

The girl went on, now answering questions, now telling bits of the story in her own way, Mr Butt, the great advocate, taking care that it should all be consecutive and clear with a due crescendo of interest. In October, 1862, it appeared Lady Wilde was not in the house at Merrion Square, but was away at Bray, as one of the children had not been well, and she thought the sea air would benefit him. Dr Wilde was alone in the house. Miss Travers called and was admitted into Dr Wilde's study. He put her on her knees before him and bared her neck, pretending to examine the burn; he fondled her too much and pressed her to him: she took offence and tried to draw away. Somehow or other his hand got entangled in a chain at her neck. She called out to him 'You are

Daniel O'Connell at home in Merrion Square; from *The Illustrated London News*, 1843.

suffocating me,' and tried to rise: but he cried out like a madman: 'I will, I want to,' and pressed what seemed to be a handkerchief over her face. She declared that she lost consciousness.

When she came to herself she found Dr Wilde frantically imploring her to come to her senses, while dabbing water on her face, and offering her wine to drink.

'If you don't drink,' he cried, 'I'll pour it over you.'

For some time, she said, she scarcely realized where she was or what had occurred, though she heard him talking. But gradually consciousness came back to her, and though she would not open her eyes she understood what he was saying. He talked frantically:

'Do be reasonable, and all will be right. . . . I am in your power. . . . spare me, oh, spare me . . . strike me if you like. I wish to God I could hate you, but I can't. I swore I would never touch your hand again. Attend to me and do what I tell you. Have faith and confidence in me and you may remedy the past and go to Australia. Think of the talk this may give rise to. Keep up appearances for your own sake. . . .'

He then took her upstairs to a bedroom and made her drink some wine and lie down for some time. She afterwards left the house; she hardly knew how; he accompanied her to the door, she thought; but could not be certain; she was half dazed.

The judge here interposed with the crucial question:

'Did you know that you had been violated?'

The audience waited breathlessly; after a short pause Miss Travers replied:

'Yes.'

Then it was true, the worst was true. The audience, excited to the highest pitch, caught breath with malevolent delight. But the thrills were not exhausted. Miss Travers next told how in Dr Wilde's study one evening she had been vexed at some slight, and at once took four pennyworth of laudanum which she had bought. Dr Wilde hurried her round to the house of Dr Walsh, a physician in the neighbourhood, who gave her an antidote. Dr Wilde was dreadfully frightened lest something should get out . . .

[113] DANCING PARTIES IN MERRION AND FITZWILLIAM SQUARES; BY EILIS DILLON, FROM *VICTORIAN DUBLIN*, EDITED BY TOM KENNEDY.

Ellis Dillon, novelist, playwright and children's author, was born in Galway in 1920. Here she describes her grandparents' household and life in Dublin before the First World War.

Every winter, the families living in and around Fitzwilliam and Merrion Squares entertained each other to dances. Each family decided on a date well in advance and the Plunketts always booked a pianist named Miss Gasparro, and her violinist, to make music. It was always the same violinist but his name has not survived. It was noticed that she kicked him on the ankle if he displeased her while they played.

Between them and some cousins in Palmerston Road, they owned enough unbleached, figured damask linen to cover the floors of the double drawing-room for dancing. The linen was tacked on to the carpets, which were too heavy to be moved out. The guests usually numbered one hundred and fifty and even then the rooms were not overfilled. Supper was laid in the study and dining-room, and the pine rafters sprang up and down visibly without cracking the ornamental plaster-work of the ceiling below when everyone leaped together during the Lancers. . . .

The entertainment began with a children's party in the afternoon and after the children had gone, dancing took over for the rest of the evening. There was no singing, no performances of any kind except from the professional musicians, unless a guest had a particularly good voice. Dances where guests of indifferent talent rendered songs at the piano or played their pieces were frowned upon. While the little dance-band had supper, an older man who was a friend of the family played the piano very willingly so long as he had a glass of whiskey beside him.

The young people found it difficult to impress upon my grandmother that the whiskey was essential to his performance. The rest of the company had wine with supper, which was by intention kept rather simple. It was served at midnight and consisted of cold dishes, chicken and ham and galantines, with home-made fruit salad, cream and ice-cream. All of this was prepared in the house by the cook and the maids, helped out by the family, and served by the parlourmaid, the house-maids and the nurses.

Dancing finished at six in the morning and then the remains of supper were eaten. If too much was left over, my mother said calmly, a small dance was held the next day. Almost all of those energetic young men went off to the war in 1914 and were very soon killed.

Dublin Theatre

Previous page:
W. B. Yeats denounces the audience at the Abbey Theatre,
early 1900s

*G. F. Handel (1685–1759) had left London for Dublin in 1741 in search of a
more appreciative audience for his music. The Messiah, probably composed
in the early spring of 1742, was put on as a surprise extra at a charity concert
on 8 April, given in Neal's Music hall (now demolished) in Fishamble Street,
near Christ Church Cathedral. The letter is to his friend, Charles Jennens,
who had written the words for the oratorio.*

Sir, it was with the greatest Pleasure I saw the Continuation of Your
Kindness by the Lines You was pleased to send me, in Order to be prefix'd
to Your Oratorio Messiah, which I set to Musick before I left England. I
am emboldned, Sir, by the generous Concern You please to take in rela
tion to my affairs, to give You an Account of the Success I have met here.
The Nobility did me the Honour to make amongst themselves a
Subscription for 6 Nights, which did fill a Room of 600 Persons, so that I
needed not sell one single Ticket at the door, and without Vanity the
Performance was received with a general Approbation. Sig^ra Avolio,
which I brought with me from London pleases extraordinary, I have
form'd an other Tenor Voice which gives great satisfaction, the Basses and
Counter Tenors are very good, and the rest of the Chorus Singers (by my
Direction) do exceeding well, as for the Instruments they are really excellent, Mr Dubourgh being at the Head of them and the Musick sounds
delightfully in this charming Room, which puts me in such spirits (and
my Health being so good) that I exert my self on my Organ whit more
then usual success. I opened with the Allegro, Penseroso, & Moderato,
and I assure you that the Words of the Moderato are vastly admired. The

Audience being composed (besides the Flower of Ladies of Distinction and other People of the greatest quality) of so many Bishops, Deans, Heads of the Colledge, the most eminents People in the Law as the Chancellor, Auditor general &tc. all which are very much taken with the Poëtry. So that I am desired to perform it again the next time. I cannot sufficiently express the kind treatment I receive here, but the Politeness of this generous Nation cannot be unknown to You, so I let you judge of the satisfaction I enjoy, passing my time with Honnour, profit, and pleasure.

[115] THE YOUNG EDMUND BURKE DESCRIBES A FIERCE BATTLE AT SMOCK ALLEY THEATRE IN 1747, BETWEEN TWO FACTIONS OF TRINITY STUDENTS; FROM *THE EARLY LIFE AND CORRESPONDENCE OF EDMUND BURKE* BY ARTHUR SAMUELS.

Thomas Sheridan (see p. 66) had taken over Smock Alley in 1747 with the avowed intention of making Dublin theatre respectable, and staged a brilliant season of Shakespeare and Restoration comedies.

Smock Alley Theatre was pulled down in 1815, but the stone stairs of the old pit can still be seen in the vaults of the Catholic church of St Michael and St John in West Essex Street.

I shall now give you some news, but not as news, for I fancy you heard it before. I mean the grand theatre squabble between Mr Kelly, Gentleman, and Sheridan the Player, which has divided the town into two parties as violent as Whig and Tory; and because the scholars of our University have engaged themselves on Sheridan's side, possibly some reports may have been spread as far as you, to our disadvantage. To prevent them from having any influence on you, I shall relate the affair as impartially as I can, and with the utmost regard to truth. First then you must know that sometime ago there was a play performed here which greatly pleased the town called 'Aesop'. During the performance Mr Kelly comes in flushed with liquor, and going into the Green room where the players dress – and began to entertain the actresses in the most nauseous bawdry and ill language calling them bitches and whores, put his hands under their petticoats and would have forced some of them if ability answered his inclinations. This was represented to Sheridan, who is Manager of the Theatre, upon which he ordered Kelly out of the house, who enraged at this, goes into the pit, and as soon as Sheridan came on the stage, pelted him with oranges &c. and called him a thousand ill names, bidding him go off the stage and quite interrupting the performance. At length Sheridan advances to the front of the stage, and tells him that unless some gentleman takes care of him he would be obliged to turn him out of the house. Ten times more enraged at this, he goes after the act to Sheridan's room and insults him again. Sheridan represented calmly to him his abuse of the female players and of himself; and he, persisting in his ill language, Sheridan gave him a flogging, which he bore with Christian patience, not, however, without vowing vengeance, which he effected the next night by bringing such a party as hindered Sheridan from playing, broke open all the doors, and would very probably have killed him had he not escaped by the usage they gave the playhouse taylor. These doings made him shut up the playhouse and indict Kelly, who also indicted him. During this time thousands of 'States of Cases,' answers, replies, &c. flew about from both parties, and a great deal of dispute concerning the word 'gentleman,' for it seems Sheridan had said he was as good a gentleman as Kelly, or (as others will have it) as any in the house. This gained Kelly a great party, who called their cause the Gentleman's quarrel, taking it extremely ill that a gentleman should be struck by a player, and insisted that Sheridan should never play till he had publicly asked Kelly's pardon. The scholars, who had till now stood neuter, seeing how ill one who was of their body was treated, and the town deprived of their diversion by private pique, took the affair on themselves, and encouraged Sheridan to open the theatre again, which he did, and acted 'Richard the Third,' where a numerous body of the scholars appeared to keep the peace. At the beginning the party began to be riotous, but by menaces they were kept quiet, and one or two of the principal turned out. Thus the play went on regularly, to the satisfaction of the audience.

[116] MRS SIDDONS DROWNS A DUBLIN AUDIENCE IN
TEARS, 1783; FROM *THE KEMBLE ERA* BY LINDA KELLY.

The celebrated actress, Sarah Siddons, was the sister of Smock Alley's lead-
ing actor of the period, John Philip Kemble, and joined him in Dublin for the
summer season of 1783. Here she is ironically described by an anonymous
critic in her most famous role, Isabella in Southerne's tragedy The Fatal
Marriage.

On Saturday Mrs S –, about whom all the world has been talking, exposed her beautiful, adamantine, soft and lovely person, for the first time, at Smock-Alley theatre . . . She was nature itself! She was the most exquisite work of art! . . . Several fainted, even before the curtain drew up . . . The very fiddlers in the orchestra, 'albeit unused to the melting mood', blubbered like hungry children crying for their bread and butter . . . One hundred and nine ladies fainted! forty six went into fits! and ninety seven had strong hysterics! the world will scarcely credit the truth when they are told, that fourteen children, five old women, one hundred taylors and six common councilmen, were actu-ally drowned in the inundation of tears that flowed from the galleries, lattices and boxes, to increase the briny pond in the pit.

[117] WILLIAM MACREADY RECALLS THE LIVELINESS OF A
DUBLIN THEATRE AUDIENCE IN THE EARLY NINETEENTH CENTURY;
FROM HIS *REMINISCENCES*, EDITED BY SIR F. POLLOCK.

William Charles Macready (1793–1873) was the son of a Dublin actor-
manager who had moved to England in the late 1780s. Originally intended
for the bar, he took up professional acting aged sixteen to save his father
from bankruptcy, and became one of the most brilliant actors of his age, a

protégé of Mrs Siddons and later, rival to Edmund Kean. His memories of
Dublin date from his two seasons in Ireland in 1815 and 1816.

The value of the principle that I had lain down as a primary duty in my
art, namely *always be in earnest*, was enforced upon me still more
strongly by my experience before a Dublin audience. Their attention
arrested, and their feelings once excited, the actor enjoyed in their
glowing sympathy the full triumph of his art. The national character
might be read with tolerable correctness in their theatre. Keenly sensi-
tive to the commanding truth of the poet's or player's passion, they
would as often find recourse in their own humour from their dullness
or inefficiency. It would not infrequently happen that the humour of
the gallery would prove the ruler of the hour, disturbing the more
sedate of the spectators and utterly discomposing the player; until,
checked by perhaps some energetic declamation, or sobered by some
touch of nature, they would surrender themselves to the potent influence of the scene, and beneath its charm no assembly could watch
more intently, with more discriminating taste, or more lavish applause,
the dream of passion passing before them.

I remember on one occasion acting the character of Pierre in *Venice
Preserved*. My friend Jaffier displayed a rotundity of person that might
have agreed with the simile to which he likened himself of 'a full ear of
corn', but certainly showed no appearance of being 'withered in the
ripening'. As if in accordance with this obesity, his delivery was drawl-
ing, and his deportment heavy. In the scene prepared for the execution
of Pierre, after he had struck me and himself with his dagger, (and gasp-
ing out the few spirited words of the defiant conspirator, I had closed
my part with the cordial plaudits of the audience), a long and rather
drowsy dying speech of my poor friend Jaffier was 'dragging its slow
length along', when one of the gallery, in a tone of great impatience,
called out very loudly: '*Ah now, die at once!*': to which another from the
other side immediately replied: 'Be quiet, you blackguard,' – then
turned with a patronizing tone to the lingering Jaffier – '*Take your time!*'

[118] THE DUBLIN THEATRE IN THE DOLDRUMS IN 1842;
FROM W. M. THACKERAY'S *AN IRISH SKETCHBOOK*.

How do the Irish amuse themselves in the capital? The love for theatrical exhibitions is evidently not very great. Theatre Royal – Miss Kemble
and the Sonnambula, an Anglo-Italian importation. Theatre Royal,
Abbey Street – The Temple of Magic and the Wizard, last week. Adelphi
Theatre, Great Brunswick Street – The Original Seven Lancashire Bell-
ringers: a delicious excitement indeed! Portobello Gardens – 'THE LAST
ERUPTION BUT SIX,' says the advertisement in capitals. And, finally, 'Miss
Hayes will give her first and farewell concert at the Rotunda, previous
to leaving her native country.' Only one instance of Irish talent do we
read of, and that, in a desponding tone, announces its intention of quit-
ting its native country. All the rest of the pleasures of the evening are
importations from cockneyland. The Sonnambula from Covent Garden,
the Wizard from the Strand, the Seven Lancashire Bell-ringers from
Islington, or the City Road, no doubt; and as for 'The last Eruption but
Six,' it has *erumped* near the 'Elephant and Castle' anytime these two
years, until the cockneys would wonder at it no longer. . . .

I was at a fine concert, at which Lablache and others performed,
where there were not a hundred people in the pit of the pretty theatre,
and where the only encore given was to a young woman in ringlets and
yellow satin, who stepped forward and sang 'Coming through the rye,'
or some other scientific composition, in an exceedingly small voice. On
the nights when the regular drama was enacted, the audience was still
smaller. The theatre of Fishamble Street was given up to the performances of the Rev Mr Gregg and his Protestant company, whose soirées
I did not attend; and, at the Abbey Street Theatre, whither I went in
order to see, if possible, some specimens of the national humour, I
heard a company of English people ranting through a melodrama, the
tragedy whereof was the only laughable thing to be witnessed.

The Abbey Theatre

[119] REVIVING THE IRISH THEATRE – GEORGE MOORE IS
TAKEN BY W. B. YEATS TO SEE 'THE GHOST OF A THEATRE
DOWN BY THE QUAYS': THE FUTURE ABBEY THEATRE;
FROM GEORGE MOORE'S *HAIL AND FAREWELL*.

*The Irish Literary Theatre set up by Yeats, Moore and Moore's cousin,
Edward Martyn, had staged its original Dublin productions in the
Ancient Concert Rooms, but the money promised by Yeats' admirer, Miss
Horniman, had made it possible to look for a permanent theatre. The
building Moore romantically describes had in fact been most recently
used as a morgue.*

The quays were delightful that day, and I wished Yeats to agree with me
that there is nothing in the world more delightful than to dawdle
among seagulls floating to and fro through a pleasant dawdling light.

'But how is it, Yeats, you can only talk in the evening by the fire, that
yellow hand dropping over the chair as if seeking a harp of
apple-wood?'

Yeats cawed; he could only caw that morning, but he cawed softly,
and my thoughts sang so deliciously in my head that I soon began to
feel his ideas to be unnecessary to my happiness, and that it did not
matter how long the clerk kept us waiting. When he appeared he and
Yeats walked on together, and I followed them up an alley discreetly
remaining in the rear, fearing that they might be muttering some great
revolutionary scheme. I followed them up a staircase full of dust, and
found myself to my great surprise in an old library.

'Very like a drawing by Phiz,' I said to myself, bowing, for Yeats and
the clerk were bowing apologies for our intrusion to twenty or more
shabby genteel scholars who sat reading ancient books under immemo-
rial spider webs. At the end of the library there was another staircase,
and we ascended, leaving footprints in the dust. We went along a

passage, which opened upon a gallery overlooking a theatre, one that I had no difficulty in recognizing as part of the work done in Dublin by the architects that were brought over in the eighteenth century from Italy. The garlands on the ceiling were of Italian workmanship, the reliefs that remained on the walls. Once the pit was furnished with Chippendale chairs, carved mahogany chairs, perhaps gilded chairs in which ladies in high-bosomed dresses and slippered feet had sat listening to some comedy or tragedy when their lovers were not talking to them; and in those times the two boxes on either side of the stage let out at a guinea or two guineas for the evening.

Once supper-parties were served in them, for Abbey Street is only a few yards from the old Houses of Parliament, and even Grattan may have come to this theatre to meet a lady, whom he kissed after giving her an account of his speech. It amused me to imagine the love-scene, the lady's beauty and Grattan's passion for her, and I wondered what her end might have been, if she had died poor, without money to buy paint for her cheeks or dye for her hair, old, decrepit, and alone . . . I looked on the plank benches that were all the furniture of this theatre, I thought of the stevedores, the carters, the bullies and their trulls, eating their suppers, listening the while to some farce or tragedy written nobody knows by whom. Grattan's mistress may have sat among such, eating her bread and onions about eighty years ago . . .

Yeats and the clerk were talking about the rebuilding of the theatre, saying that the outer walls seemed sound enough, but all the rest would have to be rebuilt, and I wandered round the gallery wondering what were Yeats' dreams while looking into the broken decorations and the faded paint. Plays were still acted in this bygone theatre. But what plays? And who were the mummers that came to play them?

As if in answer, a man and two women came on the stage. I heard their voices, happily not the words they were speaking, for at the bottom of my heart a suspicion lingered that it might be *The Colleen Bawn* they were rehearsing, and not to hear that this was so I moved up the gallery and joined Yeats, saying that we had been among dust and gloom long enough, that I detected drains, and would like to get back into the open air.

We moved out of the theatre, Yeats still talking to the clerk about the price of the building, telling him that the proprietor must never know from whom the offer came; for if he were to hear that there was a project on foot for the establishment of an Irish Literary Theatre his price would go up fifty per cent. The clerk muttered something about a hundred per cent. 'And if he were to hear that Mr Edward Martyn was at the back of it –' Yeats muttered. The clerk interjected that if he were to hear that it would be hard to say what price he would not be putting upon his old walls.

A dried-up, dusty fellow was the clerk, a man about fifty, and I wondered what manner of revolution it might be that he was supposed to be stirring, and how deep was his belief that Maud Gonne would prove herself to be an Irish Joan of Arc; not very much deeper than Yeats' belief that he would one day become possessed of a theatre in Dublin and produce literary plays in it for a people unendowed with any literary sense whatever. Yet they continued shepherding their dreams up the quays, just as if *The Countess Cathleen* had not been hissed the night before, as if Cardinal Logue were not about to publish an interdiction, as if Edward [*Martyn*] were one that could be recovered from ecclesiasticism.

[120] THE BATTLE FOR *THE PLAYBOY* – LADY GREGORY'S ACCOUNT; FROM *OUR IRISH THEATRE* BY AUGUSTA GREGORY.

Augusta Gregory (1852–1932) was, with Yeats, the chief driving power behind the Irish dramatic movement. She and Yeats had discovered the brilliant Irish playwright John Millington Synge. Two of his early plays, The Shadow of the Glen *and* Riders to the Sea, *had already aroused hostility in Dublin, but his great comedy,* The Playboy of the Western World, *staged in 1907, caused a riot.*

*　　*　　*

There was a battle of a week. Every night protestors with their trumpets came and raised a din. Every night the police carried some of them off to the police courts. Every afternoon the paper gave reports of the trial before a magistrate who had not heard or read the play and who insisted on being given details of its incidents by the accused and by the police. (Curiously like the old theatre-riots of mid-eighteenth century London – except for the part played by the police.) There was a very large audience on the first night a Saturday, January 26th. Synge was there, but Mr Yeats was giving a lecture in Scotland. The first act got its applause, and the second, though one felt the audience were a little puzzled, a little shocked at the wild language. Near the end of the third act there was some hissing. We had sent a telegram to Mr Yeats after the first act 'Play great success'; but at the end we sent another – 'Audience broke up in disorder at the word shift.' . . . On the Monday night . . . I noticed on one side of the pit a large group of men sitting together, not a woman among them. I told Synge I thought it a sign of some organized disturbance and he telephoned to have the police at hand. The first part of the first act went undisturbed. Then suddenly an uproar began. The group of men I had noticed booed, hooted, blew tin trumpets. . . . It was impossible to hear a word of the play. The curtain came down for a minute, but I went round and told the actors to go on playing to the end, even if not a word could be heard. . . . The disturbance lasted to the end of the evening, not one word had been heard after the first ten minutes.

[121] THE BATTLE FOR *THE PLAYBOY* – AN OUTRAGED CITIZEN'S ACCOUNT; FROM *JOSEPH HOLLOWAY'S ABBEY THEATRE*, EDITED BY ROGER HOGAN AND MICHAEL J. O'NEILL.

Joseph Holloway (1861–1944), an architect and famous Dublin 'character', attended every play in Dublin until his death, and recorded his impressions in journals which ran to 28,000,000 words.

* * *

Saturday, January 26. The Abbey was thronged in the evening to witness the first performance of Synge's three-act comedy *The Playboy of the Western World*, which ended in fiasco owing to the coarseness of the dialogue. The audience bore with it for two and a half acts and even laughed with the dramatist at times, but an unusually brutally coarse remark put into the mouth of 'Christopher Mahon,' the playboy of the title, set the house off into hooting and hissing amid counter applause, and the din was kept up till the curtain closed in.

On coming out, Lady Gregory asked me, 'What was the cause of the disturbance?'

And my monosyllabic answer was, 'Blackguardism!'

To which she queried, 'On which side?'

'The stage!' came from me pat, and then I passed on, and the incident was closed. . . .

'This is not Irish life!' said one of the voices from the pit, and despite the fact that Synge in a note on the programme says, 'I have used one or two words only that I have not heard among the country people of Ireland, or spoken in my own nursery before I could read the newspapers,' I maintain that his play of *The Playboy* is not a truthful or just picture of the Irish peasants, but simply the outpouring of a morbid, unhealthy mind ever seeking on the dunghill of life for the nastiness that lies concealed there. . . . Synge is the evil genius of the Abbey and Yeats his able lieutenant. Both dabble in the unhealthy. Lady Gregory, though she backs them up when they transgress good taste and cast decency to the winds, keeps clean in her plays.

Monday, January 28. . . . Henderson and I went down to the Abbey . . . and on our way spoke of Synge's nasty mind – to store those crude, coarse sayings from childhood and now present them in a play. The influence of Gorki must be upon him. Henderson also told me that the new English manager had arrived, and he was thinking of retiring before being dismissed. The new man was to get £5 a week; he was only getting 30/-.

By this time we arrived at the Abbey. Two stalwart police at the vestibule suggested trouble, and we found plenty and to spare when we

went in. The performance was just concluding amid a terrific uproar
(the piece had not been listened to, we were told). The curtains were
drawn aside, and W. G. Fay [*playing Christy Mahon, the Playboy*] stood
forward amid the din. After some minutes, in a lull, he said, 'You who
have hissed tonight will go away saying you have heard the play, but you
haven't.'

'We heard it on Saturday!' came from the back of the pit, and the
hissing and hooting were renewed.

The scene which followed was indescribable. Those in the pit
howled for the author, and he with Lady Gregory and others held
animated conversation in the stalls. Denis O'Sullivan made himself
very conspicuous railing against the noise producers, and Signor
Esposito gesticulated abundantly. Small knots of people argued the
situation out anything but calmly, and after about a quarter of an hour's
clamour, the audience dispersed hoarse. 'Heblon,' in a half-tight state,
blackguarded the Irish people and upheld the dramatist, and George
Roberts said, 'The play is the finest ever written if you had only the wit
to see it!' I wished him joy of the dungheap of a mind he must possess
to arrive at that conclusion, and Lawrence and I departed.

[122] THE BATTLE FOR *THE PLAYBOY* – A SCHOOLBOY'S MEMORY;
FROM WALTER STARKIE'S AUTOBIOGRAPHY, *SCHOLARS AND GYPSIES*.

*Walter Starkie (1894–1976) was brought up in Dublin, studied at Trinity
just before the First World War, and was a lecturer and professor there in
the 1920s and 1930s. He spent much of his later life in Spain, where he
became an expert on gipsy folklore, and finally worked at the University of
California.*

The most exciting theatrical experience of my youth took place in my
thirteenth year when J. M. Synge's play *The Playboy of the Western World*
was produced for the first time at the Abbey Theatre in January 1907. It
was my first visit to the Abbey Theatre, and Paddy Tobin, whom at

school we all considered an expert in theatrical matters as he had acted with his three cousins, the Wogan Brown girls (all of them excellent actresses, and one of them, Dorothy, so vivacious that she appealed to Bernard Shaw as the ideal embodiment of Dolly in *You Never Can Tell*), promised to bring me round to the Green Room to introduce me to Lady Gregory.

'Tonight,' he said, when I met him at Nelson's Pillar, 'my father says there will be the hell of a row as the newspapers have been publishing attacks on the play, saying that it is an insult to Ireland.' When we reached Abbey Street we found a great crowd assembled in the streets adjoining the theatre. Inside, the atmosphere was electric and there was suspense in the air, as though everyone in the auditorium expected a political revolution to break out. Instead of waiting quietly in their seats for the play to begin, many gathered together in groups talking excitedly, and I was struck, too, by the varying types I saw in the audience. In addition to the usual middle-class theatre-goers, there were numbers of workers, and here and there gentlemen and ladies in evening dress, and young men whose tousled hair and beards proclaimed them initiates of the Dublin Latin quarter. A wizened old man sitting next to me pointed out the literary and political celebrities as they took their places. 'See that long thin rake of a fellow, that's Best the Librarian arguing with Dr R. M. Henry, one of the Belfast Home-Rules. Next but two to him is a fine upstanding man with a beard: that's AE, our Irish Buddha! Over there by himself is the victim of the evening, John Millington Synge. Every one of the Irish intellectuals are present, but it's not the play they've come to see, but to spy on one another.' I longed to ask the old man for an explanation for his cryptic words, but just then the lights dimmed and I heard a dismal gong sounding the knell as it seemed to me, and the curtain rose.

Although I tried very hard to concentrate upon the play it was impossible to hear the actors after the first few minutes because of the interruptions and disturbances which took place all over the auditorium. When these reached a climax, one of the company advanced to the footlights and tried to appeal for silence. He said, as far as I could make out, that anyone in the audience who did not like the play was at liberty to get up and leave, but nobody left. Instead, pandemonium broke loose, and my wizened neighbour, whom I had considered an inoffensive old man, jumped to his feet shouting: 'Clear the decks! Down with Willie Fay!' And his shouts were taken up in chorus by the gallery. Then came shouts from the pit below and many started to sing the revolutionary song, *The West's asleep.*

While all this rumpus was going on the actors and actresses on the stage continued valiantly to act their parts, but they were puppets; I could see their lips move but hardly a word reached me. Paddy Tobin and I recognized some friends who were from Trinity College. They had come at the request of Lady Gregory's nephew with other students to support the play. Seeing that the disturbances increased in the second act they thought the best way in which they could show their support of the play would be by singing *God Save the King* in chorus. Even today, when I look back at that fateful night in the history of the Irish National Theatre, I cannot imagine how such a crazy notion as singing the British National Anthem could have entered their heads. Instead of pouring oil on troubled waters they enraged the Irish patriots in the pit by singing what the latter considered a political song.

Paddy Tobin and I enjoyed ourselves immensely in the hullabaloo. Through the tempest of shouting and hissing we heard cries '*Sinn Fein Amhain*' and 'kill the author', and from our seats at the side of the gallery we had a wonderful view of the milling mob in the pit and gallery. Then suddenly the doors of the auditorium opened and a posse of Dublin Metropolitan police entered, and many of the rowdy elements were cast out. We expected the burly giants to draw their batons and made ready to join the wild stampede, but there was a momentary lull as another figure advanced to the footlights to speak to the mob; but he was no more successful than his predecessor had been in the first act, and his voice was drowned by catcalls and the strident tones of toy trumpets. Those who thought the display of force by the police would

calm the rioters were mistaken, for Act III of the play began amidst
scenes of even greater chaos. As we were unable to hear a single word
of the play, and knowing that the fight was spreading to the street
outside, we left our seats and mingled with the crowd in the vestibule.
Following Paddy during the interval I managed to reach the back of the
stage through a side door leading into the lane, and we joined the actors
and their supporters gathered round Lady Gregory and J. M. Synge.
While to me it seemed that all the players were wringing their hands,
tearing their hair and running hither and thither, Lady Gregory stood at
the door of the Green Room as calm and collected as Queen Victoria
about to open a charity bazaar. Seeing Paddy Tobin and myself, she
beckoned us over and handed each of us a piece of the huge barmbrack
which she had baked at Coole and brought up to Dublin for the Abbey
cast. While we were munching our cake we observed the author, J. M.
Synge, mooning about among the actors like a lost soul. I had seen him
on various occasions in Kingstown, and when I passed him striding
along the Dalkey road swinging his stick I used to wonder whether he
was French or Austrian, for he had moustaches and a little goatee or
'imperial'. When I saw him on the night of the Abbey riot his face was
pale and sunken, and he looked like a ghost of the sun-tanned wanderer
I had seen walking by the sea. I watched him closely as he sat motionless through the dumb-show of his play, amidst the rioting and insults
of the mob, but not a trace of emotion could I discern in his pale mask-
like face that gazed unseeing at the raging auditorium.

[123] BACKSTAGE AT THE ABBEY – LADY GREGORY'S JOURNAL,
1908; FROM *SEVENTY YEARS* BY AUGUSTA GREGORY.

Oh, this theatre! 1.00 o'clock now, and I have been writing on its affairs
ever since breakfast time.

I came round before matinee. M. wanted to speak to me 'to tender
his resignation' in consequence of Miss N. having insulted him during
Cross Roads last night, before the stage-hands, asked him what the devil

he meant because he had missed his cue . . . Also he was knocked down in *Cross Roads* by O. instead of being choked sitting in a chair, and this he seems to think was revenge, because he had at some previous time hit O. with the pipe he throws at him in *Workhouse Ward*. I spoke to Miss N. who accuses him of a variety of small offences connected with cues . . . P. has been up a few minutes ago asking for a rise of wages. On my way back to the auditorium I met Miss Q. and asked her about the quarrel. She says M. is desperately in love with N. He has been much worse since Mr Yeats did her horoscope saying she was to marry a fair man. He walked up and down saying, 'I am that fair man'. She went to him the other day and told him he was foolish and ought to put N. out of his head, but at the end he said, 'I know very well that you are in love with me yourself!'

[124] Downstage at the Abbey – a memory of Yeats; from Austin Clarke's autobiography, *A Penny in the Clouds*.

Austin Clarke (1896–1974) poet, dramatist and novelist was brought up in Dublin and educated at Belvedere and University College, Dublin (where he was probably a student at the period he recalls here). He left Ireland during the Civil War but returned from 'exile' in 1931 and founded the Dublin Verse Speaking Society which produced verse plays for the Peacock and Abbey Theatres in the same tradition as Yeats's plays. From 1942 to 1955, he broadcast a weekly programme of poetry on Radio Eireann and died in Dublin, loaded with literary honours.

The plays of Yeats were a deeply imaginative experience, and, as the poet put on his own plays as often as possible, the experience was a constant one. On such occasions the theatre was almost empty. There were a few people in the stalls, including Lady Gregory, and just after the last gong had sounded, Yeats would dramatically appear at the top of the steps leading down into the auditorium. Perhaps the actors spoke the lyric lines in tones that had become hollow-sounding with time, borrowing the archaic voice which is normally reserved for religious services. It seemed right that the poetic mysteries should be celebrated reverently and with decorum. Moreover, the presence of the poet himself in the theatre was a clear proof that all was well.

Scarcely had the desultory clapping ceased, when Yeats would appear outside the stage curtain, a dim figure against the footlights. He swayed and waved rhythmically, telling humbly of his 'little play', how he had rewritten it, and what he had meant to convey in its lines. As the twenty or thirty people in the pit were more or less scattered, I was isolated usually in one of the back seats. On such occasions, I felt like Ludwig of Bavaria, that eccentric monarch, who sat alone in his own theatre. I enjoyed the poet's curtain-lecture, almost as if it were a special benefit performance for myself.

One night, however, my youthful and romantic illusions were suddenly shattered, and in a trice the Celtic Twilight was gone. As the poet appeared punctually outside the curtain, a dazzling light shone around him. It might have been the light of his later fame! I glanced up and saw that the brilliant shaft of illumination came from the balcony. A spotlight must have been clamped to the rail and switched on as the poet appeared. But my conclusions may have been unjust, for in youth we do not understand the complexities of human motives. I did not realize at the time that poetic drama was slowly vanishing from the Abbey Theatre. It seems to me now that, consciously or not, the poet might have been making a last despairing gesture to call attention, not to his own picturesque person, but to the struggling cause of poetry on the stage.

The Approaches to the City: Dublin on Sea

Previous page:
Monument to George IV at Kingstown (Dun Laoghaire), described by
Thackery as 'a hideous obelisk, stuck upon four fat balls, and surmounted
by a crown on a cushion' (Thackeray). An early nineteenth-century
engraving

Ringsend

[125] JOHN DUNTON ARRIVES AT RINGSEND IN 1698; FROM EDWARD MACLYSAGHT'S *IRISH LIFE IN THE SEVENTEENTH CENTURY*.

Until the completion of the North and South Walls of Dublin harbour in the late eighteenth century, Ringsend provided the main embarkation point for Dublin, cut off by treacherous sands from the main city. Many early travellers complained of the discomfort of the Ringsend cars.

After some refreshment here I looked towards Dublin but how to come at it I no more knew than the fox at the grapes, for though I saw a large strand yet twas not to be walked over because of a pretty rapid stream which must be crossed. I enquired for a coach, but found no such thing was to be had here unless by accident; but was informed that I might have a Ring's End car, which upon my desire was [got] and I got upon it, not into it. It is a perfect car with two wheels and towards the back of it a seat is raised cross-ways, long enough to hold three people, the cushion mine had was made of patchwork but of such coarse kind of stuff that I fancied they had stolen some poor beggar's coat for a covering, between me and the horse upon the cross bars of the car stood my charioteer who presently set his horse into a gallop which so jolted our sides though upon a smooth strand that I was in purgatory until I got at Lazy-hill, where I paid three halfpence for my fare of half a mile's riding, and almost as pleased as the young gentleman that drove the chariot of the sun would have been, to be rid of my seat. However they are a great convenience and you may go to Ring's End from Dublin, or from hence thither with a load of goods for three pence or a groat, and I was told there are one hundred more plying hereabouts that you can hardly be disappointed.

Dublin Bay

[126] DUBLIN HARBOUR IN 1810; FROM *AN ENGLISHMAN'S DESCRIPTIVE ACCOUNT* OF DUBLIN BY NATHANIEL JEFFREYS.

A wonderful improvement has been made in Dublin harbour by a work truly magnificent, both for its appearance and utility . . . which is called the South Wall. It was begun in 1748 and finished in seven years. It extends in a straight line into the sea the surprising length of four English miles; it is formed of large blocks of mountain granite, strongly cemented and strengthened with iron cramps.

As far as the Pigeon house, which is three miles from Dublin, there is upon this wall a noble coach road of forty feet in breadth; the passengers upon which are securely protected from the violence of the sea in tempestuous weather by parapet walls; and at the extremity of this magnificent work is the LIGHTHOUSE which is built in an appropriate style of architecture perfectly corresponding to the bold dignity of the scene. It was begun in June 1762 when from the very great depth of the water and power of the winds in such an exposed position, together with the raging of a tempestuous sea, the most serious difficulties were to be encountered. But the perseverance and great professional skill of the architect (Mr Smith) bade defiance to the obstacles, the bare mention of which were enough to intimidate persons of less merit than himself.

The Pigeon House . . . about 3 miles from Dublin and 1 from the landing place, is the customary landing place of passengers from the packets . . . The breadth of the pier at this place is 250 feet, on which are erected a magazine, arsenal and custom-house. It is a place of great strength being surrounded with heavy cannon. . . . There are also in many parts of the Bay, the Martello Towers, which were so strongly recommended by Mr Windham when in power as Secretary of War, during the administration of Mr Pitt, which an Irish sailor in one of the packets being asked the use of by a passenger replied 'The devil a use can I think of, but to please Mr Windham and puzzle posterity.'

The mode of conveying the passengers to Dublin is the LONG COACH.

This carriage is upon the plan of those *elegant* vehicles upon low wheels which are used on the road between Hyde Park Corner and Hammersmith, and from the state of its repair and external appearance, as well as its internal decoration, it bears every mark of having retired on the superannuated list from that active duty . . .

This coach is generally very crowded from the anxiety of the passengers to proceed to Dublin; and from the manner in which some of the company may easily be supposed to have been passing their time on board . . ., from the effect of seasickness, the effluvia arising from 12 or 14 persons crammed together in a very small space, like the inmates of Noah's ark, *the clean and the unclean*, is not of that description which can entitle the long coach to be considered *a bed of roses*.

Three shillings for each passenger is the price of conveyance, and this is exacted beforehand – a mode of settling accounts which is frequently the cause of great dissatisfaction.

Clontarf

*Lord Charlemont had inherited a seaside estate north of Dublin about four
years earlier, and was to spend another twenty years and a vast fortune on it
before it was finished. Only the superb Temple or Casino designed by Sir
William Chambers now survives, surrounded by housing estates. He abandoned his plan to live in the Casino itself after his marriage to Mary Hickman,
'the daughter of a decayed gentleman of his acquaintance', which in its turn
had probably been precipitated by his brother hinting tactlessly that when he
inherited the Marino estate, he would sweep most of the 'improvements'
away.*

I went in my post chaise with Mrs Graham to Ld. Charlemonts at
Marino with whom we found Lord Drogheda. We walk'd thro' the
Kitchen Garden wch. is 6½ Irish Acres to his Hot House it is 170 Feet
long; in the *Anti Room* of which we breakfasted. The Walls were all
Tapstried with Myrtle and an innumerable quantity of flowering Plants
perfumed it on every side by their Fragrance. The rest of our Company
were Lord and Ly. Stopford, Lord Tyrone and Lord Powerscourt. We
then visited the Stables which are grand and handsome, the Farm Yard
Barns &c. Then we walk'd thro' a very pretty Shrubbery to a very handsome *Gothic Room* (the Windows of painted Glass). We then went to the
Temple. The stonework is admirably well executed all of Portland Stone,
it is a beautiful Building but very ill qualified to be a Dwelling House.

[128] JOHN WESLEY FAILS TO SUCCUMB TO THE CHARMS OF THE CASINO, 1778; FROM *THE JOURNALS OF JOHN WESLEY*.

Went with a few friends to Lord Charlemont's two or three miles from Dublin. It is one of the pleasantest places I have ever seen, the water, trees and lawns so elegantly intermixed with each other, having a serpentine walk running through a thick wood on one side, and an open prospect both of land and sea on the other. In the thickest part of the wood is the Hermitage, a small room, dark and gloomy enough. The Gothic temple, at the head of a fine piece of water, which is encompassed by stately trees, is delightful indeed. But the most elegant of all the buildings is not finished; the shell of it is surprisingly beautiful and the rooms well contained both for use and ornament. But what is all this unless God is here? Unless life is known, loved and enjoyed? Not only vanity unable to give happiness but vexation of spirit.

Lord Charlemont's Casino at Marino, engraved by
Thomas Ivory, 1775

Dun Laoghaire

A long pier, with a steamer or two at hand, and a few small vessels lying
on either side of the jetty; a town irregularly built, with many handsome terraces, some churches, and showy-looking hotels; a few people
straggling on the beach; two or three cars at the railroad station, which
runs along the shore as far as Dublin; the sea stretching interminably
eastward; to the north the Hill of Howth, lying grey behind the mist;
and, directly under his feet, upon the wet, black, shining, slippery deck,
an agreeable reflection of his own legs, disappearing seemingly in the
direction of the cabin from which he issues: are the sights which a traveller may remark on coming on deck at Kingstown pier on a wet morning – Let us say on an *average* morning; for according to the statement
of well-informed natives, the Irish day is more often rainy than otherwise. A hideous obelisk, stuck upon four fat balls, and surmounted with
a crown on a cushion (the latter were no bad emblems perhaps of the
monarch in whose honour they were raised), commemorates the
sacred spot at which George IV *quitted* Ireland. You are landed here
from the steamer; and a carman, who is dawdling in the neighbourhood, with a straw in his mouth, comes leisurely up to ask whether you
will go to Dublin? Is it natural indolence, or the effect of despair
because of the neighbouring railroad, which renders him so indifferent? – He does not even take the straw out of his mouth as he proposes
the question – he seems quite careless as to the answer. . . .

Before that day, so memorable for joy and sorrow, for rapture at
receiving its monarch and tearful grief at losing him, when George IV
came and left the maritime resort of the citizens of Dublin, it bore a less
genteel name than that which it owns at present, and was called
Dunleary. After that glorious event Dunleary disdained to be Dunleary
any longer, and became Kingstown henceforward and for ever. (*It*

changed back officially in 1922.) Numerous terraces and pleasure-houses have been built in the place they stretch row after row along the banks of the sea, and rise one above another on the hill. The rents of these houses are said to be very high; the Dublin citizens crowd into them in summer; and a great source of pleasure and comfort must it be to them to have the fresh sea-breezes and prospects so near to the metropolis.

The better sort of houses are handsome and spacious; but the fashionable quarter is yet in an unfinished state, for enter-prising architects are always beginning new roads, rows and terraces: nor are those already built by any means complete. Beside the aristocratic part of the town is a commercial one, and nearer to Dublin stretch lines of low cottages which have not a Kingstown look at all, but are evidently of the Dunleary period. It is quite curious to see in the streets where the shops are, how often the painter of the sign-boards begins with big letters, and ends, for want of space, with small; and the Englishman accustomed to the thriving neatness and regularity which characterize towns great and small in his own country, can't fail to notice the difference here. The houses have a battered, rakish look, and seem going to ruin before their time. As seamen of all nations come hither who have made no vow of temperance, there are plenty of liquor-shops still, and shabby cigar-shops, and shabby milliners' and tailors' with fly-blown prints of old fashions. The bakers and apothecaries make a great brag of their calling, and you see MEDICAL HALL, or PUBLIC BAKERY, BALLYRAGGET FLOUR-STORE, (or whatever the name may be,) pompously inscribed over very humble tenements. Some comfortable grocers' and butchers' shops, and numbers of shabby sauntering people, the younger part of whom are barelegged and bareheaded, make up the rest of the picture which the stranger sees as his car goes jingling through the street.

After the town come the suburbs of pleasure-houses; low, one-storeyed cottages for the most part: some neat and fresh, some that have passed away from the genteel state altogether, and exhibit downright poverty; some in a state of transition, with broken windows and pretty romantic names upon tumble-down gates. Who lives in them?

One fancies that the chairs and tables inside are broken, that the tea-pot on the breakfast-table has no spout, and the tablecloth is ragged and sloppy; that the lady of the house is in dubious curl-papers, and the gentleman, with an imperial to his chin, wears a flaring dressing-gown all ragged at the elbows.

George IV bids farewell to Ireland from the harbour at Dunleary, September 1821, engraved from the painting by John Lushington Reilly.

Sandycove

[130] JAMES JOYCE AT THE MARTELLO TOWER IN 1903; FROM *IT ISN'T THIS TIME OF YEAR AT ALL* BY OLIVER ST JOHN GOGARTY.

Joyce's famous opening scene in Ulysses between Stephen Dedalus and 'stately plump Buck Mulligan' is, like so much of his writing, autobiographical – and was much resented by Buck Mulligan/Oliver Gogarty. Here is Gogarty's version, written in the 1950s, which still retains some of the condescension which so galled Joyce.

James Joyce said, 'Do you know that we can rent the Martello Tower at Sandycove? I'll pay the rent if you will furnish it.'

Sandycove is about seven miles from Dublin on the south side of its famous bay. It lies a little to the east of the harbor which takes the mail boat from England early in the morning and late at night. The water between Dun Laoghaire and Sandycove is called Scotsman's Bay and is bounded by the east pier of the harbor and the two-storied, thick-walled Martello Tower, with the Battery close by the Forty Foot, a resort for strong swimmers. . . .

The rent for the Tower at Sandycove was only eight pounds or about $32 per year, payable at Dublin Castle. We took it; and Joyce kept his word and stumped up the rent from a prize of twenty pounds that he had won in some examination. I did the furnishing from unmissed things from 5 Rutland Square. 'It's a poor house where there are not many things superfluous.' I learned that at school from the poet Horace. . . .

The Tower at Sandycove is built of clear granite. It is very clean. Its door, which is halfway up, is approached by a ladder fixed beneath the door, which is opened by a large copper key, for there was a powder magazine in the place and the copper was meant to guard against sparks which an iron key might strike out from the stone. There is a winding staircase in the thickness of the wall to the side that does not face the sea. On the roof, which is granite, is a gun emplacement, also of granite, which can be used for a table if you use the circular sentry walk for a seat. Over the door is a projection from which boiling oil or molten lead can be poured down upon an enemy. Beside this is a furnace for making cannon balls red hot. There were no shells in the days when it was built, but the red-hot cannon balls could burn a wooden ship if they hit it. Happily these towers were never used, though they were occupied by coast guards until quite recently.

We lived there for two years, greatly to the anxious relief of our parents. Joyce had a job at an adjoining school. I had some reading to do for my medical degree. When the weather was warm we sun-bathed on the roof, moving around the raised sentry platform with the sun and out of the wind. . . . One morning back in Sandycove I was shaving on the roof of the Tower, because of the better light – it is a good idea to shave before going into salt water – when up comes Joyce.

'Fine morning, Dante. Feeling transcendental this morning?' I asked.

'Would you be so merry and bright if you had to go out at this hour to teach a lot of scrawny-necked brats?'

Touché! He had me there: not a doubt about it. Why don't I think of other people's problems? I must develop a little sympathy: suffer with them; realize their difficulties. I am glad that he has a job, though it is only that of a teacher.

The golden down that would be a beard on a more robust man shone in the morning light. Joyce did not need a shave.

'Yes,' I said, 'that is enough to obscure the Divine Idea that underlies all life. But why be atrabilious about it?' He gave me a sour look. He turned and stooped under the low door.

'I suppose you will bear that in mind and attach it to me when you come to write your *Inferno*?' I said.

He turned and made a grave announcement: 'I will treat you with fairness.'

'Put a pint or two in the fairness and I won't complain.'

He was gone.

What would be the use of sympathy with a character like that? He would resent sympathy. He is planning some sort of novel that will show us all up and the country as well: all will be fatuous except James Joyce. . . . Presently I heard him climbing down the ladder. I went into the overhanging balcony, and called down, 'Don't stop at the Arch on your way back.' He never looked up but he raised his stick in a grave salute and loped off.

[131] GOGARTY AT THE MARTELLO TOWER; FROM JAMES JOYCE'S *ULYSSES*.

Stately plump Buck Mulligan came from the stairhead, bearing a bowl of lather on which a mirror and a razor lay crossed. A yellow dressing-gown, ungirdled, was sustained gently behind him by the mild morning air. He held the bowl aloft and intoned:

– *Introibo ad attare Dei*.

Halted, he peered down the dark winding stairs and called up coarsely:

– Come up, Kinch. Come up, you fearful Jesuit.

Solemnly he came forward and mounted the round gunrest. He faced about and blessed gravely thrice the tower, the surrounding country and the awaking mountains. Then, catching sight of Stephen Dedalus, he bent towards him and made rapid crosses in the air, gurgling in his throat and shaking his head. Stephen Dedalus, displeased and sleepy, leaned his arms on the top of the staircase and looked coldly at the shaking gurgling face that blessed him, equine in its length, and at the light untonsured hair, grained and hued like pale oak.

Buck Mulligan peeped an instant under the mirror and then covered the bowl smartly.

– Back to barracks, he said sternly.

He added in a preacher's tone:

– For this, O dearly beloved, is the genuine Christine: body and soul and blood and ouns. Slow music, please. Shut your eyes, gents. One moment. A little trouble about those white corpuscles. Silence, all.

He peered sideways up and gave a long low whistle of call, then paused awhile in rapt attention, his even white teeth glistening here and there with gold points. Chrysostomos. Two strong shrill whistles answered through the calm.

– Thanks, old chap, he cried briskly. That will do nicely. Switch off the current, will you?

He skipped off the gunrest and looked gravely at his watcher, gathering about his legs the loose folds of his gown. The plump shadowed face and sullen oval jowl recalled a prelate, patron of arts in the middle ages. A pleasant smile broke quietly over his lips.

– The mockery of it, he said gaily. Your absurd name, an ancient Greek.

He pointed his finger in friendly jest and went over to the parapet, laughing to himself. Stephen Dedalus stepped up, followed him wearily halfway and sat down on the edge of the gunrest, watching him still as he propped his mirror on the parapet, dipped the brush in the bowl and lathered cheeks and neck.

Buck Mulligan's gay voice went on.

– My name is absurd too: Malachi Mulligan, two dactyls. But it has a Hellenic ring, hasn't it? Tripping and sunny like the buck himself. We must go to Athens. Will you come if I can get the aunt to fork out twenty quid?

He laid the brush aside and, laughing with delight, cried:

– Will he come? The jejune Jesuit.

Ceasing, he began to shave with care.

– Tell me, Mulligan, Stephen said quietly.

– Yes, my love?

– How long is Haines going to stay in this tower?

Buck Mulligan showed a shaven cheek over his right shoulder.

God, isn't he dreadful? he said frankly. A ponderous Saxon. He thinks you're not a gentleman. God, these bloody English. Bursting with money and indigestion. Because he comes from Oxford. You know, Dedalus, you have the real Oxford manner. He can't make you out. O, my name for you is the best: Kinch, the knifeblade.

He shaved warily over his chin.

– He was raving all night about a black panther, Stephen said. Where is his guncase?

– A woeful lunatic, Mulligan said. Were you in a funk?

– I was, Stephen said with energy and growing fear. Out here in the dark with a man I don't know raving and moaning to himself about shooting a black panther. You saved men from drowning. I'm not a hero, however. If he stays on here I am off.

Buck Mulligan frowned at the lather on his razorblade. He hopped down from his perch and began to search his trousers pockets hastily.

– Scutter, he cried thickly.

He came over to the gunrest and, thrusting a hand into Stephen's upper pocket, said:

– Lend us a loan of your noserag to wipe my razor.

Stephen suffered him to pull out and hold up on show by its corner a dirty crumpled handkerchief. Buck Mulligan wiped the razorblade neatly. Then, gazing over the handkerchief, he said:

– The bard's noserag. A new art colour for our Irish poets: snot-green. You can almost taste it, can't you?

He mounted to the parapet again and gazed out over Dublin bay, his fair oakpale hair stirring slightly.

– God, he said quietly. Isn't the sea what Algy calls it: a grey sweet mother? The snotgreen sea. The scrotumtightening sea. *Epi oinopa ponton.* Ah, Dedalus, the Greeks. I must teach you. You must read them in the original. *Thalatta! Thalatta!* She is our great sweet mother. Come and look.

Stephen stood up and went over to the parapet. Leaning on it he looked down on the water and on the mailboat clearing the harbour mouth of Kingstown.

– Our mighty mother, Buck Mulligan said.

He turned abruptly his great searching eyes from the sea to Stephen's face.

– The aunt thinks you killed your mother, he said. That's why she won't let me have anything to do with you.

– Someone killed her, Stephen said gloomily.

– You could have knelt down, damn it, Kinch, when your dying mother asked you, Buck Mulligan said. I'm hyperborean as much as you. But to think of your mother begging you with her last breath to kneel down and pray for her. And you refused. There is something sinister in you. . . .

He broke off and lathered again lightly his farther cheek. A tolerant smile curled his lips.

– But a lovely mummer, he murmured to himself. Kinch, the loveliest mummer of them all.

He shaved evenly and with care, in silence, seriously.

Stephen, an elbow rested on the jagged granite, leaned his palm against his brow and gazed at the fraying edge of his shiny black coatsleeve. Pain, that was not yet the pain of love, fretted his heart. Silently, in a dream she had come to him after her death, her wasted body within its loose brown graveclothes giving off an odour of wax and rosewood, her breath, that had bent upon him, mute, reproachful, a faint odour of wetted ashes. Across the threadbare cuffedge he saw the sea hailed as a great sweet mother by the wellfed voice beside him. The ring of bay and skyline held a dull green mass of liquid. A bowl of white china had stood beside her deathbed holding the green sluggish bile which she had torn up from her rotting liver by fits of loud groaning vomiting.

Buck Mulligan wiped his razorblade.

– Ah, poor dogsbody, he said in a kind voice. I must give you a shirt and a few noserags. How are the secondhand breeks?

– They fit well enough, Stephen answered.

Buck Mulligan attacked the hollow beneath his underlip.

– The mockery of it, he said contentedly, secondleg they should be. God knows what poxy bowsy left them off. I have a lovely pair with a hair stripe, grey. You'll look spiffing in them. I'm not joking, Kinch. You look damn well when you're dressed.

– Thanks, Stephen said. I can't wear them if they are grey.

– He can't wear them, Buck Mulligan told his face in the mirror. Etiquette is etiquette. He kills his mother but he can't wear grey trousers.

He folded his razor neatly and with stroking palps of fingers felt the smooth skin.

Stephen turned his gaze from the sea and to the plump face with its smokeblue mobile eyes.

– That fellow I was with in the Ship last night, said Buck Mulligan, says you have g. p. i. He's up in Dottyville with Conolly Norman. General paralysis of the insane.

He swept the mirror a half circle in the air to flash the tidings abroad in sunlight now radiant on the sea. His curling shaven lips laughed and the edges of his white glittering teeth. Laughter seized all his strong wellknit trunk.

– Look at yourself, he said, you dreadful bard.

Stephen bent forward and peered at the mirror held out to him, cleft by crooked crack, hair on end. As he and others see me. Who chose this face for me? This dogsbody to rid of vermin. It asks me too.

– I pinched it out of the skivvy's room, Buck Mulligan said. It does her all right. The aunt always keeps plainlooking servants for Malachi. Lead him not into temptation. And her name is Ursula.

Laughing again, he brought the mirror away from Stephen's peering eyes.

– The rage of Caliban at not seeing his face in a mirror, he said. If Wilde were only alive to see you.

Drawing back and pointing, Stephen said with bitterness:

– It is a symbol of Irish art. The cracked lookingglass of a servant.

Buck Mulligan suddenly linked his arm in Stephen's and walked with him round the tower, his razor and mirror clacking in the pocket where he had thrust them.

– It's not fair to tease you like that, Kinch, is it? he said kindly. God knows you have more spirit than any of them.

Parried again. He fears the lancet of my art as I fear that of his. The cold steelpen.

[132] JAMES JOYCE LEAVES THE MARTELLO TOWER; FROM *SELECTED LETTERS OF JAMES JOYCE* EDITED BY RICHARD ELLMANN.

15 September 1904 7 S. Peter's Terrace, Cabra, Dublin Dear Starkey [*Seamus O'Sullivan, the Dublin poet*] My trunk will be called for at the Tower tomorrow (Saturday) between 9 and 12. Kindly put into it a pair of black boots, a pair of brown boots, a blue peaked cap, a black cloth cap, a black felt hat, a raincoat and the MS of my verses which are in a roll on the shelf to the right as you enter. Also see that your host has not abstracted the twelfth chapter of my novel from my trunk. May I ask you to see that any letters coming to the Tower for me are redirected to my address at once? Please rope the trunk as it has no lock. Faithfully Yours

JAS A JOYCE

James Joyce as a student.

Howth

[133] A CHILDHOOD IN HOWTH, IN THE 1800S; FROM MAUD GONNE MACBRIDE'S AUTOBIOGRAPHY, *A SERVANT OF THE QUEEN*.

Maud Gonne (1866–1953) was the daughter of a wealthy British army officer (the 'Tommy' in this extract). After her mother's early death from tuberculosis, she and her sister were sent to live in the healthy sea-air at Howth. She grew up to extraordinary beauty, and became the love of Yeats' life; but she refused to marry him, and spent her life in almost ceaseless revolutionary activity for the Irish cause. She married (unhappily) in 1903 John MacBride, who was to be one of the leaders of the 1916 rising.

Howth was different then from what it is today. There was no tram, and very few houses. The ugly little house we rented had been built by the enterprising man who drove the one outside car in the district to and from the station at Sutton. He and his large family lived in a little cabin near by and his mother lived in another, even smaller and smokier, cabin farther up in the heather.

Tommy used to come for weekends and Kathleen and I used to be strapped securely on to one side of the car, with our feet in a big sack of hay for the horse and a rug to keep us all compact, tucked in at each side of the cushions if the day was cold or windy; our landlord sat on the other side till we arrived at Sutton where Tommy, coming off the train, would take his place and he the driver's seat in the middle, while Tommy's bags and exciting parcels of cakes and toys filled the well of the car and the drive home seemed very long till we could get opening them.

No place has ever seemed to me quite so lovely as Howth was then. Sometimes the sea was as blue as Mama's turquoises, more strikingly blue even than the Mediterranean because so often grey mists made it invisible and mysterious. The little rock pools at the bottom of the high cliffs were very clear and full of wonderlife; sea-anemones which open look like gorgeous flowers with blue and orange spots and, if touched, close up into ugly brown humps, tiny crabs, pink star-fish, endless varieties of sea-snails, white, green, striped and bright butter-cup-yellow. Nurse must have been a wonderful climber, for she often took us down to bathe in those ready-made bathing pools where Kathleen and I boastfully declared that we were swimming, with our feet and hands firmly touching the bottom. The waves used to come splashing into them and made us feel very brave. It must have been a fairly perilous enterprise for her to convey safely two young children up and down those zig-zag narrow cliff paths among the wheeling crying sea-gulls. We were never allowed to go near the cliffs alone, but on the other side of the house far up the heather-covered hill to Granny's cabin, we were free to wander and play as we pleased. The heather grew so high and strong there that we could make cubby houses and be entirely hidden and entirely warm and sheltered from the strong wind that blows over the Head of Howth. After I was grown up I have often slept all night in that friendly heather. It is as springy as the finest spring mattress and, if one chooses the place well, so cosy and sheltered and quiet. From deep down in it one looks up at the stars in a wonderful security and falls asleep to wake up only with the call of the sea birds looking for their breakfasts.

Nurse was a sociable soul. Very soon she knew all the people who lived in the little cabins along the road to the Post Office and away in the heather, and while, over a friendly cup of tea, she chatted, Kathleen and I played with the barefooted children and shared their slices of hot griddle cake baked at the turf fire, or their potatoes out of big iron pots hung in the chimneys. No potatoes and no bread ever tasted as good. All the hospitality was on their side for nurse would never let us bring them to share our meals, carefully set out by Annie the housemaid in the little sitting-room, and woe to Annie if our silver christening mugs and spoons were not brilliantly polished. Those elaborately set-out meals and the steel hoops of her own crinoline were nurse's way of keeping up respectability.

Our feelings towards the ragged children were mixed; they were better climbers than we were and better riders of donkeys, but we could boast of our exploits in swimming pools. If we had better clothes, they had more learning, for every day they trudged off to the far-away schoolhouse, while we played all day with the kids and donkeys in the heather. On the whole honours were fairly equal. . . .

Nurse was a knowledgeable woman and gained great reputation for having saved a sick baby's life. She had a store of nursery remedies and came to be consulted whenever there was a sick child or a minor accident in Howth. She was very proud of this reputation; it gained her forgiveness for her crinoline and English accent, of which also she was proud, but which, if it had not been for her reputation as a doctor and her unfailing good nature, might have marred her popularity; all the cabins were hung with coloured pictures of Wolfe Tone, Emmet and Michael Dwyer and of Allen Larkin and O'Brien and the early Land-League heroes side by side with chromos of the Sacred Heart and of the Blessed Virgin. If nurse knew who these men were, she never said anything; but when she was not there, the old people used to say they were great men, the Lord have mercy on them, but would not say more because after all we too, as well as nurse, belonged to the other side, – the English garrison; nevertheless they made us welcome to their glowing turf fires.

Dublin in Revolution

Previous page:
Constance Markievicz surrenders outside the College of Surgeons,
Easter 1916, by Grace Plunkett

The Larkin Strike

[134] A POLICE BATON CHARGE IN O'CONNELL STREET, 1913;
FROM SEAN O'CASEY'S *DRUMS UNDER THE WINDOWS*.

*James Larkin (1876–1947) born in Liverpool of impoverished Irish
parents, came to Dublin in 1908 after successfully organizing a massive
strike in the Belfast docks, to found the Irish Transport and General
Workers Union. A superb orator and magnetic personality, he rapidly
attracted thousands of Dublin's unskilled workers (who lived and worked
in some of the worst conditions in Europe), including the young Sean
O'Casey. The Dublin employers, led by William Martin Murphy (who
owned Clery's store, the Dublin United Tramways Company and the
Irish Independent) forbade their employees to join his Union; and
when they refused, he organized a general lock-out. The bitter struggle
that followed opened with the brutal baton charge on unarmed crowds in
O'Connell Street described here by O'Casey. The Dublin workers were
eventually starved back to work; Larkin left for America in search of
support, and was eventually arrested there for 'criminal syndicalism'.
Although Larkin's strike split the rising militant Nationalist movement,
it also acted as catalyst, and while it lasted, wrote Desmond Ryan, 'the
very air of Dublin was electric with revolution'.*

The meeting of the locked-out workers, arranged for the following
Sunday, had been proclaimed by Dublin Castle. The night the proclamation had come to Liberty Hall, a vast crowd gathered to hear what
was to be done. The meeting would be held; Jim Larkin would be there
in O'Connell Street. The darkness was falling, a dim quietness was
spreading over the troubled city. Even the gulls muted their complaining cries; and the great throng was silent; silent, listening to the dark
voice speaking from the window. To Sean, the long arm seemed to
move about in the sky, directing the courses of the stars over Dublin;
then the moving hand held up the proclamation, the other sturdy hand

held a lighted match to it; it suddenly flared up like a minor meteor; in a dead silence it flamed, to fall at last in flakes of dark and film ashes down upon the heads of the workers below, fluttering here and there, uncertainly, by the wind from the mighty cheer of agreed defiance that rose to the sky, and glided away to rattle the windows and shake the brazen nails and knobs on the thick doors of Dublin Castle. Resolute and firm, thought Sean; but they have no arms, they have no arms.

Oh! O'Connell Street was a sight of people on that Sunday morning! From under the clock swinging pedantically outside of the *Irish Times* offices, across the bridge over the river, to well away behind the Pillar, topped by Nelson, the wide street was black with them; all waiting for Jim to appear somewhere when the first tick of the clock tolled the hour of twelve. . . .

There he is! suddenly shouted a dozen voices near Sean. Goin' to speak from the window of the very hotel owned be Martin Murphy himself! and there right enough, framed in an upper window, was a tall man in clerical garb, and when he swept the beard from his chin, the crowd saw their own beloved leader, Jim Larkin.

A tremendous cheer shook its way through the wide street, and Sean raised his right arm, and opened his mouth to join it, but his mouth was snapped shut by a terrific surge back from the crowd in front, while another section of it, on the outskirts, surged forward to get a better view, though now the cheer had been silenced by a steady scream in the near distance, by the frantic scuffling of many feet, and loud curses from frightened men. Twelve rows or so ahead of him, Sean saw a distended face, with bulging eyes, while a gaping mouth kept shouting, The police – they're chargin'; get back, get back, there! Let me out, let me out; make a way there for a man has a bad heart! They're batonin' everyone to death – make a way out for a poor, sick man, can't yous!

Sean made a desperate try to turn, but the jam became so close that he was penned tight to his struggling neighbour. He felt himself rising, but fought savagely to keep his feet on the ground; and try as he might, he couldn't get his lifted arm down to fend off the pressure on his chest that was choking him. He could neither get his right arm down nor his left arm up to loosen the collar of his shirt, to get more air, a little more air; he could only sway back and forward as the crowd moved. The breathing of the suffocating crowd sounded like the thick, steamy breathing of a herd of frightened cattle in a cattle-boat tossed about in a storm; and over all, as he tried to struggle, he heard the voices of the police shouting, Give it to the bastards! Drive the rats home to their holes! Let them have it, the Larkin bousys!

James Larkin at Liberty Hall during the Dublin workers' strike, 1913, pen and ink sketch by William Orpen

The Easter Rising

[135] EASTER MONDAY, 1916 IN ST STEPHEN'S GREEN;
FROM *THE INSURRECTION IN DUBLIN* BY JAMES STEPHENS.

*James Stephens (1880–1950), poet and story-teller, was brought up
in a Dublin orphanage and worked as a solicitor's clerk until his
novel* The Crock of Gold *won him recognition as a writer of genius.
At the time of the Rising, he was working in the Dublin National
Gallery. His eye-witness account, published May 1916, conveys the
bewilderment with which the Rising was greeted by most Dubliners,
and carried a plea for recognition of the idealistic motives of its
leaders.*

This has taken everyone by surprise. It is possible, that, with the exception of their staff, it has taken the Volunteers themselves by surprise;
but, today, our peaceful city is no longer peaceful; guns are sounding or
rolling and cracking from different directions, and, although rarely, the
rattle of machine guns can be heard also.

Two days ago war seemed very far away – so far, that I have covenanted with myself to learn the alphabet of music. . . . On Monday (a
Bank Holiday) I went to my office at the usual hour, and after transact-
ing what business was necessary I bent myself to the notes above and
below the stave, and marvelled anew at the ingenuity of man. Peace
was in the building, and if any of the attendants had knowledge or
rumour of war they did not mention it to me.

At one o'clock I went to lunch. Passing the corner of Merrion Row I
saw two small groups of people. These people were regarding steadfastly in the direction of St Stephen's Green Park, and they spoke occasionally to one another with that detached confidence which proved
they were mutually unknown. I also, but without approaching them,
stared in the direction of the Green. I saw nothing but the narrow street
which widened to the Park. Some few people were standing in

tentative attitudes, and all looking in one direction. As I turned from
them homewards I received an impression of silence and expectation
and excitement.

On the way home I noticed that many silent people were standing in
their doorways – an unusual thing in Dublin outside the back streets.
The glance of a Dublin man or woman conveys generally a criticism of
one's personal appearance, and is a little hostile to the passer. The look
of each person as I passed was steadfast, and contained an enquiry
instead of a criticism. I felt faintly uneasy, but withdrew my mind to a
meditation which I had covenanted with myself to perform daily, and
passed to my house.

There I was told that there had been a great deal of rifle firing all the
morning, and we concluded that the military recruits or Volunteer
detachments were practising that arm. My return to business was by
the way I had already come. At the corner of Merrion Row I found the
same silent groups, who were still looking in the direction of the Green,
and addressing each other occasionally with the detached confidence
of strangers. Suddenly, and on the spur of the moment, I addressed one
of these silent gazers.

'Has there been an accident?' said I.

I indicated the people standing about

'What's all this for?'

He was a sleepy, rough-looking man about forty years of age, with a
blunt red moustache, and the distant eyes which one sees in sailors. He
looked at me, stared at me as at a person from a different country. He
grew wakeful and vivid.

'Don't you know?' said he.

And then he saw that I did not know.

'The Sinn Feiners have seized the city this morning'.

'Oh!' said I.

He continued with the savage earnestness of one who has amazement in his mouth:

'They seized the city at eleven o'clock this morning. The Green there is full of them. They have captured the Castle. They have taken the Post Office.'

'My God!' said I, staring at him, and instantly I turned and went running towards the Green.

In a few seconds I banished astonishment and began to walk. As I drew near the Green rifle fire began like sharply-cracking whips. It was from the further side. I saw that the gates were closed and men were standing inside with guns on their shoulders. I passed a house, the windows of which were smashed in. As I went by a man in civilian clothes slipped through the Park gates, which instantly closed behind him. He ran towards me, and I halted. He was carrying two small packets in his hand. He passed me hurriedly, and, placing his leg inside the broken window of the house behind me, he disappeared. Almost immediately another man in civilian clothes appeared from the broken window of another house. He also had something (I don't know what) in his hand. He ran urgently towards the gates, which opened, admitted him, and closed again.

In the centre of this side of the Park a rough barricade of carts and motor cars had been stretched. It was still full of gaps. Behind it was a halted tram, and along the vistas of the Green one saw other trams derelict, untenanted.

I came to the barricade. As I reached it and stood by the Shelbourne Hotel, which it faced, a loud cry came from the Park. The gates opened and three men ran out. Two of them held rifles with fixed bayonets. The third gripped a heavy revolver in his fist. They ran towards a motor car which had just turned the corner, and halted it. The men with bayonets took position instantly on either side of the car. The man with the revolver saluted, and I heard him begging the occupants to pardon him, and directing them to dismount. A man and woman got down. They were again saluted and requested to go to the sidewalk. They did so.

The man crossed and stood by me. He was very tall and thin, middle-aged, with a shaven, wasted face. 'I want to get down to Armagh today,' he said to no one in particular. The loose bluish skin under his eyes was twitching. The Volunteers directed the chauffeur to drive to the barricade and lodge his car in a particular position there. He did it awkwardly, and after three attempts he succeeded in pleasing them. He was a big, brown-faced man, whose knees were rather high for the seat he was in, and they jerked with the speed and persistence of something moved with a powerful spring. His face was composed and fully under command, although his legs were not. He locked the car into the barricade, and then, being a man accustomed to be commanded, he awaited an order to descend. When the order came he walked directly to his master, still preserving all the solemnity of his features. These two men did not address a word to each other, but their drilled and expressionless eyes were loud with surprise and fear and rage. They went into the hotel.

I spoke to the man with the revolver. He was no more than a boy, not more certainly than twenty years of age, short in stature, with close curling red hair and blue eyes – a kindly-looking lad. The strap of his sombrero had torn loose on one side, and except while he held it in his teeth it flapped about his chin. His face was sunburnt and grimy with dust and sweat. . . .

When I spoke he looked at me, and I know that for some seconds he did not see me. I said:

'What is the meaning of all this? What has happened?'

He replied collectedly enough in speech, but with that ramble and errancy clouding his eyes.

'We have taken the city. We are expecting an attack from the military at any moment, and those people,' he indicated knots of men, women and children clustered towards the end of the Green, 'won't go home for me. We have the Post Office, and the Railways, and the Castle. We have all the city. We have everything.'

[136] EASTER MONDAY, 1916 OUTSIDE THE GPO; FROM THE
AUTOBIOGRAPHY OF ERNIE O'MALLEY, *ON ANOTHER MAN'S WOUND*.

*Ernie O'Malley (1898–1957) was a seventeen-year-old medical student at
the outbreak of the Rising. He joined the Republicans soon after, fighting
mainly in the Mendicity Institute on the Quays. He later fought in both the
War of Independence and the Civil War (against the Treaty) and narrowly
escaped execution (see p. 267).*

Easter Monday, a holiday, was warm and many people went to the
races, to the Hill of Howth, Killiney, or to the mountains. I walked
across the city over the Liffey to the South Side, intending to visit the
older portions of Dublin; up by Winetavern Street, through the
Coombe, and back around by Dublin Castle walls. I looked at the statue
of Justice on the upper Castle Gate. She had her back to the city, and I
remembered that it had frequently been commented on, satirically.

I passed by Trinity College; the heavy oaken doors were closed. In
O'Connell Street large groups of people were gathered together. From
the flagstaff on top of the General Post Office, the GPO, floated a new
flag, a tri-coloured one of green, white and orange, the colours running
out from the mast.

'What's it all about?' I asked a man who stood near me, a scowl on
his face.

'Those boyhoes, the Volunteers, have seized the Post Office. They
want nothing less than a Republic,' he laughed scornfully. 'They've
killed some Lancers; but they'll soon run away when the soldiers come.'

Thin strands of barbed wire ran out in front of the Post Office. Two
sentries in green uniforms and slouched hats stood on guard with fixed
bayonets. They seemed cool enough. Behind them the windows had
been smashed. Heavy mail bags half-filled the spaces, rifle barrels
projected, officers in uniform with yellow tabs could be seen hurrying
through the rooms. Outside, men were carrying in heavy bundles –
'explosives, I bet, or ammunition,' said a man beside me. Others

unloaded provisions and vegetables and carried the food inside. On the flat roof sentries patrolled to and fro. Men on motor bicycles, uniformed and in civilian clothes, arrived frequently and the sentries made a lane for them through the crowd.

I walked up the street. Behind Nelson's Pillar lay dead horses, some with their feet in the air, others lying flat. 'The Lancers' horses,' an old man said, although I had not spoken. 'Those fellows,' pointing with his right hand toward the GPO, 'are not going to be frightened by a troop of Lancers. They mean business.' Seated on a dead horse was a woman, a shawl around her head, untidy wisps of hair straggled across her dirty face. She swayed slowly, drunk, singing:

Boys in Khaki, Boys in Blue,
Here's the best of Jolly Good Luck to You.

On the base of the Pillar was a white poster. Gathered around were groups of men and women. Some looked at it with serious faces, others laughed and sniggered. I began to read it with a smile, but my smile ceased as I read.

Poblacht na hÉireann

The Provisional Government

OF THE

IRISH REPUBLIC

To The People of Ireland

Irishmen and Irishwomen

In the Name of God and of the dead generations from which she received her old traditions of nationhood, Ireland, through us, summons her children to her flag and strikes for her freedom.

. . . In every generation the Irish people have asserted their right to national freedom and sovereignty, six times during the past three hundred years they have asserted it in arms. . . . We declare the right of the people of Ireland to the ownership of Ireland and to the unfettered control of Irish destinies, to be sovereign and indefeasible. . . . The Republic guarantees religious and civil liberty, equal rights and equal opportunities to all its citizens . . .

Signed on behalf of the Provisonal Government.

Thomas J. Clarke

Sean Mac Diarmada   Thomas MacDonagh

P. H. Pearse   Eamonn Ceannt

James Connolly   Joseph Plunkett

Clarke, I had known through a friend of ours, Major MacBride, who used to come across the city to buy cigars in his little shop. Pearse I had seen for the first time a few minutes before. A man in the crowd had shouted out his name as a quiet-faced figure in uniform with a strange green, soft hat had passed slowly out through the front door of the GPO. He had talked with an officer underneath the portico beside a fluted pillar. His face was firm and composed. Connolly I had heard speak at meetings. I had seen MacDonagh in the University where he lectured on English, gayer than the other lectures. Plunkett was editor of the *Irish Review*, back numbers of which I had read. They did not mean anything – only names.

[137] EASTER MONDAY, INSIDE TRINITY COLLEGE; BY
JOHN JOLY, IN *BLACKWOODS MAGAZINE*, JULY 1916.

John Joly, who published this account anonymously, was Professor of Geology at Trinity College; and also a brilliant scientist and inventor. Although a firm supporter of the British Empire, his account lays much of the blame for the Rising on misgovernment by the English authorities.

Easter Monday, April 24, 1916 – not yet one fortnight old as I write – looked a day of peaceful thoughts if ever there was one. It was cool, bright weather. The Dublin hills stretched away to the south-west, a picture of immovable repose in the afternoon light.

Down the Dundrum road a band of the Veteran Volunteers – the 'G.R.'s – came swinging along at a steady pace, their faces towards the City. An officer on horseback led them. As he passed us, we recognised in him Major Harris of the Officers' Training Corps of the University of Dublin. He stopped us. 'Have you heard that the Sinn Feiners have risen in Dublin, and seized the General Post Office and Stephen's Green, and shot several of the police?' The Veterans passed on their way to the city, leaving us bewildered. Some of them were to meet death within an hour . . .

I was in Trinity College by four o'clock. I had already been in the city that same morning visiting a friend. There were then no signs of the fatal events proceeding elsewhere. The Post Office was actually being seized at the time I was sitting with my sick friend. But now how different! Carriage traffic had almost ceased, and crowds hurried, partly in terror, partly in curiosity, about the streets. An occasional shot was heard. But it soon became evident that the Rebels were virtually in possession of the city.

I left Trinity cautiously by one of the side gates. I was anxious to ascertain, if possible, the magnitude of the movement and to get some idea of the numbers engaged in it. I visited the General Post Office, the central building in Sackville Street. It was a wreck. Glass littered deeply the path and pavement in front of it. Armed men stood behind its shattered windows. Useless barricades had been piled up within – mail bags, evidently filled with letters, to keep out bullets! Chairs and tables through which bullets would pass almost as easily! And, peering out from their defences, the unhappy warriors threatened with their rifles the scared crowd which alternately approached and ran away. At one window a mere boy was still knocking out the glass with the butt of his rifle. Above the building floated a huge green banner with the inscription in white letters, 'Irish Republic'. Truly *Der Tag* had come! But oh, how pitiful! A fantastic chimera, and death the sure and certain wage!

The Rebels were moving about freely in the streets. All seemed armed with rifles. The police had entirely disappeared. . . .

Irish Rebellion, May, 1916.
Holding a Dublin street against the Rebels

British troops defend a barricade in Moore Street
against the rebels, May 1916

The Anzacs had been above on the roof of the College since an early hour. Owing to the strict order received from the Irish Command not to fire until attacked, many chances of 'potting' Rebels had been missed. But later in the morning this order had been withdrawn. Already before daylight a despatch-rider of the enemy had been brought down by the fire of the Anzacs. It was wonderful shooting. He was one of three who were riding past on bicycles. Four shots were fired. Three found their mark in the head of the unfortunate victim. Another of the riders was wounded and escaped on foot. The third abandoned his bicycle and also escaped. This shooting was done by the uncertain light of the electric lamps, and at a high angle downwards from a lofty building. The body was brought in.

Later I saw him. In no irreverent spirit I lifted the face-cloth. He looked quite young; one might almost call him a boy. The handsome waxen face was on one side concealed in blood. Poor boy! What crime was his? That of listening to the insane wickedness and folly preached by those older and who ought to be wiser than he. And was not he, after all, but one of those who carry to its logical conclusion the long crusade against English rule which for generations has kept peace from Irish hearts?

[138] INSIDE THE GPO, EASTER WEEK; FROM *REMEMBERING SION* BY DESMOND RYAN.

Desmond Ryan (1893–1964), son of a famous Irish nationalist who edited the Gaelic League's newspaper, had worked as Pearse's secretary before 1916. After his release from internment, he became a journalist and wrote several memoirs of the 1916 Rising and its leaders.

Marched according to orders to Liberty Hall with small company in which I drilled, little expecting to be so soon in arms against the armed forces of Great Britain. Great excitement prevailed and the surrounding area was desolate in appearance. The door is locked. Congestion of traffic has whetted our curiosity as we marched through the average holiday crowds and soldiers strolling with their girls past College Green. Admitted to Larkin's palace we swarm upstairs. The Volunteers are 'out' and Ireland is rising. It is evident from the excited shouts to keep 'a watch on the railway line' and 'fill all vessels with water.' Rifles and flushed faces. A feeling of momentary sickness, then wonder. An excited youth informs our commander that there are no longer Volunteers or Citizen Army, so Mr Connolly had said when the row started and the Volunteers had been addressed in front of the Hall, only the Army of the Irish Republic. Commandant Pearse sends down a message to us to proceed to the GPO. We hurry downstairs and at the double across Abbey Street. 'Hurrah for the Volunteers!' shouts an aged working man. 'Hammer the s— out the—!' We rush across Princes Street catching a glimpse of a girl crying and hurrying along, a well-dressed young man beside her. Kids cheer from doorways. A dim crowd up towards the Rotunda. The GPO windows loom before us, men inside with rifles behind barricaded windows. Our commander's rifle-butt smashes through glass and wood and breaks. Scramble in and over, shots ring deafeningly in our ears, a cry, 'the Lancers!' and a volley from within to stop those troops who retire, leaving two dead horses behind. Hurry. Locks blown in, men rushed to the roof, to second storey. Sacks, books, typewriters are stuffed in all hitherto not strengthened windows. Men watch grimly behind. Pearse and his brother appear and survey the scene calmly within, though the latter looks a trifle sad. Vessels are filled with water everywhere. Cooking is carried on where the GPO staff left off. The great door leading into Princes Street is eventually covered with a rough barricade. A young officer dashes in cheering, a smile on his flushed features. Later he is hurried by, the lower part of his face severely injured with a bomb explosion, his hands, chin and neck streaming blood. He is ordered at the revolver's point – for he grows obstinate – when his wounds are dressed and shock subsides – to hospital. Blood is new to us and we only learn later that he has recovered. Inside organisation proceeds. Parties come and go. The crowd outside cheers the hoisted Republican flags and the Proclamation. Pearse speaks without. Connolly, a grim, manly figure in green Commandant's uniform, grasps his hand: 'Thank God, Pearse, we have lived to see this day!' An orderly desolation has settled down within. A dazed DMP man sits in the yard, florid, his head between his hands . . .

[From the roof we can see] soldiers walk unmolested and unarmed within five yards of our guns. Nightfall. Meals of tea, rice and rumours. We laugh. No sleep. Heavy firing in distance, in Four Courts direction. No sleep. Dawn rises over the city.

Tuesday. – Roof still. Smaller crowds in streets. Rumours of Ireland ablaze. Cork, Kerry and Limerick are up and the Curragh line is held both sides. We don't care much. We get used to the bullets. 'Hurrah! Who'd miss it? Is so-and-so "out"? Who was killed? Good man, a pity. Keep under cover!' Inquiries as to advance of troops from different quarters. Our men are to be seen manning shops opposite. Organising of inside and outside defence proceeds. Telephone in good order but the wire is a nuisance when one moves across the parapet. A barricade blocks Earl Street. Looting begins. A fire opposite is put out. Another starts. Get used from then to fires. General preparations to resist siege and, if need be – make last stand. Rain falls and drenches us to the skins. We get waterproofs. News of P(earse) from the gent in the fur coat (the Yank): 'He's in good form.' (P. and B. inspect the positions next day.) No sleep. Hunger, a past and dead sensation. Night. . . . Queer faces in the sky. . . . Wireless flashes from the DBC Restaurant. Get used to stray bullets and feel good. Drunken man singing is killed by stray shots. Kids singing below: 'We are the Volunteers, we'll whack the British Army.' Fires proceed, dawn, sleepless but happy. When will we be wounded?

Wednesday. – Roof still, with an old visit below. Stoics. Firing from the quays to Abbey Street. Tap-tap-tap. Liberty Hall is gone. Artillery and machine-guns at work. Get used to it. Next sensation please! Bullets overhead and down the street. Promise of relief. Ordered below later where we see our friends. Willie: 'That fire cannot be stopped. It will catch the whole block.' Pearse calm. James (Connolly): 'Boys, they're beaten!' Fall asleep while the fires glare in. Ten hours solid rest. Good outside reports.

Thursday. – The blaze spreads along opposite block – house to house. On guard at windows. Boom! The place shakes. Gets stale with repetition. Frequent stands to arms. Snipers and heavy artillery new and prevalent excitements. Connolly wounded in sortie. Armoured car report, and rumour of contemplated advance through Imperial (Hotel's) ruins of troops. Pearse addresses us: 'Her name is splendid among the names of cities!' Fires behind in Henry St. Linenhall ablaze. A terrible and depressing night. But the songs ring out and another dawn comes.

Friday. – Morning lull. Is it arbitration? Fire gains. The street in ruins. Hasty barricade in front in three rows of coal sacks. Constant stands to arms. Keen sniping from upstairs. Men on roof struck with shrapnel. Desperate fight against the fire which has now burst out upon the GPO roof. Fire wins. One constant stand to arms and tension. The women have departed in the morning. One darkened, roaring, leaping blaze in front, above, behind. Debris crashes in. Communications entirely cut. Expectation of general assault. Rations secured. Men shoot two of themselves by mistake. Order to retreat. Dash across the bullet-swept and flame-lit street. Men fall. Henry Place to Moore St. Plunkett rallies men past a fire-swept barricade: 'Don't be cowards! Advance!' Past and into houses. All night borings and snatches of rest. Old meals. Sleep. Fires raging. Nelson looks down on blazing GPO.

Saturday. – Waiting under cover. Rumours as to fire in new position. Preparations for final charge in rear and front of barricade closing our exit. 'Postponed six hours' *perhaps*, countermanded. Waiting, waiting, waiting. Negotiations opened by English, [sic] Departure of Pearse as firm as a rock. Tears in MacDermott's eyes. Two o'clock surrender. March out. Plunkett and MacD(ermott) beside us. Corpses on pavement, ruins around us, fires smouldering still. The Last March. Officers of British Army cover us with huge revolvers as we turn into O'Connell Street, lined with troops. The disarming. We lay down everything. . . .

On the worst night of all, when the fires glared in on the ground floor of the GPO, Pearse came and sat beside me. He was seated on a barrel, his slightly flushed face crowned by his turned-up military hat. He watched the flames leaping and curling fantastically in the stillness, broken periodically by rifle volleys. Around him men slept on the floor, Connolly amongst them. Others were on guard behind loop-holed sandbags. . . . The volleys rolled away, and Pearse watched the flames. 'All the boys were safe,' he said, with a sigh of relief. Then he suddenly turned and asked me, casually but with a certain abruptness: 'It was the right thing to do, wasn't it?' 'Yes. Failure means the end of everything, the Volunteers, Ireland, all!' And the tone showed the agony of his mind, but an agony flaming to final conviction. Outside the flames grew brighter and there was a terrific burst of gunfire away in the darkness. Pearse paused and continued with deep enthusiasm and passionate conviction in his words: 'Well, *when* we are all *wiped out*, people will blame us for everything, condemn us, but only for this protest the war would have ended and nothing would have

been done. After a few years, they will see the meaning of what we tried
to do. . . . Emmet's two-hour insurrection is nothing to this! . . . They will
talk of Dublin in future as one of the splendid cities like they speak today
of Paris! Dublin's name will be glorious for ever!'

Inside the Dublin GPO, Easter Week, 1916, a contemporary recon-
struction painted by Thomas Kiersey

[139] THE AFTERMATH OF THE RISING – LOOTING IN
GRAFTON STREET AND SACKVILLE STREET; FROM *THE SINN
FEIN REBELLION AS I SAW IT* BY MRS HAMILTON NORWAY.

*Mrs Hamilton Norway was the wife of the Irish Postmaster-General whose head-
quarters, the Dublin GPO, had been at the centre of the Rising. She spent Easter
Week in the (now, sadly, demolished) Hibernian Hotel in Dawson Street, with
her husband and seventeen-year-old son, the future novelist Nevil Shute.*

Yesterday afternoon, when the firing in Grafton Street was over, the
mob appeared and looted the shops, clearing the great provision shops
and others. From the back of this hotel you look down on an alley that
connects with Grafton Street, and at the corner, the shop front in
Grafton Street, but with a side entrance into this lane, is a very large

and high-class fruiterer. From the windows we watched the proceedings, and I never saw anything so brazen! The mob were chiefly women and children, with a sprinkling of men. They swarmed in and out of the side door bearing huge consignments of bananas, the great bunches on the stalk, to which the children attached a cord and ran away dragging it along. Other boys had big orange boxes which they filled with tinned and bottled fruits. Women with their skirts held up received showers of apples and oranges and all kinds of fruit which were thrown from the upper windows by their pals; and ankle-deep on the ground lay all the pink and white and silver paper and paper shavings used for packing choice fruits. It was an amazing sight, and nothing daunted these people. Higher up at another shop we were told a woman was hanging out of a window dropping down loot to a friend, when she was shot through the head by a sniper, probably our man; the body dropped into the street and the mob cleared. In a few minutes a hand-cart appeared and gathered up the body, and instantly all the mob swarmed back . . .

In Sackville [now O'Connell] Street was a very large shop called Clery's; for some reason the looters were afraid to start on it, and old women passed up and down gazing longingly at fur coats and silken raiment and saying sorrowfully, 'Isn't Clery's broke yet?' and 'Isn't it a great shame that Clery's is not broke!' Humour and tragedy are so intermixed in this catastrophe. A very delicate elderly lady who is: staying here said to me this morning, in answer to my inquiry as to how she had slept: 'I could not sleep at all. When the guns ceased the *awful silence* made me so nervous!' I know exactly what she meant. When the roar of the guns ceases you can *feel* the silence.

Monday 2 p.m.

Behind the GPO was the Coliseum Theatre, now only a shell; and on the other side of the street was the office of the *Freeman's Journal*, with all the printing machinery lying among the *débris*, all twisted and distorted; but, worst of all, behind that was a great riding school, where all the horses were burnt to death.

James Connolly before the 1916 Rising

[140] THE EXECUTION OF JAMES CONNOLLY IN KILMAINHAM;
FROM *PORTRAIT OF A REBEL FATHER* BY NORA CONNOLLY.

*James Conolly who had been badly wounded in the GPO had been taken from
there to a military hospital in Dublin Castle and was one of the last leaders of
the Easter Rising to be executed. His death, tied to a chair in front of a firing
squad in the courtyard of Kilmainham jail, horrified Dublin opinion.*

On Tuesday [May 9] I went with mother. There were soldiers on guard
at the top of the stairs and in the small alcove leading to Papa's room.
They were fully armed and as they stood guard they had their bayonets
fixed. In the room there was an RAMC officer with him all the time. His
wounded leg was resting in a cage. He was weak and pale and his voice
was very low. Mother asked was he suffering much pain. 'No, but I've
been court-martialled today. They propped me up in bed. The strain
was very great.' She knew then that if they had court-martialled him
while unable to sit up in bed, they would not hesitate to shoot him
while he was wounded. . . .

I saw father next on Thursday, May 11, at midnight. A motor ambulance came to the door. The officer said father was very weak and wished to see his wife and eldest daughter. Mama believed the story because she had seen him on Wednesday and he was in great pain arid very weak, and he couldn't sleep without morphine. Nevertheless she asked the officer if they were going to shoot him. The officer said he could tell her nothing. Through dark, deserted sentry-ridden streets we rode. I was surprised to see about a dozen soldiers encamped outside Papa's door. There was an officer on guard inside the room. Papa turned his head at our coming.

'Well, Lillie, I suppose you know what this means?'

'Oh, James, it's not that – it's not that.'

'Yes, Lillie. I fell asleep for the first time tonight and they wakened me at eleven and told me that I was to die at dawn.' Mama broke down and laid her head on the bed and sobbed heart-breakingly. Father patted her head and said: 'Don't cry, Lillie, you'll unman me.'

'But your beautiful life, James. Your beautiful life!' she sobbed.

'Well, Lillie, hasn't it been a full life and isn't this a good end?' I was also crying. 'Don't cry, Nora, there's nothing to cry about.'

'I won't cry, Papa,' I said.

He patted my hand and said: 'That's my brave girl. . . .'

He tried to cheer Mama by telling her of the man who had come into the Post Office during the Rising to try and buy a penny stamp. 'I don't know what Dublin's coming to when you can't buy a stamp at the Post Office. . . .'

The officer said: 'Only five minutes more.' Mama was nearly overcome – she had to be given water. Papa tried to clasp her in his arms but he could only lift his head and shoulders from the bed. The officer said: 'Time is up.' Papa turned and said goodbye to her and she could not see him. I tried to bring Mama away but I could not move her. The nurse came forward and helped her away. I ran back and kissed Papa again. 'Nora, I'm proud of you.' Then the door was shut and I saw him no more. . . .

(Later) We saw Father Aloysius who had attended him in Kilmainham. 'How did they shoot him . . . how could they shoot him?' asked Mama. 'He couldn't sit up in his bed.'

'It was a terrible shock to me,' said Father Aloysius ... 'I'll always thank God as long as I live that He permitted me to be with your father until he was dead. Such a wonderful man – such a concentration of mind. They carried him from his bed in an ambulance stretcher down to a waiting ambulance and drove him to Kilmainham Jail. They carried him from the ambulance to the jail yard and put him in a chair. . . . He was very brave and cool. . . . I said to him, "Will you pray for the men who are about to shoot you?" and he said: "I will say a prayer for all brave men who do their duty." '

[141] 'SIXTEEN DEAD MEN'; FROM *THE COLLECTED POEMS OF W. B. YEATS.*

W. B. Yeats composed two of his most celebrated poems a few weeks after the execution of the 1916 leaders – 'Easter 1916' with its famous refrain, 'A terrible beauty is born', and this short ballad. They were originally printed only for friends, to avoid political controversy. He wrote at the time to Lady Gregory: 'I had no idea that any public event could so deeply move me.'

> O but we talked at large before
> The sixteen men were shot,
> But who can talk of give and take,
> What should be and what not
> While those dead men are loitering there
> To stir the boiling pot?
>
> You say that we should still the land
> Till Germany's overcome;
> But who is there to argue that
> Now Pearse is deaf and dumb?
> And is their logic to outweigh
> MacDonagh's bony thumb?

How could you dream they'd listen
That have an ear alone
For those new comrades they have found,
Lord Edward and Wolfe Tone,
Or meddle with our give and take
That converse bone to bone?

[142] A DUBLIN BALLAD BY DERMOT O'BYRNE; FROM
AN ANTHOLOGY OF 1916 BY EDNA FITZHENRY.

Well, the last fire is trodden down,
Our dead are rotting fast in lime,
We all can sneak back into town,
Stravague about as in old time,

And stare at gaps of grey and blue
Where Lower Mount Street used to be,
And where flies hum round muck we knew
For Abbey Street and Eden Quay.

And when the devil's made us wise
Each in his own peculiar hell,
With desert hearts and drunken eyes
We're free to sentimentalize
By corners where the martyrs fell.

[143] O'CONNELL STREET AFTER THE RISING; FROM
KATE O'BRIEN'S AUTOBIOGRAPHY, *MY IRELAND*.

How beautiful it looked. Sometimes now when I consider the pitiful
mess of rebuilt O'Connell Street from the Bridge to Nelson's Pillar I smile
back sadly to that other time, when this present stretch of absolutely

comical commercial vulgarity was a huge, swept-away arena of tragedy, in black and white. Wide open to the sky, to the wondering question of any stranger, and to the cold mockery of Anna Livia herself, the gashed and silent piece of ground was like some giant permanent set, vaster than in any imaginable Roman or Palladian theatre, and seeming to commemorate a finished play rather than to wait for actors. That was what we beheld, with pity and awe, of the old street our fathers used to praise. And if some of them might have cursed Sinn Fein for having brought about the destruction of their Sackville Street, I wonder what they would have said to what free prosperity has set up in its place?

[144] 'WAS HE OUT IN EASTER WEEK?'; FROM
INISHFALLEN, FARE THEE WELL BY SEAN O'CASEY.

Things had changed, but not utterly; and no terrible beauty was to be born. Short Mass was still the favourite service, and Brian Boru's harp still bloomed on the bottles of beer. But the boys were home again from prison-camp and prison cell. First the venial sinners from Frongoch; then the mortal sinners from Wakefield, Reading, Dartmoor, and other jails. . . . Nothing could be too good for the boys. When one spoke, all had to remain silent. They led at all meetings, dominated committees, won at cards, got everything anyone had to give, and were everywhere forced to lay down the law on all philosophy, patriotism, foresight, prophecy, and good manners. Was he out in Easter Week? became the touchstone of Irish life. And it was those who hadn't been out themselves who roared silence at anyone venturing to send a remark into a conversation led by a lad home from a prison or a concentration camp; for the lads, themselves, were exceedingly modest about it all, and were often embarrassed by their hangers-on, who forgot that most of Dublin, willy-nilly, was out in Easter Week; that there weren't many Dublin houses without bullet-holes in them; and that casualties were heavier among those who weren't out than among those who were. So for a long time, Easter Week became the Year of One in Irish history and Irish life.

The Civil War

[145] THE SHELLING OF THE FOUR COURTS, JUNE 1922; FROM *INISHFALLEN, FARE THEE WELL* BY SEAN O'CASEY.

After the political split following the Treaty, Republican forces had seized the Four Courts as their headquarters. The Government was eventually provoked into shelling them out.

In spite of the cool meetings held under the care of Dublin's catholic Archbishop; the dear pleading of Dan Breen, Eire's No. 1 Guerilla; in spite of pact and promise, broken ere they were understood, the day came when General Tom Ennis, a fawn trench-coat mock-modestly covering a neat green uniform, with brilliant yellow tabs on the lapels, goads his unwilling men to swing a heavy gun swiftly, so that its angry snout may point towards the Republican enemy barricaded deep in the Four Courts; hurries them into pulling the lanyard that opens the cannon's mouth to send a British shell over the walls, send it screaming over, to spread a shattering shower of sharp steel against her greying dignity, darting hither and thither in its effort to bring maiming death to angry comrades behind the walls on the far side of the river Liffey; while a great crowd of excited civilians crouch behind corners near Richmond Bridge to listen to the crack of the cannon, and watch the smoke and flame of the bursting shells. Rory O'Connor, chief of the Republicans, steadied with a few doses of phospherine, taken to tighten his nerves loosened from lack of sleep, tightens his belt, and waits; waits for a closer attack, for he has no bullying guns to answer the dinning onslaught of shells sent over, minute by minutes, by his one-time comrade, Tom Ennis, hidden behind the houses on the other bank of Anna Livia Plurabelle. Thick dust hides the body of the building, and dark smoke encircles the huge dome, making it look like the great globe itself trekking the sky through a way of stormy clouds.

The Free Staters having expended their shells, advanced to the building in a sharp trot, murmuring holy acts of contrition, finger on trigger and bayonet fixed; advanced, till a land-mine exploded under their passing feet, and brought the charge to a stop for a while, so that they could watch all the foolish wigs and gowns of Dublin sailing up into the sky; with all the records of the country, processes, cases, testimonies, bills of exchange, and sales of properties to church and private person, and all hereditaments chronicled since Strongbow came to Ireland, flying up after the wigs and gowns, to come fluttering down, scorched and tattered, into every Dublin back-yard and front garden.

[146] ERNIE O'MALLEY ESCAPES FROM THE FOUR COURTS: FROM *THE SINGING FLAME* BY ERNEST O'MALLEY.

O'Malley was captured soon afterwards from his hiding place in Ailesbury Road and badly wounded. He was reprieved from a death sentence after a prolonged hunger strike, and released in 1923.

Sean Lemass came over to me in a hurry. Normally he was very calm, but now he was excited, trying hard to keep his breath as he spoke. 'I think there's a chance of escape. The small gate here,' pointing towards the front corner of the yard, 'leads into the next house, the manager's house, and we can walk right through.' 'Let's go now,' I said. . . . We opened the small gate. There were two Staters standing near by but they did not seem to notice. We opened the back door of the house and walked through the kitchen into the hall. A man and a woman were standing at the front door looking into the street, evidently the manager and his wife. I said: 'Good-day. Please excuse us passing through your house, it's rather urgent,' and walked past into the crowd.

[147] OLIVER GOGARTY VOWS TWO SWANS TO THE
LIFFEY, 1922; FROM *IT ISN'T THIS TIME OF YEAR
AT ALL* BY OLIVER ST JOHN GOGARTY.

I was alone in the house but for a few servants. My family had gone to
the country for the Christmas holidays. I lay in the bath and steam filled
the room. I was tring to turn off a tap with my toes when I felt something cold on the back of my neck. I looked round. There was a gunman
in a belted trench coat of dark blue material.

'Out! And be quick!' He waved the gun.
'If this is murder, may I scribble a few lines to my wife?'
Pale and agitated, he again threatened me with the gun.
'For a housebreaker, you seem very nervous,' I said.

Through the door of the bathroom I could see two gunmen on the
stairs. I put a towel about me and cursed myself for leaving my gun in
the drawer of the mock Chippendale table in the dressing room. To
open that drawer it was necessary to place a foot against either leg of
the table; even then the drawer often jammed.

Oh, how I regretted that gun now! I could have blown the head off
the unsuspecting gunman and then rushed at the two guarding the
stairs. Who expects a naked man to be armed? Slowly I drew on the
trousers of my dinner suit and put on the comfortable old shoes which
were down at heel. The other two gunmen were now in the room with
me, while I dressed.

I looked in the mirror. My face was almost white. That does not
come from thought. Maybe it does; what about 'sicklied o'er'? But the
pupils were dilated. However, my thinking was unimpaired . . .

Over the fireplace I saw a pair of riding boots with trees in them. If
I could get the tree out, I would have a weapon . . .

'Put those bloody pumps in your pocket and put on these.' I was
handed a pair of skiing boots and an old coat of buffalo leather with the

furry side in. They must have found these on the back stairs. So there was probably a gunman there and I was counting on those back stairs to make a dash for it. Hopeless now.

Clad in a pair of trousers, a white shirt, a great coat and heavy shoes, I was led down. A hunchbacked woman was waiting in the hall. I noticed that the telephone wire had been dragged out. A large sedan stood at the door with a big fellow at the wheel . . .

A gunman sat on either side of me; I could feel the pressure of a gun on each kidney. Another sat in my lap and lay back. I was crushed into the cushions and completely out of sight. We started.

'If you shout when we are passing any of your bloody soldiers, you will be blown to smithereens.' . . .

We reached the last house by the Liffey Bank – at the time vacant – where the river meets the first weir at Trinity College Boat House. Here at full tide the water can be nine feet deep.

I was bundled through a small gate in the wall.

'Can I tip the driver?' I asked. That made them all angry, the driver most of all.

I was taken into a dark cellar, evidently a coal cellar, and made to stand against the wall. Seven men in two ranks stood in front of the door . . .

Somebody struck another light. I could see the pistols wavering in the front row. I remember thinking that it is more for the sake of the firing squad than of their prisoner that they bind his eyes. Now I realized why a victim gave gold to the headsman to dispatch him quickly. The match went out. I took two steps to the side. When I tried to get back so as not to show the white feather to such little jackeens, my feet were stuck to the ground . . .

The captain of the gunmen ordered, 'Soldiers, forward and seize prisoner. We are going for a lamp.' Five men came forward and led me out.

I noticed that the house was parallel to the river, which runs west to east. It was in the small cellar at the east end that I was stood against the wall. Now I was being taken to the west end of the house with the river not twenty yards away. The corner boys took me to what had evidently been a music room. Music books were scattered on the floor, which had been torn up along the wall. The torn-up planks and some of the music books were piled up to make a fire, for the night was very cold. The fire soon blazed; but the unheated chimney smoked.

'Is it a part of the Republican programme to gas a prisoner before shooting him?' I asked.

'What d'ye mean?'

'There's too much smoke in the room.'

'Ye won't notice it when they come back with the lamp.'

They were shivering from cold. I tried to lecture on small arms. 'Those automatics are dangerous. They have to have the lock drawn back before they will fire. Let me show you.' I reached for one of their guns; but there was nothing doing. With my ear on a stalk I listened for the return of the sedan with the lamp and the head gunman. Then I would be shot and my body thrown into the flooded river.

I bowed my head and groaned. 'You fellows have given me such a fright that I'll soon have diarrhoea.' I waited for the remark to soak in.

It is a vulgar notion that fright produces diarrhoea, whereas the fact is that all the secretions of the body are dried up.

Whether the remark had sunk in or not, I was terrified that the motor would return – 'Quick, a guard,' I said hurriedly. The fools seized me and stuck a gun into each side of my heavy coat. In the near darkness I slipped my arms out of the coat, while I remained inside it.

Up rushed the outside watchman, on whom I had not counted. 'What's all this?'

'He has to go out.'

It was dark outside but I feared that the eyes of the outside watchman would be accustomed to the dark. By the feel of gravel under my left foot and the smooth cement threshold about an inch above the gravel under my right, I knew that I was clear of the house. In a broken voice I said to the guards, 'Would you mind holding up my coat?'

They were still holding the coat as I was going swiftly down the river with the current. The black water had swallowed me up.

Oh, how I rejoiced in spite of the shock. Now for the Caesar act! But I had some swimming to do and the river was icy cold. I tried to grasp overhanging willows but they passed through my numbed hands.

Cross to opposite bank? What a fool I would be! The gunmen would rush over there. It would take them only some minutes to cross the bridge at Liffey Bank and to break into the grounds that went beside the stream. I floated along and I vowed two swans to the river if it bore me safe to shore.

Life, Customs and
Morals in Dublin

Previous page:
Fashionable Dublin enjoys the Beaux Walk in St Stephen's Green, aquatint by James Malton, 1797

*Much of the early history and records of Dublin deal with the protection of
the city from 'uncivilized' (literally non-city-dwelling) Irish tribes outside
the walls. This is the first hostile Norman account which set the pattern and
formed what one Irish historian has called 'the poisoned source' of Norman
and English attitudes to Ireland.*

I have thought it not superfluous to lay before the reader a brief description of this people as regards both their persons and their minds: that is
to say the external and the internal peculiarities they present.

In this country children are not, as elsewhere delicately brought
up; for everything over and above the homely and somewhat scanty
nourishment they receive from their rude parents is left to nature.
They are laid in no cradle, nor swathed in swaddling clothes; their
tender limbs know not the use of the warm bath, neither are they
adjusted with the help of art. Yet Nature, as if to show what her
unaided power can do, fails not to rear and mould them through
infancy and childhood, until in the fulness of time she leads each to
man's estate conspicuous for a tall and handsome form, regular
features, and a fresh complexion

But although adorned to the full with such natural gifts as these, still
the barbarous fashion of their garments, their shaggy beards, and their
ignorance reveal the arrant savage. For little do they wear in the way of
woollen clothing, and that little black (which is the colour of the sheep
of the country) and of ungainly cut: their habit being to apparel themselves in small closely-fitting hoods extending over the shoulders and
down to the elbow, generally made of parti-coloured scraps sewn
together. Under this instead of a coat they have a gown. Woollen trews

complete their attire, being breeches and hose in one, usually dyed some tint.

In riding they use no saddles, high boots, or spurs; but simply carry a rod crooked at the end, with which they both urge on and guide their horses. Reins indeed they have, yet they perform the double duty of bit and bridle: thus the horses, which feed on nothing but grass, can browse at any time.

An 'uncivilized' Irish chief banquets in the forest; from John Derricke's
Image of Ireland

They go to battle without armour, which they regard as an encumbrance: and in fact think it a sign of valour and an honour to fight without such protection. Of weapons they use but three kinds: short spears and pairs of darts – and in this they follow the custom of the Basques –, while they have learnt also from the Norwegians and Ostmen (of whom later) the use of the great battle-axe, and excellently well wrought and tempered their axes are. They wield them with one hand only instead of both, laying the thumb along the upper side of the heft and so directing the blow. From the stroke of one of these neither the cone-shaped helmet is sufficient to guard the head, nor a shirt of ring-mail the body. Thus in our own time it happened that a soldier had his thigh cut right through with one stroke of an axe, encased though it was all round in good steel, the amputated leg falling to the ground on one side of the horse, and its dying owner on the other. When arms fail they cast stones, with which they can inflict much damage on an enemy, as they are handier and readier at slinging than any other nation.

Verily a wild and inhospitable race: living only on the produce of their beasts, and living like beasts themselves. A race but little advanced from the primitive pastoral life. For whereas the stages of human progress are from the forest to the field, from the field to the town, and so to civic polity, this people despising agricultural labour, having little taste for the refinements of civilization, and showing a strong aversion from political institutions, knows not how to relinquish the sylvan and bucolic habits to which it has always been accustomed. . . .

Moreover they do not employ their time in the manufacture of linen, cloth, or any other ware, nor in the development of a single mechanic art. They are simply the slaves of ease and sloth: freedom from motion they esteem the height of luxury, freedom from restraint the summit of wealth.

[149] THE OSTOMEN; FROM HOLINSHED'S *CHRONICLES*.

The Ostomen – or Easterlings – were the pre-Norman inhabitants of Dublin of Viking stock. Unlike the Irish, they were recognized by Giraldus as 'civilized' men. After the Norman conquest, they migrated en masse to the north side of the Liffey to found the settlement of Oxmantown, but were gradually assimilated to the Norman settlers.

These Ostomen were not Irishmen, but yet of long continuance in Ireland. Some saie they came first out of Norwaie, and were called

Ostomen, that is to saie Easterlings, or Easterne men, bicause that coun-
trie lieth East in respect of England and Ireland. Some thinke they were
Saxons and Normans; but whatsoever they were, they were merchants
and used the trade of merchandize, and in peaceable maner they came
into Ireland; and there being landed they found such favour with the
Irishrie, that they licenced them to build haven townes wherein they
might dwell & use their trafffike. These men builded the ancientest and
most part of the cities and towns upon or neere the sea side within that
land; as namelie Dublin, Waterford, Corke, Limerike, and others. And
albeit they in processe of time grew to be mightie and strong, and for
their safetie did build townes and castels: yet they durst not to dwell
among the Irish people, but still continued and kept themselves within
their owne townes and forts, and thereof they are and were called since
townesmen. And of them were these, being the inhabitants of Dublin,
which came to meet the earle [*Strongbow*], and were thus slaine.

[150] FORTIFYING THE CITY: A ROYAL CHARTER; FROM SIR
JOHN GILBERT'S *CALENDAR OF ANCIENT RECORDS OF DUBLIN*.

*This document shows some of the main items of trade used in thirteenth-century
Dublin. Taxes levied were used to fortify and build up the medieval city walls.*

XV – 1250, May 30. Bisham. Henry III.: Permission to levy at Dublin,
during three years, tolls as follows, for fortifying and enclosing the city:
– of every crannoc of wheat, one farthing; of every crannoc of flour one
farthing; of every butt of wine, two pence; of every butt of honey, four
pence; of every weigh of wool, one penny; of every dacre of hides, one
penny; of every dacre of hides of stag, goat, or horse, one halfpenny; of
every great ship, sixteen pence; of every smaller ship, eight pence; of
every piece of English or foreign cloth, one halfpenny; of every piece of
Irish cloth, one farthing; of every crannoc of woad, two pence; of every
crannoc of salt, one farthing; of every bend of iron, one halfpenny; of
every mease of herrings, one farthing; of every ox, cow, or horse, one

penny; of eight sheep, one penny; of every hog or pig, one farthing; of one hundred boards, one farthing; of one hundred horse-shoes, one half-penny; of every weigh of tallow, butter, or grease, one halfpenny; of one hundred pounds of spice, two pence; of one hundred weight of wax, two pence; of one hundred pounds of alum, two pence; of every mill-stone, one halfpenny; of one hundred ells of linen cloth, one penny; of one hundred ells of canvas, one penny; of every load of lead, two pence; of every crannoc of beans, one farthing; of one dozen of kitchen ware, one halfpenny; of one hundred pounds of metal, one penny; of one hundred pounds of hogs' lard, one penny; of one hundred pounds of tallow, one penny; of three shillings' worth of merchandise, one farthing; of one hundred lamb-skins, one halfpenny; of one hundred squirrel-skins, one penny; of one hundred pounds of pitch, one halfpenny; of every horse-load of iron, one halfpenny; of one dozen cords of Linden wood, one farthing.—

[151] AN IRISH CHIEFTAIN RESISTS ADOPTING ENGLISH DRESS;
FROM *THE GOVERNMENT OF IRELAND UNDER SIR JOHN PERROT*.

A Parliament is now summoned to be held at Dublin (1585) where the nobility, clergy and commons being assembled, order was taken, that none were permitted to go in Irish attire (as in former times they used), but to sort themselves in such habit after the English manner, as was answerable to their several ranks and qualities. . . . He (Sir John Perrot) bestowed upon Tirlough Luineach (O'Neill), the principal lord of Ulster, and on some others, chief of the Irish, gowns and other robes fit for that place, and their degrees; which they embraced like fetters: of which being weary, one of them came to the Deputy and besought him, that one of his chaplains, which he called priests, might go with him along through the streets, clad in his Irish 'trouses': for then, quoth he, the boys will laugh as fast at him, as they now do at me, whereat though the Deputy could have smiled, yet casting a frown upon his countenance, told him, there was no cause he should think any laughed at him, for wearing those which were fit ornaments for the place he now held, and did present in Parliament; but if any did so, it was at his ill wearing of the same, which want of civil custom caused. Therefore since use would make that seemly, which was now ridiculous, he advised him to view the difference of being fit for all assemblies, and only fit for the woods and barbarous places; but, quoth the Deputy, if any idle or ill-affected person shall put the contrary into your head, believe it to be done out of an ill-meaning to the State, and worse unto your person, for contempt of order and decency will in the end be your downfall.

[152] A SIXTEENTH-CENTURY GAELIC POET LAMENTS THE
BETRAYAL OF IRISH WAYS; FROM CONSTANTIA MAXWELL'S
IRISH HISTORY FROM CONTEMPORARY SOURCES.

This poem by Laoiseach Mac an Bhaird, contrasting an 'anglicized' Irish chieftain with his hardier rebel brother, shows that the English policy of 'taming' the Gaelic lords with clothes and luxuries at Court had at least some success.

O man who follows English ways, who cut your thick-clustering
  hair, graceful hand of my choice, you are not Donnchadh's
  good son!
If you were, you would not give up your hair for an artificial
  English mode – the fairest ornament of the land of *Fódla!*
  – and your head would not be tonsured.
You think the yellow head of hair unfashionable, *he* detests both
  locks and going bald after the English style; your characters
  are different indeed.
A man who never loved English ways is Eóghan Bán, beloved of
  noble ladies. To English ways he never gave his heart: a
  savage life he chose.
Your mind is nothing to Eóghan Bán, a man who would give
  breeches for a trifle, who asked no cloak but a rag, who had
  no wish for coat and legging.

He would hate to carry at his ankle a jewelled spur on a boot, or
    stockings in the English style; he will have no locks upon him.
A blunt rapier that would not kill a fly, the weight of an awl
    sticking out behind as one goes to a hill of assembly – the
    son of Donnchadh sees no beauty in that!
Little he cares for a mantle gold-embroidered, or a high orna-
    mental collar, or a gold ring that would only be irksome, or a
    satin scarf down to the heels.
He has no longing for a feather bed, he had rather lie upon
    rushes. Pleasanter to Donnchadh's good son is a hut of rough
    poles than the *táille* of a tower.
A troop of horse at the brink of a gap, a fierce fight, a struggle
    with foot soldiers, these are some of the desires of
    Donnchadh's son – and seeking battle aginst the foreigners!
How unlike are you to Eóghan Bán – they laugh at your foot on
    the stepping-stone. Pity that you have not seen your fault, O
    man who follow English ways.

[153] THE STATE OF DUBLIN IN 1620; FROM LUKE GERNON'S
DISCOURSES, QUOTED IN *IRELAND 1607–1782* BY JAMES CARTY.

*Luke Gernon, an English judge from Munster, is one of the first settlers to
dismiss English xenophobia and paint a kindly picture of the Irish.*

Ireland Is at all poynts like a young wench that hath a green sickness . . .
She is very fayre of visage, and hath a smooth skinn of tender grasse. . . .

How shall I describe her towns . . . Dublin is the most frequented,
more for conveniency than for majesty. There resides the Deputy and
the Council. . . . The buildings are of timber and of the English form,
and it is resembled to Bristol, but falleth short. . . .

Your will expect to know the state of our State. It is not very magnificent, nor to be disregarded. There is a presence where they stand at all
times uncovered, and a cloth of State under which the Deputy sitteth.

When that he sitteth at meat, there sit of men of quality as many as the table will contayne. When he goeth abroad in solemn manner, all whom it concerns do attend him. Before him go the gentlemen, captynes, knights, and officers, all on foot. Then cometh the Deputy riding in state, and before him a knight bareheaded carrying the sword. After the Deputy, the nobles, the Council, and the Judges all in foot-clothes. His guard consists of fifty tall men, they wear not red coates, but soldier's cassocks, and halberts in theyr hands. On principal festivals, the herald goes before him in a coat of arms. So much of Dublin I may call it her Whyte hall. . . .

Let us converse with the people. Lord, what makes you so squeamish? Be not afraid. The Irishman is no Cannibal to eat you up, nor no lowsy Jack to offend you.

The man of Ireland is of a strong constitution, tall and big-limbed, but seldom fat, patient of heat and cold, but impatient of labour. Of nature he is prompt and ingenious, but servile, crafty and inquisitive after news, the symptoms of a conquered nation. Their speech hath been accused to be a whining language, but that is among the beggars. I take it to be a smooth language well comixt of vowels and of consonants and hath a pleasing cadence.

The better sort are apparelled at all points like the English only they retain their mantle, which is a garment not indecent. His brogues are single-soled, more rudely sewed than a shoo but more strong, sharp at the toe, and a flap of leather left at the heels to pull them on. His hat is a frieze cap close to the head with two lappetts, to button under his chinne.. And for his weapon he wears a skeyne which is a knife of three fingers broad, of the length of a dagger and sharpening towards the point with a rude wooden handle. . . .

The women of Ireland are very comely creatures, tall, slender and upright. Of complexion very fayre and cleare-skinned (but freckled) with tresses of bright yellow hayre, which they chain up in curious knots and devises. They are not strait-laced nor plated in their youth, but suffered to grow at liberty so that you shall hardly see one crooked or deformed. . . . I never saw fayrer wenches nor fowler calliots, so we call the old women. Of nature they are very kind and tractable.

A group of Irish soldiers drawn by Albrecht Dürer

[154] THE HOSPITABLE MAYOR OF DUBLIN, 1577, AND HOW THE DUBLIN CITIZENS MUSTER FOR THEIR DEFENCE, FROM THE *DESCRIPTION OF IRELAND* BY RICHARD STANYHURST IN HOLINSHED'S *CHRONICLES*.

There hath beene of late yeares a worshipfull gentleman, named Patrike Scarsefield, that bare the office of the maioraltie in Dublin, who kept so great port in this yeare, as his hospitalitie to his fame and renowme resteth as yet in fresh memorie. One of his especiall and entire friends entring in communication with the gentleman, his yeare being well neere expired, mooved question, to what he thought his expenses all that yeare amounted? 'Trulie Iames (so his friend was named) quoth maister Scarsefield, I take betweene me and God, when I entered into mine office, the last saint Hierome his daie (which is the morrow of Michaelmasse, on which daie the maior taketh his oth before the chiefe baron, at the excheker within the castell of Dublin) I had three barnes well stored and thwackt with corne, and I assured my selfe, that anie one of these three had bene sufficient to have stored mine house with bread, ale, and beere for this yeare. And now God and good companie be thanked, I stand in doubt, whether I shall rub out my maioraltie with my third barne, which is well nigh with my yeare ended. And yet nothing smiteth me so much at the heart, as that the knot of good fellowes that you see here (he ment the sergeants and officers) are readie to flit from me, and make their next yeares abode with the next maior. . . .

And in verie deed it was not to be marvelled: for during his maioraltie, his house was so open, as commonly from five of the clocke in the morning, to ten at night, his butterie and cellars were with one crew or other frequented. To the haunting of which, ghests were the sooner allured, for that you should never marke him or his bedfellow (such was their buxomnesse) once frowne or wrinkle their foreheads, or bend their browes, or glowme their countenances, or make a sowre face at anie ghest, were he never so meane. . . .

Some of his friends, that were snudging peniefathers, would take him up verie roughlie for his lavishing & his outragious expenses, as they tearme it. Tush my maisters (would he saie) take not the matter so hot: who so commeth to my table, and hath no need of my meat, I know he commeth for the good will he beareth me; and therefore I am beholding to thanke him for his companie: if he resort for need, how maie I bestow my goods better, than in releeving the poore? . . .

For the better training of their youth in martiall exploits, the citizens use to muster foure times by the yeare: on Black mondaie, which is the morrow of Easter daie, on Maie daie, saint Iohn Baptist his eeve, and saint Peter his eeve.

The Blacke mondaee muster sproong of this occasion. Sopne after Ireland was conquered by the Britons, and the greater part of Leinster pacified, diverse townesmen of Bristow flitted from thense to Dublin, and in short space the civitie was by them so well inhabited, as it grew to bee verie populous. Whereupon the citizens having over great affiance in the multitude of the people, and so consequentlie being somewhat retchlesse in heeding the mounteine enimie that lurked under their noses, were woont to rome and roile in clusters, sometime three or foure miles from the towne. The Irish enimie spieng that the citizens were accustomed to fetch such od vagaries, especiallie on the holie daies, & having an inkling withall by some false clatterfert or other, that a companie of them would haue ranged abrode, on mondaie in the Easter weeke towards the wood of Cullen, which is distant two miles from Dublin, they laie in stale verie well appointed, and laid in sundrie places for their comming. The citizens rather minding the pleasure they should presentlie inioy, than forecasting the hurt that might insue, flockt unarmed out of the civitie to the wood, where being intercepted by them that laie hooving in ambush, they were to the number of five hundred miserablie slaine. Whereupon the remnant of the citizens deeming the unluckie time to be a crosse or a dismall daie, gave it the appellation of Black mondaie.

The citie soone after being peopled by a fresh supplie of Bristollians, to dare the Irish enimie, agreed to banket yearelie in that place, which to this daie is observed. For the maior and the shiriffs with the citizens repaire to the wood of Cullen, in which place the maior bestoweth a costlie dinner within a mote or a rundell, and both the shiriffs within another: where they are so well garded with the youth of the civitie, as the mounteine enimie dareth not attempt to snatch as much as a pastie crust from thense.

[155] An Elizabethan soldier complains of
the price of Dublin ale in 1610; from Barnaby
Rich's *New Description of Ireland*.

*Barnaby Rich (1540–1617) was a professional Elizabethan soldier, who had
fought in Essex's Irish campaign in the 1570s. He settled in Dublin for the
next forty-seven years, supplementing a small pension with a string of popular tracts and romances – one of which gave Shakespeare the plot for*
Twelfth Night.

I might speak here of friars [and] Jesuits . . . well known to be his
Majesty's vowed and protested enemies, that are yet entertained,
upholden and maintained in Dublin, not without great contributions
allowed unto them by the Papistical sort of the citizens, that will grudge
and murmur to give a soldier a night's lodging . . . and they do not only
show an unwillingness to his Majesty in these trifling matters, but they
do likewise make manifest their ingratitude by many other means. And
whereas their corporation hath been dignified by several kings and
princes of England with many large privileges, and that they have the
whole trade and traffic amongst themselves, no man to buy or sell
within their liberties, unless he be a freeman . . . There is neither
merchandise, nor any manner of commodity that is brought from
Spain, from France, from Flanders . . . but they will have the whole
bargain to themselves, not suffering any man that is not free, to buy for
his own provision, no, not so much as a drinking glass, but it must be
had from them, and by that means he shall be enforced to pay double
the price. . . .

I am now to speak of a certain kind of commodity that outstretcheth
all that I have hitherto spoken of, and that is the selling of ale in Dublin,
a quotidian commodity, that hath vent in every house in the town every
day in the week . . . there is no merchandise so vendible (saleable), it is
the very marrow of the commonwealth in Dublin: the whole profit of
the town stand upon alehouses and selling of ale. . . . They buy malt in

Dublin, at half the price that it is sold for in London, and they sell their drink in Dublin at double the rate that they do in London: and this commodity the aldermen's wives and the rest of the women brewers do find so sweet, that Master mayor and his brethren are willing to wink at, and to tolerate those multitude of alehouses, that themselves do even know to be the very nurseries of drunkenness . . . and many other vile abominations.

[156] SUNDAY IN DUBLIN, 1725, BY D— S—; QUOTED IN *IRISH CAVALCADE* BY M. J. McMANUS.

The author of this anonymous pamphlet may be the great Dean Swift himself, although as M. J. McManus notes, during Swift's life any witty or scurrilous piece of uncertain parentage appearing in Dublin was ascribed to him 'as if by a standing affiliation order'.

Sunday, *Six in the Morning*. Old infirm letchers plagued in their beds with impracticable wishes, wrangling with their diseases and age, and repining because nature has not altered her course and exempted them from the common fate – Rakes and bullies breaking up from their nocturnal debauches, and retiring to their quarters – Petty equipages, as chaises, chairs and hackney-horses getting ready to carry declining shop-keepers and their wives to adjacent villages to divert melancholy thoughts of bankruptcy – Tailors, stay-makers, manteau-makers and milliners busy in breaking the Fourth Commandment – News-writers inventing stories of rapes, riots, robberies, etc., to fill up the Monday's newspapers – The Ministerial and anti-Court writers racking their inventions for argument and matter for their next week's essays, to transmit to London.

Seven o'clock. Officers of the army, lawyers' clerks, mercers' journeymen, and city apprentices swallowing their mercurials and water-gruel – Twelve-penny harlots rapping at pawn-brokers' doors to redeem their wearing-apparel – Servantmaids by the help of false keys pilfering their mistress's teas and sugars – Reduced officers rallied by their laundresses and denied a clean shirt – Demi-clergymen, i.e., parish-clerks, putting on their stiff bands and grave countenances – Foot-soldiers and bullies distribuing curses, black eyes and swollen faces amongst their doxies – Brandy shops opening for the reception of thieves and pickpockets – Beggars putting on their rueful countenances and crutches and managing their sores and ulcers to move compassion.

Eight o'clock. Barbers vastly busy embellishing their customers – Bawds with band-boxes, borrowed smocks, and scoured manteaus in motion about Aungier Street – Apothecaries and their apprentices trotting thro' the streets with purges and potions – Lap-dogs cleaning and dressing to go to church with their ladies.

Nine o'clock. Pampered clergymen vouchsafe to think of arising and the duty of the day – French artificers quit their garrets and exchange their greasy woollen nightcaps for swords and laced ruffles, declare for a walk to Stephen's Green and a dinner eleemosynary at a dirty alehouse – Insolvent debtors shake hands with bailiffs and appear out of the Verge with gay countenance – Poor people employed in erasing the wrinkles out of their wearing apparel and other symptoms of their having been under date and tribulation – Gentlemen's house-keepers opening their pipes upon the lower servants.

Ten o'clock. Wives, maids and widows washing, wiping, scrubbing, picking, prinking, pinning, parching, painting, trooping, lacing and scolding . . . Kept mistresses as lazy in their beds as lifeguardsmen in their quarters – Informers plaguing poor alehousemen, barbers and nosegay-women – Hackney writers, Connaught fortune-hunters, and English solicitors carefully cogging the heels of their stockings, and darning their shirt-collars in order to issue forth from the noisy instances of their landladies to borrow half-a-crown or beg a dinner – . . . Bakers and pastrycooks robbing their customers pies and puddings – Vintners and victuallers looking out their worst wines and liquors for the accommodation of such as are to dine with them gratis.

Eleven o'clock. Fine fans, rich brilliants, white hands, envious eyes and gay snuff-boxes displaying in most parish churches – Many excellent stolen sermons preaching by some clergymen who won't take pains to make worse of their own – Folks of fashion humbling themselves in rich lace and tissue and enduring the fatigue of Divine Service with wonderful seeming patience – Drunken beggars battling and breaking one another's heads in the public streets about dividing the charity of ostentatious fools and old women – Hackney coachmen and chairmen lifting up their eyes to Heaven for wet weather – Dabs and portions of beef, pork, and mutton roasting in pack-thread strings in the apartments of married cobblers, porters, pennypostmen and poor harlots.

Twelve o'clock. . . . City wives at their dram-bottles or criticising upon one another's dress and behaviour at church before dinner – Parish officers and young tradesmen vastly noisy over the dumplings in tavern kitchens – . . . Begging cripples bestowing prayers and benedictions in the streets upon their benefactors – . . .

One o'clock. Politicians dropping their two-pences upon the coffee-house bars and returning home to dinner – Hackney coaches flying about the streets with whole families, new-married couples, uncles, aunts and cousins to dine with their friends and relations . . . – All the common people's jaws in and around this great metropolis in full employment.

Two o'clock. The sexes ogling and stealing glances at one another as they sit at dinner together – Church bells and tavern bells keep time with one another – Some politicians upon the Catholic bench at the end of Stephen's Green bring the Spanish arms to Gibraltar and Great Britain and do wonders for the Pretender – Those on the Court Bench at the other end let loose a powerful army of Moors upon them and drive them out of their late conquests in Barbary . . . Pickpockets taking their stands at the avenues into public walks.

Three o'clock. Pawn Brokers' wives dressing themselves with their customers' wearing apparel, rings and watches – Prebendaries, petty canons and choristers, with much reluctancy, quit their couches, wives and bottles for cathedral exercises . . . – City cheesemongers and grocers snoring in churches and meeting-houses – The paths of Rathfarnham, Finglass and Donnybrook found much more pleasant than those of the Gospel – Citizens marching in threes, fours and fives thro' the town, in quest of sour wine and cider – Waiters at taverns and coffee-houses making vast preparations to cut a figure in the Beau Monde – Looking-glasses and – in great favour with the ladies – Women servants, half naked, at their broken bits of looking-glasses, vainly attempting, by the power of soap and labour, to alter the colour of their skins.

Four o'clock. Drunken bullies, beaus and gamesters religiously in their beds, as remembering that the Sabbath was appointed for a day of rest – People of quality picking their teeth and talking of modes and mortgages . . .

Five o'clock. A general church and meeting-house delivery for the City of Dublin – Vintners begin to yawn and quit their afternoon naps and welcome in their guests – All the pretty prating mouths sitting at tea-tables, like coroners' inquests upon the murdered reputations of their neighbours – Hired servants meeting and saluting one another in the streets, abusing the families that entertain them, and advancing the old doctrine of 'more places than parish churches' – Single men who have had their dinner given them at ale-houses begin to call to pay.

Six o'clock. People of quality and distinction drove out of the Green by milliners, manteaumakers, tire-women, sempstresses, clearsarchers, poulterers, staymakers, French peruke makers, dancing-masters, drapers, gentlemen's gentlemen, tailors' wives, starch old maids, and butchers' daughters – Assignations and malicious whisperings at the Ring in the Park – Nightwalkers washing their smocks against the close of the day – Vintners' wives and daughters dressed up behind their bars, to decoy young fellows into large reckonings – Matchmakers and fortune-hunters in full employment – Beggars converting their coppers into true sterling.

Seven o'clock. Fools and powdered fops admiring themselves in coffee-houses – City apprentices complaining to fond mothers of their masters – Foot-soldiers drunk at their posts with brandy – The Ministry severely censured in ale-houses – Few lawyers at evening lectures – Men, women and children returning from the fields drunk and hungry – Dusty chaises with shores in highcrown hats limping thro' the streets of Dublin – People of quality beginning to pay spiteful visits to one another.

Eight o'clock. Cold beef and pudding most vigorously attacked in taverns and other public-houses – Servants in gentlemen's and tradesmen's kitchens carousing the liquors stolen from their masters – Young shopkeepers, beau journeymen and lawyers' clerks sneaking into town upon brokenkneed horses . . . Hired infants, who have been lent out to beggars, restored to their real parents – Men of quality visiting their wives' chamber maids in the absence of their wives from home.

Nine o'clock. Young rakes conversing with their mothers' maids in taverns – City dames vouching for one another, for the good company they have passed the afternoon in – . . . Journeymen shoemakers taking off their wearing apparel, as holding it by no longer tenure than the opening of the pawnbrokers' shops the next morning – Children, servants, old women, and others of the same size of understanding, pleasing and terrifying themselves with stories of witches, devils and apparitions.—

[157] DUBLIN SOCIETY IN THE 1750S, AND THE VIRTUOUS DUBLIN LADIES; FROM THE *LETTERS OF CHIEF BARON OF WILLES*, EDITED BY JAMES KELLY.

The morning is generally spent in riding out or taking the Air in a Coach . . . and a bad morning in visiting, for no Gentleman ever visits in an afternoon, Most Gent being supposed (& generally are engaged) at dinner either at home or abroad with company. There is scarce such a thing as meeting a Gent & asking him to take a family dinner today, the fashion is a mutual Course of entertainment where you meet with a Table as well covered at a private Gentlemans house taking the magnificence of plate & the Garnish of ornaments & servants as at a Man of Quality or of large Fortune. The people generally dine late, Never before 4 & generally 5. I don't think considering the fashion of the place that is a prudent hour, for no Gent except of the profession of the Law ever does any business after dinner. It was the custom till within these few years that where you dined you supped, But now the Company parts generally from 8 to 10. Unless the master of the house or some of the company are hard drinkers & choose to sit later at the bottle. There is one good custom that any Gent takes up his hat & goes away when he pleases without taking Notice of the master of the House And tis reckoned rather unpolite to press anyone to stay. If there is a Lady, Generally there is a dinner & cards where you dine, If not there is scarce a Gent or Lady who has not one or more Cards for a Rout or Routs Every night in the Week.

The generality of the play is rather too high for the general circumstances of the people, The lowest players hazarding the winning or losing 3 or 4 Games a night. There are some that turn playing at cards into Gaming & lose considerable Sums. And indeed high play is too much the fashion of this kingdom . . . This usual rota of diversions, together with plays every night in Winter & publick Concerts, & in parliament Winter one Ball & one Drawing Room night at the Castle every week, And in Summer time the publick Gardens Make altogether such a round of Diversions, And the Time is so fully employed in them That it gives too trifling and disipated Ideas to the minds of Young People And is too apt to make them fancy that they were born into this world for no other purpose but like the great Leviathan to take their pastime therein.

But there is one thing I must say for the Honour of the Irish ladies, Tis very uncommon to hear of any scandal upon their Reputations Both Single & married Ladies in general behave with great Virtue, and I do attribute it to Virtue rather than to prudence & caution in concealing an Intrigue, Because Dublin is like a large Market town in England where everyone knows & is known by everybody, and there is scarce anything done by anybody But it is publickly known. . . .

Dublin society amuses itself in the Rotunda pleasure-gardens, late
eighteenth century, from Walker's *Hibernian Magazine 1790*

[150] THE FIGHTING DUBLINERS; FROM *IRELAND
SIXTY YEARS AGO* BY J. E. WALSH.

At the period we refer to [*the late eighteenth century*], any approach to
the habits of the industrious classes by an application to trade or business, or even a profession, was considered a degradation to a gentleman, and the upper orders of society affected a most rigid exclusive-
ness. There was, however, one most singular pursuit in which the
highest and lowest seemed alike to participate, with an astonishing
relish – viz., fighting – which all classes in Ireland appear to have

enjoyed with a keenness now hardly credible even to a native of Kentucky. The passion for brawls and quarrels was as rife in the metropolis as elsewhere, and led to scenes in Dublin, sixty or seventy years ago, which present a most extraordinary contrast to the state of society there at the present day.

Among the lower orders, a feud and deadly hostility had grown up between the Liberty boys, or tailors and weavers of the Coombe, and the Ormond boys, or butchers who lived in Ormond-market, on Ormond-quay, which caused frequent conflicts; and it is in the memory of many now living that the streets, and particularly the quays and bridges, were impassable in consequence of the battles of these parties. The weavers descending from the upper regions beyond Thomas-street, poured down on their opponents below; they were opposed by the butchers, and a contest commenced on the quays which extended from Essex to Island bridge. The shops were closed; all business suspended; the sober and peaceable compelled to keep their houses; and those whose occasions led them through the streets where the belligerents were engaged, were stopped; while the war of stones and other missiles was carried on across the river, and the bridges were taken and retaken by the hostile parties. It will hardly be believed that for whole days the intercourse of the city was interrupted by the feuds of these factions. The few miserable watchmen, inefficient for any purpose of protection, looked on in terror, and thought themselves well acquitted for their duty if they escaped from stick and stone. A friend of ours has told us that he has gone down to Essex bridge, when he has been informed that one of those battles was raging, and stood quietly on the battlements for a whole day looking at the combat, in which above a thousand men were engaged. At one time, the Ormond boys drove those of the Liberty up to Thomas-street, where rallying, they repulsed their assailants and drove them back as far as the Broad-stone, while the bridges and quays were strewed with the maimed and wounded. On May 11th, 1790, one of these frightful riots raged for an entire Saturday on Ormond-quay, the contending parties struggling for the mastery of the bridge; but nightfall having separated them before the victory was decided, the battle was renewed on the Monday following. It was reported of Alderman Emerson, when lord mayor, on one of those occasions, that he declined to interfere when applied to, asserting that 'it was as much as his life was worth to go among them.'

These feuds terminated sometimes in frightful excesses. The butchers used their knives, not to stab their opponents, but for a purpose then common in the barbarous state of Irish society, to *hough* or cut the tendon of the leg, thereby rendering the person incurably lame for life. On one occasion after a defeat of the Ormond boys, those of the Liberty retaliated in a manner still more barbarous and revolting. They dragged the persons they seized to their market, and dislodging the meat they found there, hooked the men by the jaws, and retired, leaving the butchers hanging on their own stalls.

The spirit of the times led men of the highest grade and respectability to join with the dregs of the market in these outrages . . . and the young aristocrat, who would have felt it an intolerable degradation to associate or even be seen with an honest merchant, however respectable, with a singular inconsistency made a boast of his intimate acquaintance with the lawless excesses of butchers and coal-porters. The students of Trinity College were particularly prone to join in the affrays between the belligerents, and generally united their forces to those of the Liberty boys against the butchers. On one occasion, several of them were seized by the latter, and to the great terror of their friends, it was reported they were hanged up in the stalls, in retaliation for the cruelty of the weavers. A party of watchmen sufficiently strong was at length collected by the authorities, and they proceeded to Ormond-market: there they saw a frightful spectacle – a number of college lads in their gowns and caps hanging to the hooks. On examination, however, it was found that the butchers, pitying their youth and respecting their rank, had only hung them by the waistbands of their breeches, where they remained as helpless, indeed, as if they were suspended by the neck.

[159] THE DUBLIN FOOTPADS; FROM *IRELAND SIXTY YEARS AGO* BY J. E. WALSH.

The footpads of Dublin robbed in a manner, we believe, peculiar to themselves. The streets were miserably lighted – indeed, in many places hardly lighted at all. So late as 1812, there were only twenty-six small oil lamps to light the immense square of Stephen's green, which were therefore one hundred and seventy feet from one another. The footpads congregated in a dark entry, on the shady side of the street, if the moon shone; if not, the dim and dismal light of the lamps was little obstruction. A cord was provided with a loop at the end of it. The loop was laid on the pavement, and the thieves watched the approach of a passenger. If he put his foot in the loop, it was immediately chucked. The man fell prostrate, and was dragged rapidly up the entry to some cellar or waste yard, where he was robbed, and sometimes murdered. The stun received by the fall usually prevented the victim from ever recognizing the robbers. We knew a gentleman who had been. thus robbed, and when he recovered, found himself in an alley at the end of a lane off Bride-street, nearly naked, and severely contused and lacerated by being dragged over the rough pavement.

[160] THE ELOQUENCE OF THE DUBLIN BEGGAR; FROM JOHN GAMBLE'S *SKETCHES OF HISTORY, POLITICS AND MANNERS TAKEN IN DUBLIN IN THE AUTUMN OF 1811*.

The address of an Irish beggar is much more poetical and animated than that of an English one; his phraseology is as peculiar as the recitative in which it is delivered; he conjures you, for the love and honour of God, to throw something to the poor famished sinner – by your father and mother's soul to cast an eye of pity on his sufferings – he is equally liberal in his good wishes, whether you give him anything or not; 'may you live a hundred years – may you pass unhurt through fire and water – may the gates of Paradise be ever open to receive you'; are common modes of expression, which he utters with a volubility that is inconceivable.

A Dublin beggar plies his trade near Capel Street bridge, detail from an aquatint by James Malton, 1797

[161] ELOQUENCE AT THE VICEROY'S SUPPER PARTY IN THE EARLY 1800S; FROM *JACK HINTON, THE GUARDSMAN* BY CHARLES LEVER. *THE VICEROY REFERRED TO HERE IS THE DUKE OF RICHMOND, A FAMOUS BON VIVEUR, WHO AFTER A DRUNKEN DINNER WOULD OFTEN TOSS A GUEST OVER HIS SHOULDER*

Amid a shower of smart, caustic, and witty sayings, droll stories, retort arid repartee, the wine circulated freely from hand to hand; the presence of the Duke adding fresh impulse to the sallies of fun and merriment around him. Anecdotes of the army, the bench, and the bar, poured in unceasingly, accompanied by running commentaries of the hearers, who never let slip an opportunity for a jest or a rejoinder. To me the most singular feature of all this was, that no one seemed too old or too dignified, too high in station or too venerable from office, to join in this headlong current of conviviality: austere churchmen, erudite chief-justices, profound politicians, privy councillors, military officers of high rank and standing, were here all mixed up together into one strange medley, apparently bent on throwing an air of ridicule over the graver business of life, and laughing alike at themselves and the world. Nothing was too grave for a jest, nothing too solemn for a sarcasm.

[162] AN AMERICAN TOURIST LOOKS AT SPLENDOUR AND MISERY
IN DUBLIN IN THE FIRST YEARS OF THE NINETEENTH CENTURY;
FROM *ANCIENT & MODERN DUBLIN* BY WILLIAM CURRY.

'This city,' says the Tourist, 'presents the most extraordinary contrast of poverty and magnificence to be met with in Europe. As you approach it, you find the suburbs composed of hovels, the sides of which are partly stone and partly earth, the roofs of turf, the whole dimensions of each not exceeding twelve or fourteen feet square. These miserable caves may or may not have a hole for a window, and an aperture on the top, to let out the smoke, if the luxury of fire can be afforded. Around the door the dirty children are huddled – not one half are decently clad; some of them still evince notions of civilization by slinking into a house, or turning their bare parts against a wall. I saw hundreds whose whole dress, consisting of a mass of rags, of all colours and all sorts of fabrics, will not furnish one piece of cloth eight inches square – and these tatters seemed to be sewed together only to prevent them deserting each other. Having passed the suburbs, the dwellings improve; and, on reaching Sackville-street, you imagine yourself in one of the most elegant cities in Europe. In walking over the city, the Irish Parliament House, (now the Bank,) the Exchange, the quay along the

Liffey, and several of the public squares, excite the stranger's admiration. There is no part of London which can compare with the centre of Dublin in beauty and magnificence. But, in turning the eye from the architectural splendour which surrounds him, upon the crowds which flow along the streets, the stranger will be struck with the motley nature of the throng. Here is a lass almost buoyant with satin and feathers; there is a trembling girl of eighteen, purple from cold, shrinking from shame, and drawing around her the poor rags which, with all her care, scarce cover her body; here is an *exquisite*, perfuming the air as he passes, with rings on his fingers, diamonds on his brooch, and a gemmed quizzing-glass at his side; there is an honest fellow who cannot afford a hat, whose feet, summer or winter, know not the luxury of shoe or stocking, and whose whole wardrobe consists of two articles, viz. a tattered jacket, and about half a pair of small-clothes; and, not to multiply pictures, while the Lieutenant dashes by in a coach and four, the stranger gazes at the gallant and costly pageant, while he empties his pocket to satisfy the throng of beggars who pray him, in the name of God, to give them a penny.'

Happily for the citizens and the traveller, the last remark does not now apply, as beggars are not allowed on the streets; the Mendicity Society [*see next extract*] providing what is at least sufficient to keep them from starvation. Should the American Tourist have again occasion to visit the metropolis he would find the state of things much improved.

[163] WILLIAM COBBETT VISITS THE DUBLIN WORKHOUSE;
FROM *NOT BY BULLETS AND BAYONETS* BY MOLLY TOWNSEND.

William Cobbett, the famous radical journalist and MP, visited Dublin in 1834 when he was seventy-one. A long-standing champion of the Irish Catholic Cause, he received a rapturous welcome. His harrowing account of the Dublin poor was published as an Open Letter to an English farm labourer. The Mendicity Institute on Ussher's Island (blithely referred to in Curry's

guide-book (see previous extract) as relieving the problem of Dublin's beggars)
was originally one of Dublin's great private houses – Moira House. Its bricked-
up entrance still survives on the Quays.

MARSHALL,

I have this morning seen more than one thousand of working
persons, men and women, boys and girls, all the clothes upon the
bodies of all of whom were not worth so much as the smock-frock that
you go to work in; and you have a wife and eight children, seven of
whom are too young to go to work. I have seen the *food* and the *cooking*
of the food, in a LARGE HOUSE, where food is prepared for a part of these
wretched people. Cast-iron coppers, three or four times as big as our
largest brewing copper, are employed to boil *oatmeal* (that is, *ground
oats) in water*, or *buttermilk*, or *skim-milk*; and this is the food given to
these poor creatures. . . . The LARGE HOUSE, of which I have spoken to
you above, is called the MENDICITY. The word *mendicant* means *beggar*,
and the word MENDICITY means *beggary*. So that this, which was formerly
a nobleman's mansion, is now the *house of beggars*. From this house
there are sent forth, every day, *begging carts*, drawn by women, who go
from house to house to collect what is called 'broken victuals.' These
carts are precisely, in shape and in size, like my *dog-hutches*, except that
the begging carts have a sort of *copper* at top to put the victuals in at,
and a locked-up door at one end, to take the victuals out of. Now mind
what I am going to say: the bones, bits of rusty bacon, rind of bacon,
scrapings of dishes and plates, left cabbage, left turnips, peas, beans,
beets, and the like odds and ends, that Mrs Kenning throws into our
hog-tub, form a mass of victuals *superior in quality* to these *mendicity-
collections*; and in proof of which I state the following facts: that the
carts, when they come in, have their contents taken out and examined
by persons appointed for the purpose, who separate all that can become
food from the mere rubbish and filth, that is, by servants at the houses,
tossed into the carts amongst it; and a gentleman has, in evidence given
by him before commissioners here, stated, that out of *seventy odd*

hundred weight taken out of the carts the examiners found only *nine hundred weight* that could by any possibility become human food, the *bones* in these nine hundred weight not being included. . . .

In another place I saw the most painful sight of all: *women*, with heavy hammers, *cracking stones* into very small pieces, to *make walks in gentlemen's gardens!* These women were as ragged as the rest; and the sight of them and their work, and the thoughts accompanying these, would have sunk the heart in your body, as they did mine.

[164] DINING-OUT IN DUBLIN IN THE 1840S; FROM W. M THACKERAY'S *AN IRISH SKETCHBOOK*.

And so having reached Dublin, it becomes necessary to curtail the observations which were to be made upon that city; which surely ought to have a volume to itself: the humours of Dublin at least require so much space. For instance, there was the dinner at the Kildare Street Club, or the Hotel opposite, – the dinner in Trinity College Hall, – that at Mr –, the publisher's, where a dozen of the literary men of Ireland were assembled, – and those (say fifty) with Harry Lorrequer himself, at his mansion of Templeogue. What a favourable opportunity to discourse upon the peculiarities of Irish character! to describe men of letters, of fashion, and university dons! . . . But the author who wishes to dine again at his friend's cost, must needs have a care how he puts him in print.

Suffice it to say, that at Kildare Street we had white neck-cloths, black waiters, wax-candles, and some of the best wine in Europe; at Mr –, the publisher's, wax-candles, and some of the best wine in Europe; at Mr Lever's, wax-candles, and some of the best wine in Europe; at Trinity College – but there is no need to mention what took place at Trinity College; for on returning to London, and recounting the circumstances of the repast, my friend B –, a Master of Arts of that university, solemnly declared the thing was impossible: – no stranger *could* dine at Trinity College; it was too great a privilege – in a word, he would not believe the story, nor will he to this day; and why, therefore, tell it in vain?

I am sure if the Fellows of Colleges in Oxford and Cambridge were told that the Fellows of T. C. D. only drink beer at dinner, they would not believe *that*. Such, however, was the fact: or may be it was a dream, which was followed by another dream of about four-and-twenty gentlemen seated round a common-room table after dinner; and, by a subsequent vision of a tray of oysters in the apartments of a tutor of the university, sometime before midnight. Did we swallow them or not? – the oysters are an open question.

[165] Dubliners take to kilts, early 1900s; from *Life and the Dream* by Mary Colum.

In those days there were many men in Dublin who returned to the wearing of Gaelic kilts, which differed from the familiar Scots kilts by being plain saffron or green in color; sometimes the kilt would be saffron and the brath green, fastened to the shoulder of the jacket with a Tara broach of silver or copper. For a tall, well-built figure the kilts are the most becoming of all forms of dress for a man, making him look both romantic and virile. Several of the writers affected them: Darrell Figgis, who wrote poetry and novels and had a career later as a politician in the new Irish state, Thomas MacDonagh, who wrote poetry and later taught in the National University, and who signed the proclamation of the Irish Republic in 1916; kilts were occasionally worn by the brothers Pearse – Padraic, who founded a bilingual school, and Willie who was a sculptor. The last three were executed in 1916 as leaders of the insurrection and signers of the proclamation of the Irish Republic. Figgis also had a violent end. He committed suicide as part of the outcome of a tragic love affair. But the most picturesque of those who arrayed themselves in kilts was Lord Ashbourne's son, William Gibson, afterwards himself Lord Ashbourne, who, when he succeeded to the title, insisted on addressing the House of Lords in Irish.

Lord Ashbourne poses in his kilt, early 1900s

[166] Brass-plate Dublin; from *Seven
Winters* by Elizabeth Bowen.

*The novelist Elizabeth Bowen was born at 5 Herbert Place by the Grand
Canal, and spent the first seven winters of her childhood there.*

Between the middle of Dublin and Herbert Place lies a tract of Georgian
streets and squares. We had a choice of two routes into the city. From
the foot of our steps we could turn right, then go along Lower Baggot
Street; or we could turn left, take the curve round St Stephen's Church
and after that go along Upper Mount Street and the south side of
Merrion Square; to this route was added the charm of going through
Leinster Lawn, between the Museum and the National Gallery; one
then followed that secretive passage, under the high flank of Leinster
House, through to the circular lawn on the other side and the gates
opening on to Kildare Street.

(When I was with my father, the glory of the Royal Dublin Society was upon us and we took the indoor short cut, through the Leinster House rooms.) . . .

The post-Union exodus of the bright-plumaged people had not (as I saw) been followed by real decay. The Irish Bar and the eminent Dublin doctors kept South Dublin witty and sociable. Judges and specialists now lived round Merrion Square. The front doors were painted, the fanlights and windows polished, the great staircases possibly better swept and the high-ceilinged double drawing-rooms heated and lit for *conversazioni*. In the winters of my childhood this second society was still in full, if not at its fullest, force. The twentieth century governed only in name; the nineteenth was still a powerful dowager. Between England and Anglo-Ireland a time-lag is, I think, always perceptible. Any transition into Edwardian dashingness would have been seen in the Castle set. But the Castle seasons left my father and mother cold. The world my parents inhabited, and the subworld of its children, was still late-Victorian. Their friends were drawn from the Bar, from Trinity College, from among the prelates of the Church of Ireland or landed people quietly living in town.

In fact, the climatic moodiness of South Dublin (a bold Italianate town-plan in tricky Celtic light) must have existed only in my eye. All here stood for stability. The front doors were, as I say, fresh painted – crimson, chocolate, chestnut, ink-blue or olive-green. One barrister friend of my father's had a chalk-white front door I found beautiful. And each door – to this my memory finds no single exception – bore its polished brass plate. Daughter of a professional neighbourhood, I took this brass plate announcing its owner's name to be the *sine qua non* of any gentleman's house. Just as the tombstone says '*Here Lies*' the plate on the front door (in my view) said '*Here Lives*.' Failure to write one's name on one's door seemed to me the admission of nonentity. The house-holder with the anonymous door must resign himself to being overlooked by the world – to being passed by by the postman, unfed by tradesmen, guestless, unsought by friends – and his family dwelt in the shadow of this disgrace.

The fact that I could not read made these plates with writing still more significant. The first time I did see a town front door of unmistakable standing *without* a plate, I remember being not only scornful but hostile. Why should the dweller here envelop himself in mystery? On that occasion, my mother explained to me that plates were not, after all, the rule. If not, why not? I said hotly: how very silly. How else was one to know who lived in a house? In the light of this fixed idea (which I still think a good one) I remember my first view of London – street after street of triste anonymity. So no one cares who lives in London, I thought. No wonder London is so large; all the nonentities settle here. Dublin has chosen to be smaller than London because she is grander and more exclusive. All the important people live in Dublin, near me.

[167] DUBLIN, AFTER THE 'CROSSNESS'; FROM *IN SEARCH OF IRELAND* BY H. V. MORTON.

H. V. Morton was one of the first travel-writers to describe Dublin after the establishment of the Free State; and his delightful book, first published in 1930, is still in print. The 'crossness' is, of course, the War of Independence or Anglo-Irish War which began with the Rising of 1916 and was ended by the Treaty of 1921; followed by the Civil War between the Free State army and the Republicans which ended only in 1923. All in all, Dublin had had seven years of fighting.

Why has Dublin been called 'dear dirty Dublin'? This surely is an ancient libel. The roads outside Dublin are apparently dirty on the evidence of the omnibus wheels, to which are attached small hanging brooms of stiff bristles. These brooms tickle the tyres when the wheels are in motion and brush off the mud. But the city itself is as clean as a Dutch dresser.

In the streets stand amongst the taxicabs many of the oldest horse-cabs on earth, objects of remarkable antiquity which surely, by some virtue of the Irish temperament, continue to function, and there is also that strange but famous vehicle, known to the English as a 'jaunting-car', but called in Ireland an 'outside-car'. I imagine that the outside-car is to Dublin what the few remaining hansom cabs are to London – a sentimental refuge for Americans. When you hire one of them and sit sideways to the world, Dublin smiles indulgently at you from the pavement. I went round behind a spanking bay pony while the jarvey pointed out the sights with his whip.

In O'Connell Street he indicated a line of shattered buildings, and remarked that they had been destroyed during the 'crossness'.

'You mean,' I said, 'the fighting.'

'Och, sure,' he replied, 'it was the crossness, I said.'

I thought this description quite the kindest and most generous I had ever heard!

Sentries, smart in green uniforms and brown leggings, marched before the Government building, which flies the tricolour of the Free State. A hefty young man, armed with a revolver, stood on the steps. In a barrack square we saw a company of young soldiers at bayonet drill, practising a lunge and parry, which looked to me something new in warfare.

The crowds in the Dublin streets are vastly different from English crowds. You do not see the haggard money look which is becoming characteristic of all large English cities. There is more laughter. There is no painful rushing about. There is a cheerful ease about Dublin, a casual good temper, which makes it difficult to realize the dark times through which this city has passed. There are certain apparent superficialities which, however, possess a deep significance. The English red has vanished from the streets; the pillarboxes are green. So are the envelopes in which telegrams are delivered. So are the mail vans. And the names of the streets are written in Gaelic, which not one in a thousand Dubliners can read! Still this proves a change in ownership and a striving to be Irish.

When we came to the end of the journey the jarvey said, when I asked how much he wanted:

'I'll leave it to yourself.'

A Frenchman would have taken my enormous bribe with a surly doubtfulness, but he was quite frankly overpaid, and showed it with Irish candour. 'God bless ye,' he said. 'And now what about a bit of a drive tomorrow?'

Bibliography

BAGWELL, RICHARD, *Ireland under the Stuarts*, London, 1909

BARNARD, F.P., *Strongbow's Conquest of Ireland*, London, 1888

BARRINGTON, SIR JONAH, *The Rise and Fall of the Irish Nation*, Dublin, 1833

BEHAN, BRENDAN, *Brendan Behan's Island*, London, 1962

BIRRELL, AUGUSTINE, *Things Past Redress*, London, 1932. *Blackwoods Magazine*, July 1916

BOWEN, ELIZABETH, *Seven Winters*, Dublin, 1942

—— *The Shelbourne*, London, 1951

CAMPBELL, REVD THOMAS, *A Philosophical Survey of the South of Ireland*, Dublin, 1777

CARLETON, WILLIAM, *Autobiography*, ed. D. Masson, London, 1896

CARLYLE, THOMAS, *Reminiscences of My Irish Journey in 1849*, London, 1882

CARTE, THOMAS, *An History of the Life of James, Duke of Ormonde*, London, 1735

CARTY, JAMES, *Ireland 1607–1782, A documentary record*, Dublin, 1951

CHART, D.A., *The Story of Dublin*, London, 1907

CHURCHILL, WINSTON, *My Early Life*, London, 1930

CLARKE, AUSTIN, *A Penny in the Clouds*, London, 1962

COLUM, MARY, *Life and the Dream*, London, 1947

CONNOLLY, NORA, *Portrait of a Rebel Father*, Dublin, 1935

COOPER, GEORGE, *Letters on the Irish Nation*, Dublin, 1799

CROKER, JOHN WILSON, *The Croker Papers 1808–57*, ed. R. Pool, London, 1967

CURRAN, W.H., *Sketches of the Irish Bar*, Dublin, 1855

CURRY, WILLIAM, *A New Picture of Dublin*, London, 1820

—— *Ancient & Modern Dublin*

DE BOVET, ANNE, *Three Months in Ireland*, London, 1891

DELANY, MARY, *Autobiography and Correspondence of Mary Granville, Mrs Delany*, ed. Lady Llanover, London, 1861

DE QUINCEY, THOMAS, *Autobiographic Sketches*, London, 1890

Desiderata Curiosa Hibernica, Dublin, 1772

DE VERE, AUBREY, *Recollections*, London, 1897

Dublin Historical Record, The, Vol. 20, Dublin, 1964

Dublin Penny Journal, The, Dublin, 1840

EVERETT, KATHERINE, *Bricks and Flowers*, London, 1949

FITZHENRY, EDNA, *An Anthology of 1916*, London, 1935

GAMBLE, JOHN, *Sketches of History, Politics and Manners taken in Dublin in the Autumn of 1811*, Dublin, 1811

GERARD, FRANCIS, *Picturesque Dublin*, London, 1898

GILBERT, SIR JOHN, *The History of the City of Dublin*, Dublin, 1854–59

—— *Calendar of Ancient Records of Dublin*, Dublin, 1889–1907

—— *The History of the Parliament House*, Dublin, 1896

GOGARTY, OLIVER ST JOHN, *As I was going down Sackville Street*, London, 1937

—— *It isn't This Time of Year at all*, New York, 1954

—— *Government of Ireland under Sir John Perrott, The* [by E.C.S.] London, 1626

GRATTAN, HENRY, *The Life and Times of Henry Grattan by his son*, London, 1839–46

GREGORY, AUGUSTA, *Our Irish Theatre*, London, 1914

——. *Seventy Years, the autobiography of Lady Gregory*, New York, 1976

GWYNN, STEPHEN, *Dublin Old and New*, London, 1938

HALL, MR AND MRS S. C., *Ireland, its Scenery, Character, etc*, London, 1841

HANDEL, G. F., *Autograph Letters of Handel and Jennens*, ed. Edward, 6th Earl of Howe, Christie's Catalogue, London, 1973

HARDY, FRANCIS, *Memoirs of the Earl of Charlemont*, London, 1810

HARRIS, FRANK, *The Life of Oscar Wilde*, London, 1937

HERBERT, J. D., *Irish Varieties*, Dublin, 1836

HOLINSHED, RALPH, *Chronicles of England and Ireland*, London, 1808

HOLLOWAY, JOSEPH, *Joseph Holloway's Abbey Theatre*, ed. Roger Hogan and Michael J. O'Neill, Illinois, 1967

HOPKINS, GERARD MANLEY, *Letters of Gerard Manley Hopkins to Robert Bridges*, London, 1935

HYDE, DOUGLAS, *The Literary History of Ireland*, London, 1899

Illustrated London News, The, London, May 1882 and August 1847

JEFFREYS, NATHANIEL, *An Englishman's Descriptive Account of Dublin*, London, 1810

JOYCE, JAMES, *Portrait of the Artist as a Young Man*, New York, 1916

—— *Ulysses*, Paris, 1922

—— *Selected Letters of James Joyce*, ed. Richard Ellmann, Oxford, 1975

KELLY, LINDA, *The Kemble Era*, London, 1980

KENNEDY, TOM, (ed.), *Victorian Dublin*, Dublin, 1980

LEVER, CHARLES, *Charles O'Malley*, Dublin, 1842

Jack Hinton, the Guardsman, Dublin, 1847

LOCKHART, J.G., *The Life of Sir Walter Scott*, London, 1847

LONGFORD, CHRISTINE, *A Biography of Dublin*, London, 1938

MACBRIDE, MAUD GONNE, *A Servant of the Queen*, London, 1938

MCCARTHY, MURIEL, *All Graduates and Gentlemen*, Dublin, 1980

MACREADY, WILLIAM CHARLES, *Reminiscences*, ed. Sir F. Pollock, London, 1875

MACDONAGH, MICHAEL, *The Life of Daniel O'Connell*, London, 1903

MACLYSAGHT, EDWARD, *Irish Life in the Seventeenth Century*, Dublin, 1939

MCMANUS, M. J., *Irish Cavalcade*, London, 1939

MCPARLAND, EDWARD, *James Gandon: Vitruvius Hibernicus*, London, 1985

MACNEILE DIXON, W., *Trinity College, Dublin*, London, 1902

MADDEN, R.R., *Ireland in '98*, London, 1888

MALTON, JAMES, *A Picturesque and Descriptive View of Dublin*, London, 1792–99

MAXWELL, CONSTANTIA, *Irish History from Contemporary Sources*, London, 1923

—— *Dublin under the Georges*, London, 1936

—— *History of Trinity College, Dublin, 1591–1892*, Dublin, 1942

MOORE, GEORGE, *Parnell and his Island*, London, 1886

—— *Hail and Farewell (Ave, Salve, Vale)*, London, 1900

MORTON, H.V., *In Search of Ireland*, London, 1930

MULVANEY, T. J., *The Life of James Gandon*, London, 1847

NEWBOLT, HENRY, *Froissart in Britain*, London, 1900

NORWAY, MRS JAMES HAMILTON, *The Sinn Fein Rebellion as I saw it*, London, 1918

O'BRIEN, JOSEPH, *Dear, Dirty Dublin, A city in distress, 1899–1916*, California, 1982

O'BRIEN, KATE, *My Ireland*, London, 1962

O'BRIEN, WILLIAM, *Recollections*, London, 1905

O'CASEY, SEAN, *Pictures in the Hallway*, London, 1942

—— *Drums under the Windows*, London, 1945

—— *Inishfallen, Fare Thee Well*, London, 1949

O'CONNOR, CYNTHIA, *The Pleasing Hours*, Cork 1999

O'KEEFE, JOHN, *Recollections*, London, 1826

O'MALLEY, ERNIE, *On Another Man's Wound*, London, 1936

—— *The Singing Flame*, Dublin, 1978

ORRERY, LORD, *The Orrery Papers*, ed. the Countess of Cork and Orrery, London, 1903

PILKINGTON, LETITIA, *The Memoirs of Letitia Pilkington*, London, 1748

Recollections of Dublin Castle and Dublin Society, Anon, Dublin, 1902

RICH, BARNABY, *New Description of Ireland*, London, 1610

RYAN, DESMOND, *Remembering Sion*, Dublin, 1934

SAMUELS, ARTHUR, *The Early Life and Correspondence of Edmund Burke*, London, 1923

SHELLEY, PERCY BYSSHE, *Letters to Elizabeth Hitchener*, London, 1908

SHERIDAN, THOMAS, *The Life of Doctor Swift*, London, 1770

STARKIE, WALTER, *Scholars and Gypsies*, London, 1963

STEPHENS, JAMES, *The Insurrection in Dublin*, London, 1916

SWIFT, JONATHAN, *The Correspondence of Jonathan Swift*, ed. Elrington Ball, London, 1911–14

THACKERAY, WILLIAM MAKEPEACE, *An Irish Sketchbook*, London, 1843

TOWNSEND, MOLLY, *Not by Bullets and Bayonets*, London, 1983

TOWNSHEND, DOROTHEA, *The Life and Letters of the Great Earl of Cork*, London, 1904

VICTORIA, QUEEN, *The Collected Letters of Queen Victoria*, ed. G. E. Buckle, London, 1926

WALSH, J.E., *Ireland Sixty Years Ago*, Dublin, 1847

WESLEY, JOHN, *Wesley, His Own Biographer*, London, 1891

—— *The Diaries*, edited by J. Carnock, London 1906

WILLES, CHIEF JUSTICE BARON, Add MSS 29 252, British Museum, London

WINSTANLEY, JOHN, *The Poems of John Winstanley*, London, 1748

YEATS, WILLIAM BUTLER, *The Collected Poems of W. B. Yeats*, London, 1950

Index

Numbers in *italics* refer to illustrations